A
Handbook
of
Theological
Terms

VAN A. HARVEY

A TOUCHSTONE BOOK
Published by Simon & Schuster

TOUCHSTONE
Rockefeller Center
1230 Avenue of the Americas
New York, NY 10020

First Touchstone Edition 1997

TOUCHSTONE and colophon are registered
trademarks of Simon & Schuster Inc.

Manufactured in the United States of America

3 5 7 9 10 8 6 4

Library of Congress in Publication Data is available.

ISBN: 0-684-84644-6

PREFACE

Some time ago, the newspapers carried the story of a church conference in Europe in which the theologians were derided by the laymen present because of their use of technical theological jargon. Some commentators obviously sympathized with the laymen and ominously pointed out that there was a revolutionary spirit abroad in the churches, a spirit reflecting a new resolve by the laymen not to leave theology to the professionals. I hope it will not be taken as defensiveness on the part of a professional, or as an apology for the obscurantism theologians too frequently indulge in, if I raise a question about this. Is the road to a responsible lay theology to be a one-way thoroughfare? Is the condition for discourse between lay and professional theologians to be that professionals must always speak in the language of the street while the layman, in turn, feels no responsibility for rigorous and disciplined study of theology and, therefore, some mastery of its technical and traditional vocabulary? To answer that question in the affirmative rests on certain assumptions about language and about the relationship of faith to theology that will not, I believe, bear much analysis and will ultimately destroy whatever rigor and intellectual integrity theology may claim to have. It may be that the traditional terminology is outmoded or needs to be rejected. But surely this can be judged only after it has been understood and not simply on the grounds that the common man is not familiar with it.

My purpose here, however, is not to argue this matter but to give the reader some indication of why I spent the time I have writing this wordbook and to cast some light on the principles of selection and interpretation which guided me.

My aim has not been to provide definitions of obscure theological terms but to indicate how such terms, ancient and modern, have been variously used in differing circumstances and what is at issue in these various uses. It is a wordbook, not a dictionary. It was clear from the outset that this would necessarily involve an exercise of my own judgment, which, in turn, would reflect my own theological perspective. This judgment is involved not only in the inclusion of certain terms and the exclusion of others but in what I choose to say about the terms themselves. Because of this, the wordbook will inevitably appear slanted and nonobjective to many who have different perspectives. I do not see any way of doing what I wanted to do and avoiding this criticism. The only comfort I have is that I have yet to find a philosophical or theological dictionary, not to speak of a wordbook, which does not have a definite point of view (and most have several conflicting points of view) and which, therefore, escapes this criticism; although editors of Christian theological dictionaries are more prone to think that they have because they unconsciously equate objective and orthodox.

Several considerations governed the selection and explanation of the terms in the wordbook. First of all, I decided to limit it primarily to those terms employed in systematic and philosophical theology. This necessarily and regretfully meant the exclusion of many other important kinds of theological terms, for example, liturgical, Biblical, ethical, and ecclesiological. This will seem incredible to those who view theology primarily as a criticism of the life and practice of the church. Regrettable, though not incredible, it may be. Something can be said for a wordbook that concentrates on systematic and philosophical terms, if only because the more inclusive sorts of dictionaries are available while the theological wordbooks are not. At any rate, it was impossible to include all these types of words without violating the conception of the book.

Secondly, I decided to try to illumine, where possible, the fundamental issues between Protestantism and Roman Catholicism, generally, and among Protestants, specifically. I chose to do this by placing the emphasis on the difference between the Reformers and the medieval theologians and on contemporary Protestant theology. This necessarily involved a certain degree of rough generalization. It will also seem unbalanced and arbitrary to many readers. The wordbook, for example, rarely deals with the doctrines and traditions of the Eastern Orthodox churches. This, also, is regrettable but not completely indefensible, because I do not see how it can be denied that the renaissance in modern theology, both Catholic and Protestant, is in large part due to the influence of the so-called neo-Reformed theologians like Karl Barth, Emil Brunner, Rudolf Bultmann, the Niebuhrs, and Paul Tillich. And surely one of the natural expectations of most laymen who will pick up this book will be that it may shed some light on the language and problems of these thinkers.

In addition to these general considerations, there were more specific guidelines. (1) I have treated primarily those basic categories and terms which are fundamental to the understanding of Christian theology as well as of its relationship to classical philosophy, e.g., atonement, being, christology, attributes of God, natural theology, proofs for the existence of God, revelation, the doctrine of the Trinity, grace, justification, theism, and the like. These articles were written in "systematic clusters" in order to integrate the volume and to avoid repetition. At the end of most of the articles are references to other articles to which they are related and which may make them more intelligible. Furthermore, the first use in an article of a term explained elsewhere is in small capitals. (2) I have devoted considerable attention to the somewhat technical problems and terminology that occur in the doctrine of God, christology, the doctrine of the Trinity, etc. (3) I have included those terms related to the articles above which have arisen out of a specific historical context but which now have a looser meaning in polemics, e.g., adoptianism, Arianism, Pelagianism, semi-Pelagianism, etc. I have found it necessary to exclude, however, a description of general historical positions like Thomism, Calvinism, Molinism, Lutheranism. (4) I have included a number of terms that are peculiar to modern Protestant theology or which are essential for understanding the present situation, e.g., Biblical criticism, form criticism, I-Thou, myth, etc. (5) I have included a few Latin or Greek words that occur quite frequently in theological discourse both classical and modern, like *actus purus*, *agape* and *eros*, *apocatastasis*, *causa sui*, *communicatio idiomatum*, *donum superadditum*, etc. (6) I have included a number of words which border on jargon but do have a somewhat technical meaning in the works of important contemporary theologians, e.g., alienation, authentic existence, boundary situation, demythologization, *Geschichte*, *Heilsgeschichte*, existential, *Historie*, historical Jesus, self-understanding, etc. (7) I have thought it important to say something about those schools of modern philosophy that have had such an influence on the contemporary scene, such as analytic, process, existentialist, and positivistic philosophy. The only abbreviations, incidentally, that occur are Prot., R.C., and E.O. for Protestant, Roman Catholic, and Eastern Orthodoxy respectively; O.T. and N.T. for Old and New Testaments; and the standard abbreviations for books of the Bible.

This brief statement will, I hope, give the lay reader some idea of what he may expect. Only the wordbook itself, however, is intended to convince him that the language is worth learning because men have used it to talk about matters of consequence.

In closing, I'd like to express my gratitude to my typist, Mrs. Anne Norris, who labored under difficult circumstances; to my colleagues, Professors David Coldwell, Schubert M. Ogden, Klaus Penzel, and James F. White, who helped me at various stages along the way; and to my wife, Margaret, who was patient enough to play the role of the mythical "common man" to whom I tried to be intelligible.

Dallas, Texas   Van A. Harvey
January 1, 1964

A
Handbook
of
Theological
Terms

A

Abba is the word for father in Aramaic when used in more intimate and familiar speech. Jesus evidently used it (Mark 14:36) as did the earliest Christians (Rom. 8:15; Gal. 4:6). Some scholars have seen special significance in this fact, claiming that it presupposes a radical new conception of the relationship of man to GOD that may be symbolized in the more intimate and familial symbolism of father-son rather than in the more remote one of king-subject or master-servant.

Absolute (The) is a concept that was particularly popular with philosophers of religion in the last century. In its most abstract sense, it referred to ultimate BEING or reality. Its specific meaning, however, was a function of the particular METAPHYSICS of the philosopher. Generally signifying self-subsistence, unconditionedness, ultimacy, first cause, it naturally seemed to many philosophers and theologians to be peculiarly appropriate as a term for deity. (See Attributes of God; Being; God; Perfection, Theological; Theism.)

Absolution. Broadly speaking, the declaration of the forgiveness of sins; more narrowly, the official act of declaring the sins of a PERSON or persons to be forgiven after suitable penitence. In the R.C. tradition it is an essential part of the SACRAMENT of penance. Certain Prot. confessions, the Augsburg Confession and Smalcald Articles, also stress its importance as a function and power of a truly Christian CHURCH.

Accident. In classical and Scholastic philosophy, an A. is something which a SUBSTANCE (a unified and enduring subject which remains essentially unchanged throughout its states) possesses but which does not belong to its inherent nature. Whether a man (a composite substance of body and SOUL) is large or tall is, for example, an A. In this sense, A. is also to

11

be distinguished from attribute or property, which refers to those things inherent to a being. The classification of A.s (proper/common, intrinsic/extrinsic) was a subject of lively debate in SCHOLASTICISM, although the substance-A. distinction itself was rarely challenged. The distinction also played an important theological role in the doctrines of IMMORTALITY, GOD (it being argued that God was not subject to the distinction), and of TRANSUBSTANTIATION. Some modern philosophers reject the notion of substance and, therefore, the distinction. (See Being; Essence; Existentialism; Process Philosophy; Substance; Theism; Transubstantiation.)

Accommodation. In the interpretation of Scripture, A. occurs when a meaning that was not originally intended by the author is attached to a verse or verses; for example, when an O.T. reference to Israel is applied in some fashion to Christ. In CHRISTOLOGY, the term is sometimes used to refer to the theory that Jesus accommodated his teachings to his 1st-century listeners, although he, being omniscient, knew they were not strictly true. (See Exegesis; Hermeneutics.)

Acosmism is the metaphysical view that the physical world does not exist but is only a manifestation of the absolute SPIRIT which alone is real. So considered it is a peculiar form of PANTHEISM.

Actuality is the technical term in classical Aristotelian METAPHYSICS for the realization of potentiality. Potentiality refers to the inherent powers a thing possesses by virtue of its being the kind of thing it is. A man, for example, possesses intrinsic capacities by virtue of being a man rather than a tree. Potentiality is differentiated, then, from both A., the realization of potentiality, and possibility, the mere conceivability of an idea. In Aristotelian metaphysics, which had an important influence on Thomas Aquinas (c.1225-74), all change was regarded as the passage from potentiality to A. All finite beings are compounded, therefore, of potentiality and A. GOD, by contrast, is pure A., containing no potentiality. From this definition follow many important conclusions concerning the nature of God. (See *Actus Purus*; Being; God; Theism.)

Actus Purus. A Scholastic term for deity. Because the divine being was regarded as essentially unchanging and all change was, by definition, regarded as the transition from potentiality to ACTUALITY, it followed that the divine must be pure actuality (A.P.). Such a being contains no unrealized potentiality and can be affected by nothing other than itself. This idea has been attacked by many Prot. theologians for various reasons: Some argue that the idea is unbiblical and an illegitimate speculative notion; others argue that it is an inadequate philosophical conception and incompatible with perfection. (See Aseity; Attributes of God; Being; God; Impassibility; Perfection, Theological; Proofs for the Existence of God; Theism.)

Adoptianism. In its strict sense, the term refers to the christological beliefs of certain theologians in Spain in the 8th century who wished to emphasize the complete humanity of Jesus. They argued that although the second PERSON of the TRINITY may be said to be the only-begotten Son (of one nature with GOD), the human man, Jesus, "was adopted through GRACE" into sonship. In other words, only the adopted Son of Man could be said to have suffered and been buried.

Since this theory resembles in some way still earlier views, Adolf von Harnack (1851-1930), the great historian of doctrine, used the term "adoptionist" to denote those christologies in which Jesus was regarded essentially as human but as elevated to divine sonship at some point in his life. The term is now often applied to any such view. (See Arianism; Christology; Ebionite; *Logos*; Pre-existence of Christ; Subordinationism; Theandric Acts; Trinity.)

Agape and *Eros.* A. is the Greek word most often used in the N.T. to signify GOD's love for man and the love which should bind men to one another, especially Christians in the CHURCH (see *Koinonia*). Its classical description is found in I Cor. 13. A. is the selfless commitment of the lover to the one loved, to the enrichment and enhancement of the beloved's being. The Christian believes that such an A. is made manifest in Jesus Christ, in whom God gives himself to man.

In R.C. THEOLOGY, A. or CHARITY is the queen of the supernatural VIRTUES infused into the SOUL by SANCTIFYING GRACE. It is the highest of the virtues because it elevates man above the natural order of BEING into the supernatural order of the love whereby God loves himself. For most men, it is believed, its perfect realization is not to be found in this life but waits for the BEATIFIC VISION in ETERNITY; nevertheless, through FAITH and hope it may be, in part, enjoyed in this life. It is nothing but the love for God, and, secondarily, the love for all those creatures whom God loves.

A. is often contrasted with E., another Greek term used to signify longing and desire and, hence, viewed by the Greeks as a "daemon" driving man beyond himself to fulfillment and completion. This fulfillment could only be achieved, according to Plato (c.427-347 B.C.), in a final vision of truth, beauty, and goodness by the soul in eternity. E. stems from the feeling of incompleteness, the longing of the lower for the higher. A. is the binding of the perfect to the imperfect, the condescension of the higher to the lower.

It was the Swedish scholar, Anders Nygren (1890-), who systematically pointed out the differences between the two ideas and traced their influence on Western Christian thought. He argued that A. is the unique and basic motif in Christianity because it points to God's act of condescension in Christ, his binding of himself in community with man not out of need or desire but simply out of his spontaneous, gratuitous love for man. Wherever the idea of E. has been permitted into the Christian understanding, Nygren went on, the basic motif of A. has been threatened and destroyed, because E. assumes that love is motivated by worth in the object and, therefore, denies the spontaneous and gratuitous nature of A. Nygren's work has had an important influence on contemporary Prot. theologians, although some of these, like Paul Tillich (1886-), believe the case has been overstated. Although A. and E. may be distinguished, Tillich writes, they cannot be ultimately separated. Neither the O.T. nor the N.T. completely eliminates the elements of E. from the divine A., just as E. is not completely lacking in A. In the O.T., God's love for Israel has elements of desire, just as the N.T. assumes that the only true fulfillment of man's E. is to be found in the divine being who is A. (See Ethics, Christian; Ethics, Contextual; God; Grace;

Justice; *Koinonia*; Perfection, Christian; Righteousness of God; Sanctification.)

Agathology. The inquiry into the nature of the good. (See Ethics, Christian; Ethics, Social; Natural Law; Perfection, Christian; *Summum Bonum.*)

Agnosticism means generally the denial of the possibility of knowledge and is, therefore, usually synonymous with skepticism. Since knowledge is a sweeping word that embraces numerous different kinds of statements and claims, A. is more usually found to be a rejection of some specific type of claim (historical, ethical, religious) rather than a rejection of the possibility of knowledge as such. Since the rise of modern science, the most common and pervasive A. has been concerning the possibility of knowing anything not capable of scientific description and verification, hence skepticism about the knowledge of GOD, the self, moral values, etc. (see Positivism). Sometimes this A. is a deeply felt skepticism about all religious claims, but sometimes it is but a theoretical A. and may actually go hand in hand with religious conviction or belief. One frequently finds, for example, a very sophisticated theoretical A. used by some philosophers and theologians as a justification for making certain claims "on FAITH." In this sense, A. need not to be equated with unfaith. Such a theological or philosophical defense was quite characteristic of Prot. THEOLOGY in the 19th century. Theology, it was argued, is not a knowledge of a supernatural object so much as it is (1) the analysis of man's religious affections for an ineffable reality (Schleiermacher, 1768-1834), (2) the clarification of man's ultimate value judgments (Ritschl, 1822-89), or (3) the analysis of an individual's EXISTENTIAL commitments (Kierkegaard, 1813-55).

Agrapha. Generally, unwritten words or sayings; more specifically, those words and sayings of Jesus not contained in the canonical writings.

Alienation. A term often used by Prot. theologians influenced by EXISTENTIALISM to refer to the estrangement of the self

15

from itself, others, and GOD; hence a synonym for the consequences of unfaith or sin. The word has a history in 19th-century German idealistic philosophy, especially in Hegel (1770-1831), Feuerbach (1804-72), and Karl Marx (1818-83). (See Authentic Existence; Conscience; Existentialism; Faith; Fallenness.)

Allegorical Interpretation is a type of EXEGESIS that minimizes the literal or plain meaning of a text in favor of an alleged and hidden spiritual meaning. The Apostle Paul practiced it when he interpreted the story of the two sons of Abraham to be a symbolic depiction of the two COVENANTS. The method was widely used in ancient and medieval times to interpret difficult passages in the O.T. Some typical examples of A.I. are: (1) when passages in the O.T. are believed to refer to Christ and the CHURCH; (2) when they are believed to be concerned with the SOUL and its VIRTUES; (3) when they are believed to refer to heavenly realities of different sorts. The Prot. Reformers rejected A.I. and this attitude persists among contemporary Prot. exegetes. (See Accommodation; Biblical Criticism; Exegesis; Hermeneutics.)

Altruism. As contrasted to egoism, or self-centeredness, A. denotes a selfless concern for the well-being of others. The term was used by certain militant humanistic writers in the 19th century, especially Comte (1798-1857), to refer to a selfless devotion to humanity for its own sake, and, hence, was also to be contrasted with Christian CHARITY, which had a supernatural or theological meaning. (See *Agape* and *Eros*.)

Analogy, Way of (*via analogia*), refers to a particular way of attributing characteristics to GOD that has played an important role in R.C. THEOLOGY in particular and in philosophical theology and APOLOGETICS in general. The significance of this role may be seen when it is understood that the theory of A. has been regarded as providing the answer to two knotty theological questions: (1) How can one make significant statements about the infinite in concepts that are derived from the finite? (2) How can one draw inferences about the nature of the Creator from the created, and thus provide the basis for a NATURAL THEOLOGY that requires no special appeal to REVELATION?

The first question may be put in the form of a dilemma: either the predicates we apply to God are applied in exactly the same way that we apply them in experience (univocally), in which case we in effect deny that God is different in kind from the creatures, or the predicates we apply to God are applied to him in a different way than we apply them in experience (equivocally), in which case we do not know what the meaning of our language is. If, for example, we say that God is wise, we mean either that he is wise in the same sense this word has in our experience (in which case we deny that there is any difference between human and divine WISDOM), or the word is being used in a sense different from its normal one (in which case we can't be sure of what we are saying). The method of A. tries to avoid this dilemma by claiming that even though two things may be radically different, they may have such a relation or likeness to one another (an analogy of being or *analogia entis*) that terms applicable to one may be applied to another in a related though not identical, hence analogical, fashion.

The second use of A. does not merely seek to establish that theological concepts have a significant meaning; it is used as a basis for inferences about the divine nature. Because of the alleged likeness of the creatures to the Creator, it is said that the human mind can reason from the nature of the effects (creatures) to the nature of the cause (Creator). Thus, the A. of being (*analogia entis*) is a crucial factor in a natural theology or theological apologetics. If, for example, person-ality is regarded as the highest manifestation of BEING, then it has been alleged to follow that personality provides the best analogue for the nature of God.

The doctrine of A. was made into a fine theological tool in the medieval period, especially by Thomas Aquinas (*c*.1225-74) and his successors. Thomas distinguished between two types of A.: (1) the A. of proportion, (2) the A. of proportion-ality. By the former, Thomas meant that, by virtue of the likeness (A. of being) between two subjects, predicates applied to one of them could be applied in a slightly different but related sense to the other. By the latter, Thomas meant that a similarity of relationship exists between two pairs of things so that the same term may be used of this relationship; for example, vision stands in relation to the eye as intellectual understanding stands in relation to the mind, so that the word "see" is appropriate in both cases. An already technical issue is confused somewhat by the fact that the first type of A. is often called by later scholars the "A. of attribution" while the second is called the "A. of proportion." At any rate, the important point is that A. rests on the presupposition that the creatures bear a sufficient likeness to God so that the perfections or attributes of the former may be applied in an eminent way to the latter; for example, although God's wisdom eminently exceeds man's wisdom, nevertheless, enough likeness exists to justify applying the word "wise" in its perfect sense to God and in a secondary imperfect sense to man. So, too, one may say "God exists," even though God's EXISTENCE is of a different sort than man's existence, because there is an A. between the two types of being.

The doctrine of A. was a matter of considerable debate among non-R.C. philosophers of religion in the 18th and 19th centuries. Those philosophers under the influence of Immanuel Kant (1724-1804) tended to argue that the finite mind is utterly incapable of knowing the nature of the ABSOLUTE, and they based their apologetics, as far as they were inclined to defend the Christian faith, on philosophical skepticism. Other philosophers under the influence of Hegel (1770-1831) and the idealists thought that mind or reason provided the crucial A. for understanding the nature of God.

The doctrine of A. has once again been vigorously attacked by the Prot. theologian Karl Barth (1886-), who sees it as the crucial point at issue between Prot.s and R.C.s. In order to understand his rejection of A., it is necessary to keep in mind the two different questions A. is supposed to answer, which were distinguished at the beginning of this article: (1) How is it possible to make significant statements about God? (2) How can one make inferences about the nature of the Creator from the created and thus have a natural

18

theology? Barth objects to the second use of A., i.e., as the basis for a natural theology. His objections are complex, but he thinks there is no basis for believing that God bears a likeness to man except the FAITH in the revelation in Jesus Christ. He argues, then, that one cannot honestly base a natural theology, which professes not to make an appeal to revelation, on a concept that is itself derived from revelation. Furthermore, he argues that when theologians try to do this they create an intolerable division between a general knowledge of deity and the knowledge of his action as revealed in Jesus Christ. Barth, therefore, argues for an A. of faith (*analogia fidei*), but deplores the *analogia entis* as the basis for a natural theology. (See Apologetics; Attributes of God; Being; God; Natural Theology; Perfection, Theological; Proofs for the Existence of God; Theism.)

Analytic Philosophy designates not so much a school of philosophy characterized by a shared body of systematic doctrine and belief as it does a widespread and common conviction concerning the proper aims of philosophy and the method to be used to attain those aims. It is currently the dominant philosophy in England and has had a great impact on America. Traditionally, the aim of philosophy has been synthetic, to construct a comprehensive account of human experience and reality, a world view or *Weltanschauung*, and philosophers have employed many methods to secure that aim. More recently, philosophers have argued that the aim of philosophy is not to establish such a *Weltanschauung* but to clarify the logical status of the various kinds of utterances human beings make and to eliminate the PARADOXES and confusions arising when the limits and function of language are not observed. The method of such a philosophy is analysis, the painstaking clarification of the crucial words and phrases used in any field (science, common sense, ethics, religion) in order to see how those words and phrases normally function. Since the claims human beings make are varied and can be classified in different ways, the subject matter of A.P. is also correspondingly varied. It is this that forms the point of contact between A.P. and Christian THEOLOGY, for these philosophers have been increasingly interested in the meaning and use of theological terms. What does it mean to say, for example, that GOD is merciful? Is this the same kind of claim as "the king is just"? If analysis shows that it is not—that in the one case "just" functions to describe a set of conditions an alternative to which can be imagined, whereas "merciful" used in this way does not so function—then what kind of a claim is it? Are there any rules to control the use of "merciful"? What problems arise by using "merciful" in this way? Under what conditions would one be willing to admit such an assertion to be false? In short, what is the logic of such religious claims? A.P. poses the difficult question whether there are any means of controlling theological discourse and of providing some norms for settling theological disputes. For this reason, A.P. is increasingly making an impact on the younger Prot. theologians in America.

Anathema. In the history of the Christian CHURCH since the 4th century, this Greek word has been used to refer to the exclusion of heretics from the community of the faithful. Sometimes it has been distinguished from the term "excommunication," although for most purposes they coincide. Among R.C. theologians there are differences of opinion concerning the effects and finality of A., which, in turn, reflect deeper differences concerning the nature of the church. The term has not been of great importance in Protestantism, although this is not to say that early Prot.s tolerated heretics. St. Paul seems to have used the term (Gal. 1:8; I Cor. 16:22) in the less specific sense of calling down the wrath of GOD on the heads of the faithless. It does not seem to suggest specific disciplinary measures or ceremonies as in later practice. (See Apostasy; Blasphemy; Dogma; Heresy; Schism.)

Angelology is that part of Christian THEOLOGY devoted to clarifying and systematizing belief concerning the EXISTENCE, nature, and various functions of supernatural beings called angels. The term "angel" comes from the Greek word meaning messenger, and this name was given to the heavenly beings that were believed to be intermediaries between GOD and man. In the earliest strata of the O.T., the comparable Hebrew word may have been a way of speaking of what was believed to be an appearance of God himself in human form. At any rate, there are enough allusions to such intermediary beings throughout the O.T. to support the conclusion that the existence of such beings was a widely held popular belief. Some scholars argue that this belief reflects the influence of non-Hebraic religion. Sometimes angels are called "sons of God" or "heavenly hosts" or "God's ministers." Many diverse functions are attributed to them. This popular Jewish belief naturally carried over into the N.T. Most theologians of the early CHURCH were so preoccupied with christological and theological problems that they did little to refine and develop the doctrine, and the first really major work on the topic was *On the Celestial Hierarchy* by Pseudo-Dionysius the Areopagite (fl. A.D. 500). He developed an elaborate system of degrees and ranks of angelic powers that was very influential on later medieval theology. Medieval theologians debated at great length whether angels were composed of both form and matter, constituted a species, possessed IMMORTALITY, and were capable of occupying space or not. Although A. has been a part of traditional Christian teaching, it is notable that Roman Catholicism has not made any important doctrinal pronouncements on the matter. Prot.s, except for some fundamentalists, have tended to ignore the issue. Karl Barth (1886-) is perhaps the only contemporary Prot. theologian who has reflected systematically on this issue, and this part of his thought is often regarded as "quaint" by Prot. theologians otherwise impressed by his work.

Anhypostasis. A technical term denoting the christological theory which claims that the divine LOGOS assumed human nature in general but was not incarnate in a real, concrete, individual man. The human nature was abstract or logical rather than individual and concrete, hence the phrase "the impersonal humanity of Christ." The position is often attributed to Cyril of Alexandria (*c.*376-444) and is said to have been anticipated by Apollinaris, whose teaching was condemned in A.D. 381. Modern versions of this ancient view are alleged to be found in the works of some modern Prot. theologians, i.e., Leonard Hodgson (1889-) and Emil Brunner (1889-). (See Apollinarianism; Christology; Docetism; *Enhypostasis*; Hypostatic Union; *Kenosis*; *Logos*; Monophysitism; Nestorianism.)

Animism. The belief that all natural phenomena are possessed of SOULS or SPIRITS that animate them and explain their special characteristics.

Annihilationism. A view that the SOULS of the wicked are not everlastingly punished in HELL but are, rather, destroyed or annihilated. This doctrine appeared to some 19th-century philosophers of religion as a happy compromise between eternal damnation, which seemed to prejudice the redemptive love of GOD, and UNIVERSALISM, which seemed to prejudice the freedom of man to reject that love. The presupposition of this view is that the IMMORTALITY of the soul is a gift and not intrinsic. The theory was condemned by the Fifth Lateran Council in 1513. (See *Apocatastasis*; Conditional Immortality; Eschatology; Hades; Hell; Immortality; Intermediate State; Judgment, Final; Limbo; Purgatory; Resurrection of the Dead; Soul.)

Antelapsarianism. See Predestination.

Anthropocentric. An adjective frequently used to characterize any type of philosophy, THEOLOGY, or theory of the universe in which man's needs or values are made the center.

Anthropology. Most generally, the science of which man, his biological origins and his cultural behavior, is an object. In THEOLOGY, it denotes that part dealing with man as a creature of GOD, what it means to say that he is made in the IMAGE OF GOD (*imago dei*), is free, and is a sinner. Christian theology, both R.C. and Prot., has been preoccupied with A. during the last century, partly because of the problems raised by the theory of evolution and by modern psychology, and partly because of the emergence of rival philosophies like Marxism, idealism, and EXISTENTIALISM, which also were attempts to come to terms with the implications of science for the understanding of man. R.C. theology was particularly concerned to combat the DETERMINISM implicit in Marx's (1818-83) views as well as the implication that the theory of evolution made the belief in man's possession of an immortal SOUL untenable. Prot. theology, especially NEO-REFORMED, was preoccupied with the denial of man's freedom, on the one hand, and the excessive optimism characteristic of liberalism and idealism, on the other. (See Authentic Existence; Conscience; Creationism; Depravity, Total; Determinism; Existentialism; Freedom of the Will; Historicity of Human Existence; Image of God; Natural Law; Sin, Actual; Sin, Original; Soul; Traducianism.)

Anthropomorphism. The attribution of human characteristics, activities, or emotions to GOD. Philosophical theologians, both R.C. and Prot., have traditionally argued that in so far as such language is used it is to be considered analogical or symbolical or metaphorical. (See Analogy, Way of; Attributes of God; God; Panentheism; Perfection, Theological; Person; Symbol.)

Anti-Christ is the word used by the author of the Johannine Epistles for those who deny Christ (I John 2:18-22; II John 7). This author can, therefore, speak of many A.s. The term early became identified with the demonic forces of evil that would appear shortly before the second coming or PAROUSIA of Christ and that were often personified. So understood, the term has played an important part in MILLENNIALISM, and the A. has at one time or another been identified with Caligula, Nero, ARIANISM, the Pope, Hitler, Stalin, and communism.

Antinomianism. On the grounds that the Christian is saved by GRACE and not by works or moral effort, some Christians have claimed that the saved man is free from all moral obligations or principles. The term is applied to this view. (See Casuistry; Conscience; Decalogue; Ethics, Christian;

Ethics, Contextual; Law and Gospel; Natural Law; Perfection, Christian; Sanctification; Social Gospel; Vocation.)

Antinomy is a technical term in the philosophy of Immanuel Kant (1724-1804) that designates two contradictory assertions both of which seem equally rational, e.g., (1) the world had a beginning in time and is finite, and (2) the world had no beginning in time and is infinite. Kant delineated four sets of such antinomies. The fact that the reason can legitimately defend both sides of an A. indicates, Kant argued, that the reason is functioning beyond its inherent limits. Furthermore, the fact that these antinomies have to do with metaphysical issues indicates that METAPHYSICS is attempting to resolve matters that are impossible for reason to do in the nature of the case. The upshot of Kant's argument was that reason is limited to dealing with sense experience and that metaphysics is impossible. This argument had a powerful influence on subsequent Prot. THEOLOGY, for it was taken for granted that metaphysics could be of no aid to theology. (See Paradox.)

Anxiety is a technical term in existential philosophy that has played an important role in the ANTHROPOLOGY of certain Prot. theologians, especially Rudolf Bultmann (1884-), Reinhold Niebuhr (1892-), and Paul Tillich (1886-). A. is regarded by these theologians as more than a passing psychological mood. It is viewed as the basic concomitant of being both finite and free in the way these are united in human EXISTENCE. Being aware of his finitude (his limitations and death) man is conscious of NON-BEING. Being aware of his ability to act (his freedom), man is conscious of the "non-being of possibility." Both occasion A. This basic or ontological A. is to be distinguished, Tillich insists, from neurotic or pathological A., which is an aberration of ontological A. FAITH is the courage to accept this A. and to use it creatively. The concept of A. was first used by Kierkegaard (1813-55) in his highly imaginative interpretation of the MYTH of Adam's fall, and the basic elements of this interpretation also appear in the writings of Reinhold Niebuhr and Tillich. (See Authentic Existence; Existence; Existentialism; Fallenness; Freedom of the Will; Sin, Original.)

Apocalyptic Literature. A genre of literature distinguished principally by its ascetic and mysterious allusions to the signs preceding the events to occur in the last days of world history. It usually is written in times of extreme persecution and suffering. Since A.L. was prevalent before and during the life of Jesus, it is thought to be extremely important as one of the keys to understanding the language and Messianic symbols of the N.T. writers, not to mention Jesus himself. In the O.T., the Book of Daniel is often classified in this genre, as is the Book of Revelation in the N.T. There are also A. elements in the prophetic books of the O.T. and in the Gospels in the N.T., e.g., Matt. 24, 25; Mark 13; Luke 21. (See Eschatology.)

Apocatastasis is a Greek word referring to the final and complete salvation of all beings. It suggests universal REDEMPTION or UNIVERSALISM. It is to be found in the works of those theologians, like Clement (*c.*150-*c.*215) and Origen (*c.*185-*c.*254) of Alexandria, who emphasized the perfection of the divine love and who could not believe that the wrath of GOD is the final expression of that love. Origen's teachings were later condemned. There are those who claim to detect the idea in the work of Karl Barth (1886-). (See Decrees, Eternal; Election; Eschatology; Immortality; Judgment, Final; Perfection, Christian; Predestination; Resurrection of the Dead; Soteriology.)

Apollinarianism. Specifically, the term refers to the christological beliefs of Apollinaris (fl. *c.*350) and his followers that were condemned at the Council of Constantinople in 381. The Apollinarians argued that the immutable and perfect BEING of GOD could have existed in union with the mutable and imperfect being of humanity in Jesus Christ only if that humanity had been present in an incomplete way. Employing the ancient conception that human nature was constituted by three principles, body, SOUL, and rational SPIRIT, they insisted that the body and soul of Jesus were human but that his rational spirit was replaced by the divine LOGOS. Generally, the term is applied somewhat loosely to those christological views that stress that the center of the human personality of Jesus was replaced by the divine LOGOS. (See *Anhypostasis*;

25

Christology; Docetism; *Enhypostasis*; Hypostatic Union; *Kenosis*; *Logos*; Monophysitism; Nestorianism.)

Apologetics traditionally denotes the reasoned defense of the Christian religion against intellectual objections, the attempt to establish certain elements of that FAITH as true or, at least, not demonstrably untrue. In Roman Catholicism, A. has usually assumed the form called NATURAL THEOLOGY, which has as its function the PROOFS FOR THE EXISTENCE OF GOD. In revealed theology, a R.C. theologian is required only to demonstrate that the supernatural doctrines are not irrational. A. has assumed many forms in Protestantism: the argumentation for the existence of God, the recommendation of religion as the enhancement of human life, the defense of the Bible against its critics, and the attack against secular views of man and his nature. In contemporary NEO-REFORMED THEOLOGY, the term "A.," in so far as it denotes the attempt to establish THEISM as true, has fallen into disrepute, although this same theology has itself often been characterized by the aggressive attempt to show the relevance of the SYMBOLS of Christian faith for the understanding of life. (See Analogy, Way of; Attributes of God; Culture, Theology of; Demythologization; Metaphysics; Natural Theology; Philosophy of Religion; Theism.)

Apostasy comes from the Greek word meaning "to desert a post" and refers generally to the abandonment of Christianity for unbelief. (See Anathema; Blasphemy; Dogma; Heresy; Schism.)

Apostolicity is one of the traditional marks or NOTES of the true CHURCH along with unity, holiness, and catholicity. The so-called CATHOLIC communions (R.C., E.O., and to some extent, Anglican) interpret A. to mean an unbroken continuity with the original apostles in doctrine, tradition, and church order, a continuity preserved by an unbroken succession of bishops. Prot.s generally interpret A. to mean a continuity of message, of the Gospel, with the apostles, and, therefore, not necessarily preserved by an unbroken ecclesiastical structure.

(See Church; Dogma; Ecumenical; *Ekklesia*; *Koinonia*; Laity; Notes of the Church; Protestant Principle; Sacrament; Word of God.)

Apotheosis refers to the deification of a mortal at some point in his life. It was believed, for example, that certain Roman emperors became divine when they assumed their thrones.

Appropriations. R.C. and Prot. Scholastic theologians have traditionally argued that the only real distinctions between the PERSONS of the TRINITY consist in their relationships to one another. The relationship of paternity, for example, distinguishes the Father from the Son and the Holy Spirit, and the relationship of FILIATION distinguishes the Son from the Father and the Spirit, and the relationship of spiration distinguishes the Holy Spirit from the Father and the Son. Because all three persons possess one common ESSENCE, however, all ATTRIBUTES and activities of GOD (OMNISCIENCE, OMNIPRESENCE, CREATION, REDEMPTION, SANCTIFICATION) are shared by all three. Nevertheless, piety often feels it appropriate to ascribe some property or character to one of the persons that really belongs to all three, i.e., one person appropriates some quality that is common to all. A. may be classified in three ways: (1) those having to do with God's internal nature apart from his activities, (2) those having to do with God's activities, and (3) those having to do with God's effects. Since tradition has also held that each person of the Trinity shares fully in all of the divine works (in Latin, *opera trinitatis ad extra indivisa sunt*), a doctrine of A. seems to reduce itself finally to a theory of the relationships within the divine nature, i.e., the doctrine of PROCESSIONS. (See Filiation; *Filioque*; Generation; *Logos*; Modalism; Monarchianism; *Perichoresis*; Person; Procession; Spirit–Holy Spirit; Subordinationism; Trinity.)

Arianism. Strictly, the term refers to the christological theories of Arius (*c*.250–*c*.336), a priest at Alexandria, which were condemned as heretical at the First Council of Nicaea in A.D. 325 and again at the First Council of Constantinople in 381. These views and the subsequent debate concerning them shook the Roman Empire for over half a century and badly divided the churches.

Arius' views can only be reconstructed from a few remaining fragments and the writings of his opponents. He seems to have argued that since only GOD the Father may be said to be the absolute, unbegotten, eternal Unity (Monad), the "only begotten Son" is in some sense subordinate and inferior because derived from the absolute Unity. This inferior or subordinate nature of the Son or LOGOS was expressed in the Arian formula "there was a time when the Son was not." By this Arius did not mean that the Son was a mutable creature among the other creatures; on the other hand, he could not say that the Son was essentially divine. Consequently, the *Logos* was regarded as a sort of intermediate being who was neither fully divine nor fully a creature. The anti-Arians believed that this view attributed salvation to a half-divine, half-creaturely being.

Constantine, the emperor, called a council to deal with the issue, and after considerable and often unseemly debate a creedal statement was agreed upon by the majority. This creed asserted that the Son of God was "true God from true God," of "one ESSENCE or BEING (HOMOOUSION) with the Father," the latter phrase being unacceptable to the strict Arians, who insisted that the Son was not of one essence with the Father. To this creed, some ANATHEMAS were added against those who said that "there was a time when he was not" or that "the eternal Son is a creature." Arius and two others refused to sign the creed and were excommunicated and banished by the emperor. After a few years and for complex reasons, Arian sentiment returned, until in 336 Arius was restored to communion with the CHURCH and the orthodox leader, Athanasius (*c*.295-373), was forced into exile. The Arian party then began to proliferate creedal statements among which three distinct christological positions are discernible: (1) the Anomoean (from the Greek word meaning "dissimilar"), which affirmed that the Son was unlike the Father; (2) the Homoean (meaning "similar"), which affirmed that the Son is similar to the Father; (3) the Homoiousian (meaning "like in essential being"), which affirmed that the Son was like the Father in essential being but was not identical in being (*homoousion*). After the death of the Arian emperor, Constantius, Athanasius was able to reconcile the Homoiousian and the orthodox (*homoousion*) party, and this culminated finally in 381 with the reaffirmation of the original Nicene Creed by the Council of Constantinople.

The term "A.," like many other terms arising out of specific historical situations, has accrued a more general meaning and is often used to denote any christological view that subordinates the *Logos* to God the Father. (See Christology; Docetism; Ebionite; *Homoousion*; *Hypostasis*; *Logos*; Person; Subordinationism; Trinity; Wisdom.)

Arminianism. Strictly understood, A. refers to the doctrines of Jacob Arminius (1560-1609), a Dutch Reformed theologian and professor at Leyden. More loosely understood, it refers to those views that stress the ability of man to respond to divine GRACE. Chosen to refute the idea that GOD elects some men to be damned, Arminius himself became convinced that this doctrine inevitably makes God the author of sin. Skilled in argument and dialectic as well as being a man of exemplary character, Arminius attracted a large following. They set forward their views in a document known as *The Remonstrance* (1610). This document rejects the five main points of Calvinist teaching and sets forward five alternative doctrines. It rejects (1) supralapsarian PREDESTINATION, (2) infralapsarian predestination, (3) the idea of a limited ATONEMENT (that Christ died only for the elect), (4) the idea of IRRESISTIBLE GRACE, and (5) the doctrine of necessary PERSEVERANCE. Positively, the document asserts that the unconditional decree of God establishes the principle that whoever believes on Jesus Christ will be saved, and not that some particular men will be saved and others damned. Second, it affirms that the atonement was intended for all men, not in the sense that all men inevitably will be saved (UNIVERSALISM) but in the sense that salvation is possible in principle for all men. Third, it declares that man is not saved by his own efforts or without the grace of God working in him. Fourth, it says that this grace is not irresistible but that it is possible for men to reject it. Finally, it states that the question whether grace once granted can be lost requires further study and discussion.

A synod was called to meet at Dort in order to deal with the Remonstrants. Those delegates with Arminian views were refused seats. Not surprisingly, the Arminian position was condemned and a form of "single" predestination affirmed, i.e., the view that from all ETERNITY God willed that some should be elected to salvation while the remainder are simply "passed over."

Many historians of doctrine see the significance of A. to lie in its attempt to think through the relationship between God and man in personal terms. At any rate, Arminian views had a profound effect on the subsequent development of Prot. thought, especially on evangelical theologians such as John Wesley (1703-91). (See Decrees, Eternal; Election; Perseverance; Predestination.)

Articuli Fidei Fundamentalis refers to those doctrines which traditional THEOLOGY held must be believed if one were to gain eternal salvation. (See Faith; Revelation.)

Articuli Fidei Mixti refers to those doctrines which are derived partly from REVELATION and partly from one's natural knowledge of GOD.

Articuli Fidei Puri means literally "articles of pure faith" and in classical THEOLOGY refers to those doctrines believed to be supernaturally revealed. (See Faith; Revelation.)

Ascension refers to departure of the Christ into heaven after his resurrection. Traditionally, the A. was believed to have taken place forty days after the resurrection and so was regarded as a distinct event, this being the account given in the Book of Acts (1:3-11). However, other passages in the N.T. (Acts 2:32 f.; Rom. 8:34; Eph. 1:20; Phil. 2:9; Col. 3:1; I Tim. 3:16; I Pet. 3:22) indicate that the resurrection and the A. may originally have been regarded as the same event, although each term had a different emphasis in meaning. The resurrection points to the victory over death, the A. to the exaltation of Christ to "the right hand of the Father." Traditionally, the exaltation has had several meanings: (1) that the exalted Christ is the priestly advocate who intercedes on behalf of the faithful; (2) that Christ shares in the sovereignty of the Father; (3) that no earthly authority can exhaustively represent Christ, since he is free. The issue concerning the mode of Christ's presence with the Father became a matter of controversy between Calvinists and Lutherans in the debate over the EUCHARIST, the former insisting on a circumscribed local existence of Christ in heaven, the latter insisting that Christ was ubiquitous. (See Consubstantiation.) Modern Prot. theologians tend to regard this controversy as an irrelevant speculative issue and interpret the exaltation as a SYMBOL for the confession "Christ lives," that is, that Jesus of Nazareth has been designated as the eternal WORD OF GOD and that the power of GOD is the power of Jesus Christ set free from the limitations of time and space. (See Christology; *Communicatio Idiomatum*; Consubstantiation; Eucharist; *Logos*; *Parousia*; Real Presence; Resurrection of Christ; Trinity; Word of God.)

Aseity. A characteristic of being self-derived in contrast to being derived from or dependent on another, hence predicable only of GOD in classical THEOLOGY. It is a technical term for the judgment that the EXISTENCE of God is necessary in contrast to CONTINGENT. Karl Barth (1886-) interprets A. as the freedom of God. (See *Actus Purus*; Attributes of God; *Causa Sui*; God; Necessary Being; Ontological Argument; Perfection, Theological; Theism.)

Assent. See Faith.

Assumption comes from the Latin word meaning "to take to" and refers to the bodily ascension of some PERSON into heaven. Enoch, an ancient Hebrew patriarch, as well as Elijah and Moses, was often said to have undergone assumption. In 1950, the A. of the Virgin Mary was proclaimed to be a R.C. DOGMA.

Assurance has traditionally referred to the confidence of the believer that he is a recipient of GOD's redemptive GRACE. In Roman Catholicism, grace is so bound up with the SACRAMENTS that this problem of confidence does not arise as it does in Protestantism, which puts such an emphasis on personal FAITH. Luther (1483-1546) insisted that because faith is confidence in God's graciousness in Jesus Christ, it is accompanied by an experience of joy and the certitude of one's salvation (*certitudo salutis*), and he contrasted this with having confidence in one's works. Nevertheless, Luther did not regard faith as a static certainty but as something to be renewed every day against doubts and temptations. When speaking in this context, Luther wrote as if faith could not be identified with a feeling of A. To doubt this, however, inevitably raised the more insidious doubt that one's feeling of A. was not valid. Calvin (1509-64), even more than Luther, permitted a gulf to exist between A. and one's actual ELECTION to eternal life, because Calvin contended that some people who felt assured of their faith were actually only enlightened "for a season" and would slip away into damnation. This observation could not avoid raising in the believer's mind the question of whether his subjective confidence of faith was really evidence of a genuine election or not, and this haunting doubt permeates much Calvinist piety. John Wesley (1703-91), especially in his early writings, attacked this Calvinistic idea and insisted that A. is the confidence in the pardon of one's sins and inevitably accompanies true faith. In fact, lacking this confidence, one cannot be sure of having received God's favor. Wesley later modified his views, recognizing degrees of faith and corresponding degrees of A., but the doctrine of A. tended to become a hallmark of Methodism. Later Methodists tended to so broaden the idea of A. that it pertained not only to the confidence of forgiveness but to the certitude that one had read the Scriptures properly or had the correct doctrinal beliefs or had acted morally. (See Election; Faith; Infusion; Justification; Perfection, Christian; Perseverance; Sanctification.)

Atheism is a term designating the denial of the EXISTENCE of deity. Its concrete meaning, therefore, varies widely, depending on the accepted conception of deity. If the word "god" is used to refer to one transcendent, perfect, and personal subject, then A. will include all those systems (PANTHEISM and polytheism) that, though professing belief in the existence of a divine principle, deny the existence of a personal god. On the other hand, if the word "god" is used in its broadest possible sense, then A. will be strictly limited to the denial of the existence of any principle or being worthy to be called divine. This wide range of usage accounts for why the term "atheist" has been employed at one time or another in history as a charge against Socrates, Christians, Jews, pantheists, deists, and Marxists. In Western culture since Constantine, where THEISM has been the predominant theological tradition, A. has been often applied to the theoretical denial of the existence of a transcendent source of goodness and WISDOM, hence to unbelief in the Christian god. In so far as Christian FAITH has been identified with assent or theoretical belief, A. has been regarded as sin. In so far as faith has been regarded as one's deepest commitment, however, theoretical A. has been regarded less seriously, and a distinction has been made between a theoretical and a practical A. In this view a professed Christian believer could be a practical atheist, while a theoretical atheist might be a practical believer.

Atonement. Generally, the term refers to the reconciliation (at-one-ment) of two parties. In Christian THEOLOGY, it refers to the restoration of the broken relationship between GOD and man that was accomplished in the life and death of Jesus Christ. So understood, the concept belongs to SOTERI-OLOGY. How the state of estrangement is to be conceived and how it can be overcome has been variously interpreted in the history of Christian thought, and it is interesting that there exists no DOGMA of the A. as there does a dogma of the INCARNATION.

The SYMBOLS used by the earliest Christian community were naturally rooted in Hebraic religious practice, especially sacrifice. The sacrificial ritual was believed to be ordained by God so that the believer might participate in and realize the forgiveness of Yahweh. The sinner seeking reconciliation laid his hand upon the head of the sacrificial animal, signifying his own identification with it. In the shedding of the blood, the sinner symbolized the giving up of his own life. The blood was taken into the Holy of Holies, the offering burned and the meat eaten, once again signifying identification with the sacrificial victim. In calling Jesus the "lamb slain from the foundation of the world," the early Christians expressed their understanding that the sinner must become identified with the life and death of Jesus Christ. In so far as this sacrificial system was presupposed, it is doubtful if the idea that the victim was paying a penalty on behalf of the sinner was at all important. Nor was the idea that an angry God must be appeased significant. The word PROPITIATION probably refers to the mercy seat or covering of the Ark which was the place of propitiation, i.e., where God's mercy was disclosed.

In the history of Christian thought, there have been three main ways of conceiving of the A. (1) Man is regarded as enslaved by sin, death, and the devil, all of which are regarded as objective powers. God in Christ accomplishes the work of defeating these powers. Gustaf Aulen (1879-), who calls this view the "classical view," insists that the crucial idea here is that God himself is the chief actor in the drama and that the reconciliation does not take place from man's side. Aulen thinks this view was characteristic of the early Greek Fathers, Paul, and Luther (1483-1546). (2) The disobedience of man is regarded as nothing less than an affront to the infinite majesty or honor of God. Such an affront requires an infinite SATISFACTION. But since no creature can offer such a satisfaction, God himself must offer it, although in the form of a man, since it is on behalf of man. God becomes man in order to satisfy his own offended honor. This view is closely identified with the thought of St. Anselm (1033-1109). It has been determinative so far as R.C. and Prot. ORTHODOXY are concerned, although in the latter tradition a penal element is added and stressed, i.e., Christ is believed to have taken upon himself the punishment properly due man and thus satisfied God's just demands. (3) The basic problem of man is how he can be freed from the fear of God and respond personally to God's love. This is made possible, this view argues, by the embodiment of God's sacrificial love in the life and passion of Christ, an event which grasps the imagination and moves the heart in a way no transaction or doctrine can do. This theory is often identified with Abélard (1079-1142) and is somewhat unfairly called the "moral influence" theory. (See Faith; Grace; Imputation; *Kerygma*; Law and Gospel; Patripassianism; Propitiation; Recapitulation; Satisfaction; Soteriology; Theopaschites.)

Attributes of God. An attribute in general is a defining characteristic of a thing, and the A.O.G. refer to those characteristics uniquely applicable to the divine being. The means of arriving at the A.O.G. as well as classifying them have been the object of much theological controversy and discussion. Two classical ways of arriving at the A.O.G. have been (1) the way of negation (*via negativa*), (2) the WAY OF ANALOGY (*via analogia*), of which there are several variations: the analogy of being (*analogia entis*), the analogy of faith (*analogia fidei*) and the way of eminence (*via eminentia*), which is really a form of *analogia entis*. The way of negation tries to specify what God's nature is by stating what GOD is not. By ridding the idea of God of all finite characteristics, it is believed that some meaningful positive idea can be reached. For example, God is not complex, therefore absolutely simple; God is not finite, therefore infinite; not in time, therefore eternal; not subject to change, therefore immutable; not spatially limited, therefore omnipresent; not caused, therefore possesses ASEITY. The way of analogy is discussed elsewhere. Some theologians have divided the A.O.G. into the metaphysical and moral; others have distinguished between those which apply to God apart from his relation to the world and those having to do with this relation to it. Some claim no real distinction can be made between the A.O.G.; others argue that only in the light of such distinctions is an intelligible idea of God at all possible. (See *Actus Purus*; Analogy, Way of; Being; God; Immensity; Natural Revelation; Omniscience; Omnipotence; Panentheism; Pantheism; Perfection, Theological; Theism.)

Attrition is regarded by R.C. theologians as an imperfect sorrow for sin in that, unlike contrition, it does not proceed from the love of GOD but from the fear of HELL or the loss of heaven. The Council of Trent (1545-63) declared that although A. is an impulse from the Holy Spirit it alone does not serve to justify the sinner. The interpretation of this declaration has been the subject of debate among R.C. theologians. Most of them now hold that A. together with the SACRAMENT of penance is sufficient to secure pardon.

Authentic Existence is a somewhat technical term in EXISTENTIALISM and theological literature influenced by it. It refers to the specifically human possibility of being able to resolve to be oneself in certain fundamental situations. For example, although death is the universal fact, *how* one chooses to face death may be either authentic or unauthentic. Or again, life in relationship to others is a structure of all human EXISTENCE, but *how* one understands and chooses to be with others is either authentic or unauthentic. Choice or decision, therefore, is the necessary condition for selfhood, and how one chooses determines the kind of self one will be in the moment. A great deal of existentialist philosophy is devoted to analyses of the two possibilities of authenticity and unauthenticity as they appear in the fundamental BOUNDARY SITUATIONS that qualify human existence. Although Martin Heidegger (1889-) and his interpreters insist that A.E. is not to be equated with what theologians call FAITH, some theologians have insisted that faith cannot be viewed merely as one form of authenticity but must be considered A.E. itself. (See Anxiety; Conscience; Existence; Existentialism; Fallenness; Faith; Historicity of Human Existence; Phenomenology; Self-Understanding.)

Autonomy. See Heteronomy.

Axiology is that part of philosophy having to do with the EXISTENCE, nature, and criteria of value. It attempts to answer such questions as: (1) What constitutes anything as valuable? (2) What are the various types of value? (3) Are there any objective criteria by means of which values can be arranged on a scale or a conflict of value adjudicated? (4) What is the relation of value to BEING?

B

Baptism is derived from the Greek word *baptizein*, which means "to be dipped," and is the initiatory rite and SACRAMENT of the Christian CHURCH. The origins of B. are obscure, but by the time of the writing of Paul's letters in the N.T., it is plain that it already was established as a Christian practice. The original mode of B. was probably immersion. Because it involved a direct threat to life by drowning and a sudden deliverance from this death, it was a powerful SYMBOL of the structure of FAITH, of being buried with Christ (the dying of the old man) and of being raised to new life (the birth of the new man).

Theological controversy has surrounded the sacrament of B. almost from the beginning. Three such controversial issues, all related, are worth touching upon: (1) whether the B. performed by heretical churches or ministers should be acknowledged to be valid; (2) whether B. has some intrinsic potency, and if so, what; (3) whether children should be baptized. The first problem arose in the 3rd century and again in the 4th with the Donatist controversy. It was finally decided, and it remained as part of R.C. teaching, that so long as the proper form and matter of B. are present, it is valid regardless of the worthiness or the views of the minister involved. This solution presupposed (2) that B. in itself has some special potency or power. In general, Roman Catholicism holds that to be the power of conveying SANCTIFYING OR HABITUAL GRACE, which removes the stain and guilt of ORIGINAL SIN, and entitles the baptized person to further graces. This constitutes, in turn (3) the reason for baptizing infants, for without B. they are not participants in sanctifying grace nor have they been regenerated.

The Prot. Reformers rejected the R.C. view of sacramental grace because they believed it alien to the Biblical teaching concerning JUSTIFICATION through faith. On the one hand, Luther (1483-1546) and Calvin (1509-64) wanted to say that B. had some intrinsic power, but, on the other hand, they wanted to make sure that this power was conceived as the power of the WORD OF GOD, the aim of which was to awaken faith. In emphasizing the first point, Luther occasionally argued that B. was necessary for salvation and that the Holy Spirit effects REGENERATION through B. When emphasizing the second point, however, he could write that "B. is no more than an outward sign that the divine promise ought to admonish us. . . . If a man cannot have it or refuses it, he is not condemned, so long as he believes the Gospel. For where the Gospel is, there is B. and all else that a Christian man needs." The tension between these two emphases is most clearly seen in the Reformers' attempt to justify infant B. For in what sense is it intelligible to talk about an infant's faith in the Reformers' sense of that word? Luther's effort to justify it is plainly inconsistent with his central position. Calvin appealed to the covenantal idea that the children of believers were sanctified by their parents. The problem of infant B. versus "believers B." has continued to plague Protestantism. Karl Barth (1886-) has argued that the entire THEOLOGY of the sacraments needs rethinking in the light of evangelical principles. He says that the power of the sacrament lies in the fact that as an element in the churches' message it is a "free word and deed of Jesus Christ Himself." B., then, sums up the entire movement of sacred history. But this does not mean that because the church is required to perform it the power of Jesus Christ is dependent on it. B., as such, has no intrinsic power, and R.C., Lutheran, and Anglican attempts to say that it does, Barth argues, finally obscure the freedom of GOD. B. is no cause of redemption; it should be the recognition and seal of its true basis. Given this understanding, Barth offers powerful arguments against the practice of infant B. Oscar Cullmann (1902-), a N.T. scholar, has tried to refute these. (See Church; Covenantal Theology; *Ekklesia*; Eucharist; *Ex Opere Operato*; Faith; Grace; Protestant Principle; Sacrament; Word of God.)

Beatific Vision refers to the unhindered and immediate vision of GOD that traditionally has been viewed as the ultimate destiny of the redeemed. It plays an important role in R.C. doctrine and its nature and conditions were matters of deep concern and discussion in medieval times. Although Prot. theologians, on the whole, have retained the notion, they have denied that the B.V. is merited and, therefore, that there are degrees of final perfection. (See Eschatology; Faith; Immortality; Judgment, Final; Ontologism; Perfection, Christian.)

Being is perhaps the most important single concept in the history of Western philosophy; and yet no concept has been so debated or variously defined. For the metaphysician, B. is, in the last analysis, the object of all philosophy. For the critic of METAPHYSICS, B. is the most empty of all general concepts and one that ought to be abandoned.

The origins of the idea of B. and of the enterprise of metaphysics go back to the earliest Greek philosophers. B. was at first contrasted with becoming or change, it being believed that only what resisted change and decay could be said to be real and not illusory. Plato (*c.*427-347 B.C.) suggested, however, that B. is power, the power either to act or to be acted upon by something else. Aristotle (384-322 B.C.) modified this to read that B. (*ousia*) is activity (*energia*). This led both Plato and Aristotle into an exhaustive analysis, not always successful, of the relationships between the form, or pattern, of power and change, and between class names and their particular embodiments. They argued that for anything to be it had to be structured, and it was this structure or form that also made it capable of being talked about and, hence, conceptualized. There was, therefore, a very close connection between B. and being conceptualized, so close a relation that it is not difficult to misunderstand Plato as having said that only the conceptualizable is truly real.

In an effort to explain the primordial facts of B., i.e., form and motion and their peculiar unity, Plato was led to a THEOLOGY of sorts. He postulated a transcendent source of motion, a cosmic SOUL or *demiurge*, who molded and shaped the world in the light of certain eternal or intelligible patterns, much as a craftsman seeks to mold his clay into the form of his ideal for it. This general framework of ideas had a profound influence on early Christian philosophy and theology. But it was possible to read Plato in two different ways: (1) as saying that GOD was really the principle of form (the Form of the Good) who is so utterly transcendent as to be "beyond B. in dignity and power," as Socrates is made to say in *The Republic*; (2) as saying that God is the *demiurge* or cosmic soul or mind or reason which is the source of motion in the world. The latter view makes it possible to be a theist in a way the former does not. The Christian idea of God as creator complicated the matter. On the one hand, to say God is creator is to say that he is the fount of all B. and not just one being among other beings, and this idea seemed to make the first way of reading Plato most favorable to the Christian point of view. On the other hand, the cosmic mind or reason, who is spoken of as a soul, seemed to fit in well with the anthropomorphic language of the Bible. In the former view, God was the ineffable, transcendent one; in the latter view, he was the perfect, harmonious soul or spirit. In the ancient Christian world, these two basic ideas of God struggled with one another, and this struggle lies behind a number of controversies in the early CHURCH about the nature of God.

The idea of CREATION required, in effect, a distinction Greek philosophy did not make, a distinction between two radically different kinds of B., finite and infinite. The Scholastic theologians attempted this. Finite B. was characterized, they were fond of saying, by a discrepancy between ESSENCE and EXISTENCE, that is, no creature had as its very nature to be. Creatures came from nothing and would go to nothing. It was the very essence of God, on the other hand, to exist. God was B.-itself, the only one who could not not be. This idea was coupled with another: namely, that the essence of finitude was change or the passage from potentiality to ACTUALITY. Perfect B. (God) therefore, would have no potentiality or receptivity of any kind. Perfect B., in other words, was changeless B., an idea that hearkens back to earliest Greek thought. The difficulty with this concept is that it makes the Biblical language about a deity who creates, acts, wills, feels sympathy with, knows, and loves somewhat problematical, because all of these terms necessarily involve receptivity and the capacity to be affected, both of which are resolutely denied by Scholastic theologians. This language had either to be explained away as the language of piety or as analogical language, the language of piety not being fitted for precise theological use and analogical language always being so interpreted that it need not be taken strictly.

It is not surprising, therefore, that there were voices of protest against this identification of God with B.-itself. The classic protest against this identification is perhaps contained in Pascal's (1623-62) famous statement to the effect that his God was the God of Abraham, Isaac, and Jacob, not the God of the philosophers. The Prot. Reformers protested also, and their rejection of speculative metaphysics as a substitute for theology has been taken up again and again by other Prot. theologians, so much so that "Greek metaphysics" has often been tantamount to an epithet in that tradition. The rejection of the science of B. (ontology) as a vehicle for theology has particularly characterized liberal Prot. as well as neo-Reformed thought, although the work of Paul Tillich (1886-) constitutes a noteworthy exception. Tillich defines God as B.-itself.

It is difficult to avoid a metaphysics of one sort or another, however, even if one claims to reject the enterprise. Therefore, other philosophers have argued that it is not metaphysics as such which is at fault but the peculiar kind of metaphysics characteristic of the Western tradition. The difficulty with traditional metaphysics, it is argued, is that it makes God or infinite B. an exception to all the basic structures of our experience rather than the perfect exemplification of them. Instead of saying that God is perfect receptivity *and* activity, which are two poles exemplified in all B., receptivity is denied and only activity is affirmed by the classical tradition. What is required, therefore, it is argued, is a more adequate description of the structures of B. and what it means to say "God is B.-itself." (See Analogy, Way of; Creation; Essence; Existence; God; Metaphysics; Necessary Being; Ontological Argument; Perfection, Theological; Process Philosophy; Substance; Theism.)

Biblical Criticism is a name commonly but loosely applied to a type of historical inquiry that seeks answers to an extraordinary number of different kinds of questions: What are the most reliable and trustworthy texts of the O.T. and N.T.? What are the relationships between the various books? When and by whom were the texts written and for what purpose? What are the sources, if any, the authors used? What is the relationship of these sources to other oral and written materials of the time? What light does the use of the sources cast on the authors' purposes? What structure and style does the text have and what does it reveal about the beliefs and intentions of the author or about the community that used the text? What are the crucial ideas in the document? How are these ideas related to other ideas of the same sort in the cultural environment? To what degree are the historical reports reliable or true?

Any simple classification of such diverse questions as these will inevitably be inadequate and restrictive. To call those questions having to do with the authenticity of a text "lower criticism" and to lump all other questions under the rubric "higher criticism" is not very illuminating. It is also artificial to make a sharp differentiation between literary criticism (the analysis of the form and style and the uses of sources) and historical criticism (questions concerning the historical character of the work), because the analysis of the form, style, and sources of an author inevitably involves historical interpretation. It would be better, then, simply to acknowledge that B.C. involves numerous sorts of questions and correspondingly numerous sorts of ways of going about answering those questions.

Some of the questions noted above have been asked by Biblical scholars from the beginning of Christendom, and in this limited sense B.C. is not new. Nevertheless, B.C. in its precise sense is a product of the 18th and 19th centuries and is unintelligible apart from the development of modern secular historiography. In this sense, B.C. is simply the application of general historical principles to the Bible. This utilization of general historical principles, however, necessarily presupposed that the Biblical documents are human and that in so far as they purport to report events, it is possible to ask whether those reports are really true. The question, Is that report true?, however, itself presupposes some standard of judgment, and this standard is necessarily influenced by present knowledge and the sciences. It was only when present knowledge was used as the criterion for judgments about the past that historians were able to sort out the fantastic, legendary, and mythological elements from the probably true ones. These two presuppositions, however, challenged the belief in the verbal INSPIRATION and inerrancy of the Scriptures; hence, B.C. became a center of controversy, particularly in the late 19th century. This controversy was aggravated by the fact that the work of the first Biblical critics inevitably involved many negative judgments about traditional beliefs. The critics judged, for example, that (1) the first five books of the O.T. were not written by Moses but were the products of many hands; (2) the book of Isaiah was not one but at least two books; (3) the book of Daniel was not written in the period it describes; (4) the Fourth Gospel differs radically from the first three Gospels and cannot provide a dependable framework for the life and thought of Jesus; (5) the authors of Matthew and Luke probably copied the work of Mark (see Synoptic Problem); (6) it is impossible to reconstruct a history of Jesus' ministry; (7) Paul probably did not write several of the letters attributed to him.

Fundamentalists attacked the "higher criticism" and the R.C. CHURCH established a Biblical Commission in 1902 to make sure that no R.C. scholar advocated historical views alien to church DOGMA. Liberal Prot. theologians, on the other hand, welcomed B.C., and Biblical scholarship owes its existence in large part to their efforts. Neo-Reformed theologians, though critical of LIBERAL PROTESTANTISM in many respects, praised the honesty of the liberal scholars and continued to support this tradition. More recently, Roman Catholicism has generally softened its attitude toward B.C. and many of its scholars accept all or most of the conclusions of the critics cited in the previous paragraph.

The new affirmative attitude toward B.C. on the part of more conservative scholars is due in part to the fact that the modern critic is less concerned to measure the past by the present and to criticize traditional belief than he is to show how the authors of various books used past traditions and sources to create a distinctive religious point of view. As a result, the critic has shed extraordinary light on the life and thought of the Hebrews, the N.T. world, and on the creativity of the writers themselves. Source criticism, FORM CRITICISM, and tradition criticism (*Traditionsgeschichte*) have made clear how the Biblical authors used materials already circulating in their cultural environment but how creative they were in synthesizing them into new perspectives.

B.C., nevertheless, raises a host of issues concerning the authority of the Bible and its interpretation, and much of modern Prot. THEOLOGY is an attempt to come to grips with them. There are two major alternatives. One view argues that the authority of the Bible consists in its witness to the "mighty acts of God," beginning in ancient times and culminating in Jesus Christ (see *Heilsgeschichte*). Although there may be errors of fact here and there and many primitive forms of expression, nevertheless, the central core of history in the Bible cannot be reasonably doubted, it is argued, and FAITH must interpret this as REVELATION. Another view argues that the authority of the Bible consists in its witness to the Gospel of God's graciousness that is primarily revealed in Jesus Christ but that is the inner meaning of the O.T. tradition as well. The Bible contains the WORD OF GOD, a Word that admittedly was conveyed in quite human and historically conditioned ways—legends, MYTHS, history, poetry, wise saying, letters— but that still confronts man with decision. Fundamentalist scholars still cling to the inerrancy of the Bible. R.C.s, on the other hand, are considerably freer than before, but it is not yet clear how far they will be permitted to go. (See Accommodation; Allegorical Interpretation; Apocalyptic Literature; Biblicism; Demythologization; Exegesis; Form Criticism; *Heilsgeschichte*; Hermeneutics; Historicism; Inspiration of the Bible; Liberal Protestantism; Miracle; Modernism; Myth; *Religionsgeschichtliche Schule*; Revelation; Synoptic Problem; Virgin Birth of Christ; Word of God.)

Biblicism is that view which accepts as true all that is to be found in the Bible in its literal meaning and which will accept no truth as Christian that cannot find explicit warrant in it.

Sometimes called bibliolatry. (See Biblical Criticism; Fundamentalism.)

Bilocation is the capability of being in two places at one and the same time. This idea was sometimes resorted to in the THEOLOGY of the SACRAMENTS to explain how the body of Christ could be present in many places at one time. Some R.C. theologians believe this capability to have been granted to a few saints at specific times.

Binitarianism is the belief that there are only two PERSONS in the godhead, in contrast to three, the orthodox doctrine. It is sometimes loosely used to characterize any THEOLOGY in which the doctrine of the Holy Spirit is relatively ignored or undeveloped. (See Trinity.)

Blasphemy refers technically to any speech, act, or thought which dishonors or defames the nature or name of GOD. In the N.T. it is associated with those who revile the name of God, Jesus, or the Holy Spirit. Since it is said in the N.T. (Matt. 12:31 f.; Mark 3:28 f.; Luke 12:10) that B. against the Holy Spirit is the one unpardonable sin, theologians and ministers have often been preoccupied with the interpretation of these passages. Generally, these verses are taken to mean that sinning against the Holy Spirit is a rejection of the spirit of truth and is, therefore, unrepentance, which makes forgiveness impossible.

Body. See Person; Resurrection of the Dead; Soul; Spirit–Holy Spirit.

Body of Christ. See Church.

Boundary Situation. A somewhat technical term in the EXISTENTIALISM of Karl Jaspers (1883-) and used also by Paul Tillich (1886-), this refers to certain unavoidable realities that peculiarly qualify or define human EXISTENCE and which pose for man the question whether he will live authentically or unauthentically. Such B.S.s (*Grenzsituationen*) are death, chance, suffering, conflict, and guilt. (See Anxiety; Authentic Existence; Existentialism; Self-Understanding.)

C

Cardinal Virtues. See Virtues.

Casuistry means quite loosely the application of general principles to particular cases. In THEOLOGY and ethics, however, it usually refers more specifically to the application of general moral principles to concrete matters of ethical decision or "cases of CONSCIENCE." The origins of C. in Christendom are complex and obscure, although they probably lie in the need of the earliest theologians and priests to give counsel to Christians faced with decisions in the midst of an explicitly pagan society. With the rise of the SACRAMENT of penance and the accompanying penitential discipline, there was increasing demand for the systematization and coordination of the various decrees, canons, and sentences of the CHURCH on these matters. As a result penitential books were widely used. Around the 13th century, Scholastic theologians gave increasing attention to interpretation of the teachings of the church in the light of the principles of natural and revealed law. As a result, the next two centuries witnessed a large number of systems of C. Characteristic was the four-volume work of Raymond of Peñafort (c.1175-1275) which treated of sins against GOD, sins against the neighbor, the rights and duties of ecclesiastics, and marriage. The Scholastics frequently differed among themselves, however, and there developed basically different interpretations of the matter, each of which involved further and more elaborate hair-splitting distinctions. One of the most influential of these was called probabilism, which became the subject of two centuries of subsequent debate. With his characteristic bluntness and sense for the essential, Luther (1483-1546) rejected the whole idea of C. as alien to the idea of the freedom of the Christian man. He was concerned primarily with sin as unfaith, not as transgression of particular laws. C. became identified, in the Prot. mind, with legalism and Pharisaism. For all that, however, ethical decisions continued to arise for Christians, and something more was required than appeals to the Ten Commandments or the law of love. The Calvinist tradition, generally, was better able to provide insights in ethical matters than the Lutheran. General theological principles applicable to social, political, and personal life were developed but never with the particularity that is associated with the word "C." (See Antinomianism; Conscience; Decalogue; Ethics, Christian; Ethics, Contextual; Ethics, Social; Justice; Law and Gospel; Moral Theology; Natural Law; Perfection, Christian; Sins, Mortal and Venial; Social Gospel; Virtue; Vocation.)

Catholic is derived from the Greek word meaning universal. Very early in the history of the CHURCH it was used as an adjective to refer to that which was universally shared among the various churches, whether belief or practice, and was given a normative significance. Whatever was C. was regarded as orthodox and true. Increasingly, C. came to be synonymous with the traditional FAITH and practice; hence when the Prot. Reformers questioned the validity of much of that tradition, the term Prot. was naturally opposed to C. As Protestantism itself developed a historical tradition of belief and practice centered around preaching and interpretation of the Bible, C. came to be a loose designation for a style of religious life, one marked by stress on the SACRAMENTS, liturgy, visible continuity in the apostolic succession of the episcopate, and a hierarchical ecclesiastical structure. With the recent concern for union among all Christian churches, however, there has been a new interest in reappropriating the word C. on the part of Prot.s, just as some C. churches have acknowledged the legitimacy of many Prot. insights. This has led to attempts to define the ESSENCE of Catholicism, which, in turn, has tended to center attention on the problem of the relation of Scripture to tradition and of preaching to sacramental worship. (See Apostolicity; Church; Communion of the Saints; Dogma; Ecumenical; *Ekklesia*; Faith; Grace; Heresy; Justification; Laity; Notes of the Church; Orthodoxy; Protestant Principle; Righteousness of God; Sanctification; Word of God.)

Causa Sui means literally "cause of itself" and is sometimes used as a technical term for GOD. Since nothing can literally cause itself, the idea refers to that which does not depend for its EXISTENCE on something else or whose very nature it is to exist. (See Aseity; Attributes of God; Being; God; Necessary Being; Ontological Argument; Perfection, Theological; Proofs for the Existence of God; Theism.)

Charity is the traditional word used by R.C. theologians to translate the Greek word AGAPE (love) and, along with FAITH and hope, is regarded as one of the three supernatural VIRTUES. (See *Agape* and *Eros*; Grace; Habit; Infusion; Original Righteousness; Perfection, Christian; Sin, Original; Virtue.)

Chiliasm comes from the Greek word meaning "a thousand" and is a synonym for MILLENNIALISM. (See Apocalyptic Literature; Dispensationalism; Eschatology; *Parousia*.)

Christocentric. Generally, it refers to those types of THEOLOGY in which the PERSON and work of Christ are the bases for all theological and ethical propositions. (See Christology.)

Christology is that part of Christian doctrine concerned with the REVELATION of GOD in Jesus Christ. Traditionally, this has been expressed in the doctrine of the INCARNATION, the doctrine of the union of the divine and human natures in the one PERSON. Technically, C. is to be distinguished from SOTERIOLOGY, which has been limited to the saving work of Christ, i.e., the ATONEMENT, although most contemporary Prot. theologians find this distinction misleading if not false.

Properly speaking, there is no doctrine of the incarnation as such in the N.T. There are, rather, a number of SYMBOLS drawn from the Jewish and Hellenistic religious cultures that are used as vehicles to express the conviction of the early Christians that God had acted uniquely and decisively in the life and death of Jesus of Nazareth. As the Christian community expanded into the Graeco-Roman world, these symbols required clarification and interpretation, for the symbols rooted in Jewish religious soil (like "Messiah," "Son of Man,"

"Son of God," "Son of David") could scarcely have any meaning to a Roman citizen or to a Greek. The earliest theologians of the CHURCH attempted to clarify and interpret these symbols, and the most readily available tool of communication was the language of the Greek philosophic schools, especially the Platonic school.

There were tensions within this latter tradition which led to grave problems (see Being; God). There was also the formidable problem of getting agreement on the appropriate Latin terms for rendering the Greek. In general, however, there was a consensus that two errors of interpretation should be avoided: (1) the error that emphasized the human nature of Jesus to the neglect of the divine action at work in his life, and (2) the error that emphasized the divine character of his life to the point of denying his essential humanity. The task of avoiding these errors was not as simple as it seems. It was complicated by (1) a political situation of extraordinary complexity in the Roman Empire; (2) a corrosive jealousy between rival ecclesiastical authorities, especially between Alexandria and Antioch; (3) the lack of any fixed philosophical and theological terminology, complicated, in turn, by the necessity of having to get agreement in two languages; (4) deeply rooted metaphysical presuppositions alien to Biblical thought that clung to the very words chosen to communicate the nature of that thought. Consequently, each theological position could be stated in a number of ways, the meaning of which was not clear until the terminology was agreed upon—an almost comic situation when one realizes how easy it was to confuse the matter further with political and ecclesiastical intrigue.

A number of possible statements concerning the relation of Christ to God and to man were explored between the Council of Nicaea (325) and the Council of Chalcedon (451), the latter council having fixed the main creedal lines for the future. At Chalcedon, it was affirmed that Jesus Christ was one person in two natures, divine and human, "inconfusedly, unchangeably, indivisibly, inseparably, the distinction of natures by no means being annulled through the union, but rather the peculiarity of each nature being preserved, and concurring in one person and one substantial individual, not

49

parted or divided into two powers, but one and the same Son . . . the Lord Jesus Christ. . . .,"

Since the Chalcedon formula merely excluded certain alternatives and did not really solve the problem of how one person could combine both human and divine natures, debate naturally arose over this problem. The monophysites insisted that there was only one nature in Christ, and it was divine. The monotheletes insisted that there was only one will in Christ and it was divine. The defenders of Chalcedon continued to insist on two natures and two wills in perfect harmony. After long and sterile controversy, the 2nd and 3rd Councils of Constantinople (553 and 680) judged both MONO-PHYSITISM and MONOTHELITISM to be heretical and reaffirmed the two natural wills concurring in Christ for the salvation of the race.

The Prot. Reformers did not challenge the orthodox creeds; they stressed, rather, the saving work of Christ (see Soteriology). They shifted the emphasis to the benefits of FAITH in Christ and minimized technical discussion concerning the two natures and the like. By insisting that the important thing was not a correct metaphysical theory about Christ's nature but the confidence that God was revealed as gracious and merciful in him, the Reformers prepared the way for a different type of C. with a different type of conceptualization. The implications of this were not really seen until the 19th century, however, when certain Prot. theologians, like Schleiermacher (1768-1834), and Ritschl (1822-89), argued that the graciousness of God and faith were only obscured by the traditional language. Ritschl, especially, called for a break from the metaphysical language of the Greeks. To say Jesus was divine, Ritschl insisted, is not an objective statement but a value judgment that one has found the KINGDOM OF GOD for oneself through Jesus and his preaching. Although contemporary neo-Reformed theologians reject much of liberal THEOLOGY, they accept the premise that not only is there nothing sacred about the traditional language but it may in fact hinder a true understanding of the Gospel, and, hence, be a bad C. for our time. (See Adoptianism; *Anhypostasis*; Apollinarianism; Arianism; Atonement; Binitarianism; *Communicatio Idiomatum*; Docetism; Dyophysitism, Dyothelitism;

Ebionite; Grace; *Hypostasis*; Hypostatic Union; Justification; *Kenosis*; *Logos*; Monophysitism; Monothelitism; *Parousia*; Person; Pre-existence of Christ; Recapitulation; Resurrection of Christ; Righteousness of God; Soteriology; Trinity; Virgin Birth; Word of God.)

Church is used to translate the Greek word EKKLESIA employed in the N.T. to designate the community of those who have accepted the preaching of the Gospel of Jesus Christ, participated in the symbolic rite of death and resurrection (BAPTISM), received the gift of the Holy Spirit (the new life), and gathered together for common worship and the celebration of the EUCHARIST. This community of the "new COVENANT" was believed to be in close relationship with the community of the "old covenant" (Israel), the difference being that the Messiah had come and the promises of GOD thereby had been fulfilled. This continuity and discontinuity account for the images of the C. used by the N.T. writers, some of which presupposed Judaism and some of which are entirely new.

In the last decade there has been a revived interest in the doctrine of the C. There are many reasons for this, but two especially deserve noting: (1) the struggles of the churches with secularism in general and with National Socialism and communism in particular, struggles which necessarily required some clear idea of the C. and its relation to the world; (2) the discussions among the different churches that believe a divided Christendom is not only tragic but blasphemous in the face of the united confession of belief in "one HOLY, CATHOLIC, and apostolic C."

These discussions have made clear that the various Christian churches have far more in common with one another than is often believed and that many differences arise from misunderstandings or cultural and historical differences. Almost all Christian churches believe that the C. was called into being by the REVELATION of God in Christ and sustained by the Holy Spirit and, therefore, that its real unity is invisible. So, too, almost all Christian churches believe that, in God's PROVIDENCE, this invisible unity is linked to certain visible rites or SACRAMENTS and necessarily requires an ecclesiastical structure (polity) of some sort. Most accept the major creeds and desire to be catholic and apostolic.

Nevertheless, these discussions have also made plain that there are certain fundamental conflicts concerning the nature of the C. that cannot be attributed to misunderstandings or to cultural differences. Perhaps the most fundamental of these exists between the R.C. and E.O. churches, on the one hand, and the churches stemming from the Reformation on the other. The former regard the C. fundamentally as a supernatural sphere, not simply in the sense that the C. possesses the divinely ordained means of salvation, but in the sense that this salvation itself consists in a supernatural participation in the divine life, a participation made possible through the sacramental system. The sacraments literally are "the medicine of immortality." Consequently, the whole understanding of salvation and the entire structure of these churches and their doctrines are ordered around this sacramental understanding. A corollary of this is that the sacraments and a legitimate priesthood become the visible marks of the unity of the C. and demand, in turn, an unbroken succession of ecclesiastical authority with the original apostles as well as the supernatural guidance of the C. in all matters of FAITH and morals. In short, the C. is the representative of Christ on earth and it must have the infallible authority of the one it claims to represent.

The Prot. Reformers did not originally intend to break with the R.C. C. They also believed that the C. possesses the divinely ordained means of salvation, but they conceived of salvation in radically different terms (see Justification; Grace). In their view, man was saved by faith alone, i.e., a wholehearted confidence in God's mercy, and this faith was not supernaturally caused by the sacraments. It was a personal response to the WORD OF GOD that was given in Jesus Christ and given again and again in preaching. The authority for this understanding of the Gospel, the Reformers believed, was Scripture, and it was only in subsequent debate with R.C. theologians that they were forced to pit Scripture against the alleged infallibility of the C. But once this was done and the tradition of the C. was required to justify itself against Scripture, the Reformers were able to draw the most radical consequences. It was argued that: (1) the visible C. consisting of canons, councils, and Pope was fallible; (2) the Roman Bishop has no scriptural claim to primacy; (3) the office of preaching should supplant the sacramental office of priesthood; (4) every Christian possesses the "keys" of teaching and preaching, although for the sake of public order some persons may be set aside; (5) the sacramental system as conceived in Roman Catholicism is unbiblical. In short, not only the SOTERIOLOGY of the R.C. tradition was questioned but also its infallibility and authority.

Faced with developing a conception of the C. on what they believed to be a true Biblical foundation, the Reformers argued, with only minor differences in emphases, that the C. is essentially the community of those who have faith, which is but their way of saying that the unity of the C. is Christ. In this sense, the true C. was believed to be invisible. But since faith itself is a response to the Word, and both Luther (1483-1546) and Calvin (1509-64) insisted that, in the providence of God, God speaks through the Word rightly preached, the C., from an external point of view, is closely associated with preaching and the sacraments, both of which are understood, however, as the presentation of the Gospel. Preaching, therefore, becomes the center of worship and all ecclesiastical organization was regarded as but a human means of securing obedience to preaching. The notion of an invisible C. did not refer to a C. outside of the visible C. but was a way of pointing to the hidden character of faith within the visible structures.

After the Reformers dared to break with the R.C. C., others broke also and, in effect, created a third model for understanding the C. The Anabaptists argued that the Reformers had not gone far enough, that the C. itself ought to be composed only of those who were visibly regenerated and lived a disciplined Christian life. The Reformers did not try to separate true from false believers within the C. but argued that the visible C. necessarily contains hypocrites among its members. The Anabaptists, however, believed this compromised the purity of the C. They emphasized the importance of testing whether a believer was truly Christian and they often barred errant members from the community. They also refused to make any distinction in function between clergy and LAITY, believing that all who had the SPIRIT were capable of teaching and preaching.

These three types of conceptions of the C. rest on fundamentally different self-understandings. This has become clear in ECUMENICAL discussions. The fundamental issues, then, appear to be these: (1) the relation of the authority of the Bible to the authority of the C.; (2) whether salvation is to be regarded as supernatural participation in the divine life given through the sacraments or is to be viewed as confidence in the divine graciousness; (3) whether the C. is fallible and, therefore, really subject to criticism and reformation not only in marginal matters but in matters of belief and practice. (See Apostolicity; Baptism; Communion of the Saints; Dogma; *Ekklesia*; Faith; Grace; Heresy; Infusion; *Kerygma*; *Koinonia*; Laity; Notes of the Church; Orthodoxy; Priesthood of All Believers; Protestant Principle; Sacrament; Schism; Soteriology; Word of God.)

Church Expectant. R.C. theologians distinguish among the C.E., which refers to the faithful undergoing purification in PURGATORY, and the church militant, which is the visible CHURCH on earth, and the church triumphant, the final culmination of the Christian life in the BEATIFIC VISION of GOD. (See Church.)

Church Militant. See Church Expectant.

Church Triumphant. See Church Expectant.

Circumincession. See *Perichoresis.*

Communicatio Idiomatum means literally "communion of the properties" and is a technical term in CHRISTOLOGY. The theory is that, because of the intimate union of the two natures of deity and manhood in Jesus Christ, the attributes of the former may in a loose sense be predicated of the latter, so that it is possible to say "GOD suffered" and "Christ was active in creation." Luther (1483-1546) interpreted the idea radically, insisting that God so completely became man in Christ that human attributes, like suffering and dying, became indissolubly fused with the divine, and the divine, in turn, stamped the human. This enabled Luther to say that the man Jesus is the omnipotent and omnipresent Lord of the world. This became the basis for Luther's interpretation of the EUCHARIST. This idea was rejected by Calvin (1509-64) and was the central point of contention in the arguments with Luther over the mode of Christ's presence in the Lord's Supper. (See Ascension; Christology; Consubstantiation; Eucharist; Theandric Acts.)

Communion of the Saints is a phrase that appears in the Apostles' Creed and is the usual translation of the original Latin phrase *communio sanctorum*, which first appears in the creed in the early 5th century. Since the Latin term *sanctorum* could refer to either persons or things, it is not perfectly clear whether the creed refers to the communion Christians share in "holy things" (the EUCHARIST), and thus is a creedal statement about the visible nature of the CHURCH, or whether it refers to the communion (KOINONIA) Christians share with one another living and dead. The phrase plays an important role in the Reformers' doctrine of the church, for Luther (1483-1546) insisted that the church is nothing but the C.O.S. and, therefore, spiritual and invisible in its ESSENCE, although brought about by the visible means of preaching and the SACRAMENTS. (See Church.)

Concomitance. See Transubstantiation.

Concupiscence. In the CATHOLIC tradition, it is any desire or appetite of the lower faculties of human nature not brought under the dominion and control of the rational faculties; hence a love of some lesser good that upsets the God-given (natural) pattern for human life. Although frequently associated with sexual lust, Augustine (354-430) and others have interpreted lust itself as a consequence of a misplaced love rather than a cause of it. Catholic theologians have tended to interpret C. as the result of God's deprivation of SANCTIFYING GRACE and integrity and, therefore, not strictly speaking, sin, although it tends to sin. Prot. theologians, rejecting the division between supernatural and natural endowments, have almost universally interpreted C. as sin. (See *Donum Superadditum*; Image of God; Original Righteousness; Sin, Original.)

Concursus. See Providence.

Conditional Immortality is that view in which IMMORTALITY is not regarded as an intrinsic property of the SOUL but as given, if at all, as a divine reward. Immortality is conditional upon the character of the soul in its earthly life. It is compatible with ANNIHILATIONISM, that view in which the souls of the wicked simply lapse into NON-BEING rather than being everlastingly punished in HELL. C.I. was condemned at the Fifth Lateran Council in 1513. (See Annihilationism; *Apocatastasis*; Immortality; Intermediate State; Judgment, Final; Resurrection of the Dead; Soul.)

Conscience is derived from the Latin *conscientia*, which originally possessed the double meaning of "to know with another" and "knowledge within oneself." At first almost synonymous with "consciousness," C. only gradually acquired its now popular and moralistic meaning, the faculty which judges one's own actions to be right or wrong.

The concept of the C. in theological literature has had a varied history and reflects generally the ANTHROPOLOGY of the theologian in question. Although the Greek term *syneidesis* occurs in the N.T., a systematic interpretation of C. did not appear before the medieval period. Scholastic theologians defined C. as the application to a particular action or situation of principles perceived by the *synteresis*, a faculty or organ which enables man to discern infallibly the inherent NATURAL LAW, a faculty not damaged by Adam's fall. Since the C. only applies the basic principles of the *synteresis*, however, C. can err, and it was the task of the CHURCH to educate and train the C. and to give its counsel in cases where the C. is in doubt (see Casuistry).

Since the Reformers' theological position in general was based in part on a criticism of R.C. anthropology, it necessarily involved also a criticism of the R.C. concept of C. This may be most dramatically illustrated by noting that whereas the R.C. sees *synteresis* as a remnant of man's ORIGINAL RIGHT-EOUSNESS, Luther (1483-1546) almost always equates SATAN, the law, God's wrath, despair, and C., on one side, and puts Christ, the Gospel, and joy, on the other. This unexpected juxtaposition is rooted in Luther's own religious experience. The more he had tried to gain a good C. by doing moral or religious works, the more he had realized that he was deeply alienated from GOD and, furthermore, that this ALIENATION preceded any action the C. might judge to be good or bad in itself. Man is driven to despair by his C. JUSTIFICATION by God's GRACE meant to Luther that God, the judge, actually and miraculously defends man against his own C. He accepts man as guilty and, thereby, enables man to accept himself. Thus he receives a joyful C. He is free from the despair of trying fruitlessly to gain a good one. The good C. is a gift and not something acquired by one's own efforts.

In the groups composing the "left wing" of the Reformation, C. was often interpreted as the voice of the Holy Spirit speaking in the depths of the SOUL, an idea also to be found among the Quakers. And it is this idea together with those derived from German idealism that has more or less determined modern popular Prot. belief. C. is regarded as the "voice of God" telling one what is right or wrong. The rise of the biological sciences, sociology, and modern psychology has posed severe problems for this conception of C., since it has been argued that C. is sociologically or environmentally determined and, hence, its demands vary from culture to culture.

The rediscovery of Luther and the Reformers, and the reflections of the existentialist philosophers, have been determinative for many contemporary Prot. theologians. The philosopher, Martin Heidegger (1889-), particularly, has interpreted the C. not in moral terms but as something in man calling him back to his proper relatedness to BEING and to himself. The C. calls man back to his own authentic possibilities. But this means, Heidegger argues, that man is called to accept guilt, since every action necessarily involves guilt. Certain theologians, especially Paul Tillich (1886-), have seen affinities between Heidegger's and Luther's view, so that Tillich writes "the good, transmoral C. consists in the acceptance of the bad, moral C." Luther's view of acceptance, unlike Heidegger's, however, is predicated on the conviction that God accepts the guilty and, thereby, frees man from trying to establish his own righteousness. So liberated, man can serve and love the neighbor and be free from having to judge his own actions as good or bad. (See Authentic Existence; Existentialism; Faith; Grace; Justification; Sanctification; *Simul Iustis et Peccator*; Word of God.)

Consubstantial literally means "to be of the same SUBSTANCE" and was the Latin translation of the Greek term HOMOOUSION used in the creed adopted at Nicaea in 325 to describe the relationship between the eternal Son or LOGOS and the Father in the triune godhead. (See Christology; *Logos*; Person; Trinity; Wisdom.)

Consubstantiation is the term usually applied to Luther's (1483-1546) teaching concerning Christ's presence in the EUCHARIST in contrast to the R.C. DOGMA of TRANSUBSTANTIATION, even though it is doubtful whether Luther himself ever used the term. If transubstantiation means the changing of the SUBSTANCE of the bread and wine into the substance of the body and blood of Christ, C. means that Christ is "bodily" present "in, with, and under" the elements, although they are not essentially (substantially) altered. The theory is only intelligible if one keeps Luther's CHRISTOLOGY in mind. He argued that the unity of the divine and human in Christ was so intimate that the divine assumes the attributes of the human and the human those of the divine (see *Communicatio Idiomatum*). This meant for Luther that the man Jesus could be said to be omnipresent, which is what he interpreted the creedal phrase "seated on the right hand of God" to mean. (See Ascension; Eucharist; Real Presence; Transubstantiation.)

Contextual Ethics. See Ethics, Contextual.

Contingent is the technical predicate applied to whatever was, is, or will be that is neither impossible nor necessary. Since it is neither impossible (it can be conceived without self-contradiction) nor necessary (it could have been otherwise) that any particular being or thing comes to be, all finite being is to be regarded as C. BEING. Classically, theologians have regarded any being as C. whose ESSENCE does not include its EXISTENCE. Only GOD, it follows by definition, is non-contingent. (See Analogy, Way of; Attributes of God; Being; Creation; Metaphysics; Necessary Being; Non-Being; Ontological Argument; Perfection, Theological; Proofs for the Existence of God.)

Contrition in R.C. THEOLOGY is heartful sorrow for having sinned against the divine goodness together with the resolution never to sin again. It is usually understood to include ATTRITION, which is defined as an imperfect type of sorrow for sin. According to the Council of Trent, C. "perfected by CHARITY," if accompanied by a desire for confession and ABSOLUTION, may reconcile a man to GOD even before he receives the SACRAMENT of penance.

Cosmological Argument. See Proofs for the Existence of God.

Cosmology is derived from Greek words meaning "doctrine of the world" and refers to that part of METAPHYSICS which deals with the origin and structure of the universe. The earliest and most influential cosmologies were those of Plato (c.427-347 B.C.) and Aristotle (384-322 B.C.). Although Christian theologians modified them in the light of their own doctrines of CREATION and PROVIDENCE, the problems discussed by the two great Greek philosophers—the origins of matter, the relationship of time to ETERNITY, the laws of the world, etc.—remained the standard problems for centuries. With the rise of the sciences of astronomy and of physics and the accompanying skepticism concerning the possibility of solving cosmological problems by speculative reasoning (in contrast to scientific reasoning and experiment), many of the old problems of C. became scientific problems, and those that remained, like the problems of evil (see Theodicy), were generally made metaphysical or ontological problems. C., in general, is no longer a concern of most modern philosophers, and what is sometimes called C. is not a theory of the origin and structure of the universe so much as it is a scheme of categories said to be applicable to everything that is, i.e., it is ontology. (See Creation; Metaphysics.)

Covenant. A C. is a relationship between two parties, i.e., man and wife, or ruler and ruled, in which each party voluntarily agrees to certain conditions of the relationship and gives his word to uphold it. C. provides the central analogy in the O.T. for the bond between Yahweh and Israel. Although the origins of the idea are obscure, subsequent tradition regards the C. as established by the REVELATION of GOD to Moses, the redemption of Israel out of bondage in Egypt, the giving of the LAW, and the leading of the Israelites through the wilderness into "the land." Other traditions in the O.T. carry back the idea of the C. to Noah.

The idea of C. easily degenerates into the idea of a mere legal relationship contracted for the mutual benefit of both parties. The O.T. avoids this, for the most part, because of its emphasis on the mercy of God in his ELECTION of Israel, an election that is entirely gratuitous. Moreover, the Law, which is the visible seal of the C., is not regarded as a set of legal obligations that, once obeyed, becomes the basis for a reward claim. The Law, too, is a gracious revelation of the conditions necessary for a truly authentic life, which is to say, JUSTICE in the community. To be sure, there are elements of legalism which appear in this conception, especially in the elaborate development of the ceremonial parts of the Law, but the prophets themselves warned against this. The C. forms the background, therefore, for the understanding of the prophets' denunciation of Israel's APOSTASY and their frequent choice of such basic images as marriage and adultery to illustrate the meaning of C. The message of the prophets is not that Israel has broken a legal contract but that Israel has forsaken the gracious God who originally redeemed them and who still remains faithful to the C., although Israel has repeatedly ignored and broken it.

There is considerable evidence that the legalistic conception of the C. began to predominate in post-Exilic Judaism. Instead of the C. being a living, dynamic relationship symbolized outwardly by a visible bond (the Law), the visible bond became the basis for one of the parties to legalistically measure its obligations and rights. This understanding is revealed by the identification of the C. with "the ordinances," the stress on the ceremonial details of the Law, and the detailed CASUISTRY that grew up in order to define precisely the limits of one's obligations. It is against this legalistic understanding that Jesus' protest against the Pharisees is to be understood. The Pharisee is technically righteous but inwardly his heart is selfish. Moreover, Jesus radicalizes this protest by virtue of his attitude toward those whom the legalists exclude from the C., i.e., the "sinners," or those who have broken the Law.

The earliest Christian community naturally found the imagery of the C. appropriate for expressing the meaning of Jesus Christ. He, like the redemption of Israel from Egypt, is the act in which God's mercy and election are disclosed. So, too, there is given in him a new Law or pattern for authentic life, although, paradoxically, it is no Law at all since its meaning is AGAPE, and *agape* cannot be legalistically understood. This new C., then, both fulfills and yet shatters the old C., especially in so far as the latter is identified with external works. This is why the early Christian writers can at once claim that the Law is annulled for the Christian and, at the same time, argue that the whole Law is fulfilled in love (Rom. 13:8; Gal. 5:14), a love which God makes possible by virtue of his JUSTIFICATION of the sinner. (See Covenantal Theology; Decalogue; Election; *Heilsgeschichte*; Law and Gospel.)

Covenantal Theology. The idea of COVENANT is a central idea in the O.T. and N.T. and, to that extent, all Biblical THEOLOGY is, in the loose sense, C.T. This term, however, refers quite specifically to a type of theology prevalent in the Reformed or Calvinistic tradition in which everything is systematically organized around the idea of covenant. Sometimes called federal theology, C.T. first arose in the late 16th century and came to fruition in English Puritanism in the last half of the 17th century.

According to C.T., GOD entered into a covenant with Adam,

who was the "federal" head or representative of the race of man. This covenant required absolute obedience on man's part. If this condition were met, God promised, in turn, to grant man (through Adam as his representative) eternal life. Adam failed to keep the terms of the covenant and the fall of man resulted. God resolved, then, to covenant with Jesus Christ, who is the second representative or second Adam, and to grant forgiveness and eternal life in consideration of his perfect obedience and sacrificial death. The first covenant was called the "C. of works," the second, "the C. of GRACE." Federal theologians frequently developed quite elaborate distinctions within those two general categories. The time of the old covenant was divided into the period from Adam to Abraham, from Abraham to Moses, and from Moses to Christ, and the time of the new covenant was divided into the period from the ADVENT to the resurrection, from the resurrection to the second coming (PAROUSIA), and from the second coming to the final consummation.

C.T. not only provided a scheme of salvation but something like a philosophy of history as well. Indeed, it constituted a most inclusive system of thought. Furthermore, it had important ethical and social consequences. The idea of covenant, it has been argued, lay deep in the consciousness of the Puritan fathers in America and probably informed their ideas of constitutional government and of the significance of civil and ecclesiastical law. The idea of two radically different covenants, however, had within it the seeds of its own dissolution, because it suggested that God once dealt with man in terms other than grace. Indeed, it raised the question whether FAITH itself ought to be considered as a command or law. Some theologians were quick to see the dangers to the Reformation insight concerning the graciousness of God in the notion of a covenant of works, and the course of federal theology was subsequently marked by acrimonious debate over this matter and, finally, all but disappeared.

Creation. In Christian THEOLOGY, the doctrine of C. has to do primarily with the ultimate dependence of all things on one transcendent reality. Although the doctrine has been variously interpreted by theologians, it has generally been used in two ways. Negatively, it has been used as a defense against (1) any attempt to identify GOD with the world (see Pantheism), and (2) any view that attributes evil to MATTER or that regards the world as evil. Positively, C. means (1) that God is the ultimate source and sustainer of the world, (2) that he transcends it or, otherwise expressed, that creatures have been given an independent existence "alongside of" the creator, and (3) that the C. is good and that man is responsible for it.

The classical formula of traditional Christian theology has been *creatio ex nihilo*, which means C. out of nothing, a formula which radically emphasizes that God alone is to be regarded as the only ultimate source of all that is. C. *ex nihilo* is not explicitly taught in the Bible, although it could be argued that it is implied in certain passages appearing in Isaiah, Jeremiah, and Job. In fact, some of the earliest Christian theologians interpreted Genesis 1:1-3 to mean that God formed the world out of a pre-existent and chaotic matter, a view held by many later Jews, as can be seen in the Wisdom of Solomon. This view is similar to Plato's (*c.*427-347 B.C.), and these same theologians accounted for this similarity with the unlikely suggestion that Plato had taken the idea from Moses. This Platonic idea, however, lent itself too easily to the denial that God was the sole source of all that exists, and it was ultimately rejected. It was held that C. was an absolutely free and unnecessitated act that has no conceivable human analogy and is, therefore, a mystery.

This view necessarily raises many problems, not the least of which is whether C. is an act in time or, differently expressed, whether there was a time when God was not creating. Origen of Alexandria (*c.*185-*c.*254) and John Scotus Erigena (*c.*810-*c.*877), to mention two great theologians, argued that God is essentially creative and that this implies that there must have always been some created order or other. Origen believed that this present world had a beginning in time but that it was preceded by others *ad infinitum*. Erigena believed that God precedes the world not in time but ontologically, that is, he is the eternal sustainer of whatever is. Augustine (354-430), on the other hand, insisted on the doctrine of C. out of nothing. He avoided the conclusion that there was a time when God was not creator by arguing that time comes into existence with C. so that it is meaningless to ask whether there was a time before C. Thomas Aquinas (c.1225-74) had the best of both worlds, so to speak, arguing that Origen's position was rationally tenable but that *creatio ex nihilo* was to be believed on FAITH. Luther (1483-1546) and Calvin (1509-64), for the most part, accepted the formula *ex nihilo* but were far more concerned with its religious significance than its speculative meaning. To say God was the creator was to say that all blessings proceed from God alone and that men's hopes should depend on no other.

With the rise of modern science, theologians have tended to argue that the doctrine is a religious and metaphysical one and not a quasi-scientific idea about the origins of the world. It refers at once to the contingency of all things, the intelligibility and goodness of the world, and to the freedom and responsibility of human life. To this extent, the idea of C. *ex nihilo* has lost any precise meaning and, in fact, is often regarded as a mythological SYMBOL for preserving the affirmations noted above. (See Attributes of God; Being; *Causa Sui*; Contingent; Cosmology; Emanation; Eternity; God; Immanence; Matter; Necessary Being; Perfection, Theological; Proofs for the Existence of God; Providence; Theism; Theodicy.)

Creationism is the doctrine that each individual SOUL is created out of nothing (*ex nihilo*) by GOD and implanted at birth or conception in the body. It stands opposed to TRADUCIANISM, on the one hand, and emanationism, on the other. (See Creation; Emanation; Pre-existence of Souls; Soul; Traducianism.)

Culture, Theology of. This name has been coined and used by Paul Tillich (1886-) for the analysis and criticism of a culture in the light of the Christian message. By culture, Tillich means all the expressions of the human spirit in a given time and place—language, art, science, architecture, philosophy, technology. Every culture, Tillich believes, represents a peculiar way of looking at life. It is a unique synthesis of value judgments, beliefs, purposes, hopes, aspirations, and loyalties. It expresses what Tillich calls "ultimate concern," which is what he means by religion. It follows that religion is the meaning-giving substance of culture and culture is the form of religion. If one can read the style of a culture, therefore, he can discern its ultimate concern. To analyze and criticize that concern in the light of the Christian message is the task of the T.O.C. Although Tillich has so analyzed previous cultural periods, he has been especially concerned with contemporary culture. He sees its special spirit to consist in its unbounded confidence in the domination of nature and man by technology and the protest against the resulting depersonalization and loss of depth by modern artists and existentialist philosophers. (See Existentialism; Heteronomy; I-Thou; *Logos*; Neo-Reformed Theology; Protestant Principle.)

D

Decalogue is the name given to the Ten Commandments traditionally believed to have been given to Moses on Mt. Sinai. Similar versions of them are found in the books of Exodus, Chap. 20, and Deuteronomy, Chap. 5. Whether the D. as we have it stems originally from Mosaic times has been the subject of much discussion among O.T. scholars (see Biblical Criticism). In Christian ethical theory, the issue has been the relationship of the D. to the radical ethic of love (AGAPE) in the N.T., on the one hand, and to the NATURAL LAW capable of being grasped by ordinary human reason on the other. Most generally, R.C. theory influenced by Thomas Aquinas (*c*.1225-74) has interpreted the D. as a statement of the natural law and, hence, binding on all men. The super-natural VIRTUE of love does not contradict but goes beyond the virtues set forward in the commandments. Luther (1483-1546) also insisted that the D. represented the natural, inborn law and requirements of GOD, but he argued that its purpose was to drive men to realize they could not fulfill these require-ments so that they would throw themselves on God's mercy in Christ. Nevertheless, both Luther and Calvin (1509-64) used the D. as a vehicle for catechetical instruction in the meaning of Christian life and conduct, thereby expressing their conviction that love is the true fulfillment of the law. (See *Agape* and *Eros*; Antinomianism; Ethics, Christian; Ethics, Social; Justice; Law and Gospel; Natural Law; Perfection, Christian; Sanctification.)

Decrees, Eternal. Associated with Calvinism and the Reformed tradition, this term refers to the eternal and irrevocable decision by which GOD has "from the remotest eternity, decreed what he would do, and now, by his own power, executes what he has decreed. . . ." (Calvin). So understood, the E.D. are the bases for the Calvinists' belief in foreordination as well as PREDESTINATION. Critics of the idea protest that it necessarily leads to DETERMINISM, the denial of the FREEDOM OF THE WILL, and to the logical conclusion, therefore, that God is responsible for evil. Contemporary neo-Reformed theologians, especially Karl Barth (1886-), argue that the doctrine cannot be isolated from God's REVELATION in Jesus Christ in which FAITH perceives that God has eternally decreed to bring man into EXISTENCE as a free partner and to be a loving companion to him. There is no absolute decree (*decretum absolutum*) different from the will of God revealed in Christ. (See Election; Foreknowledge; Freedom of the Will; Omniscience; Omnipotence; Predestination.)

Deism is the view that regards GOD as the intelligent creator of an independent and law-abiding world but denies that he providentially guides it or intervenes in any way with its course of destiny. Reason is the sole instrument through which God's EXISTENCE and nature can be deduced from the perfectly rational workings of the universe. D. especially flourished in England in the 18th century. Those called deists argued that this view was the most intelligible interpretation of Christianity, once that religion was stripped of its claim that God acts supernaturally and miraculously in history. (See Attributes of God; Creation; God; Immanence; Miracle; Natural Theology; Panentheism; Pantheism; Proofs for the

Existence of God; Providence; Theism; Theodicy; Transcendence.)

Demythologization refers to a type of interpretation of the N.T. first systematically proposed in 1941 by Rudolf Bultmann (1884-), a German N.T. scholar and theologian. He argued that the message of the N.T. was couched in the language of a primitive and prescientific mentality that, from the standpoint of the history of religions, must be called mythological. In this mentality, demons and angels are at war in the spirits of men, and all unusual events are directly caused by supernatural powers. So pervasive is this type of thinking in the N.T., Bultmann insists, that it is useless to select certain MIRACLE stories (for example, the resurrection narratives) as more probable than others (for example, Jesus walking on water). Rather, THEOLOGY should accept the entire message as having a mythological form and seek to interpret the whole consistently. This interpretation is possible, Bultmann continued, because mythology also has certain elements of truth, even though that truth is stated in an outmoded form. MYTH expresses certain fundamental intuitions about human existence and its relation to the powers that man experiences as the ground and limit of his life. In order to understand these intuitions, however, it is necessary to separate them from their outmoded form, that is, it is necessary to demythologize. This type of interpretation, Bultmann insisted, is faithful to the real intention of the GOSPEL, because the N.T. authors themselves were primarily concerned to bring man to an awareness of himself in relation to God and not to perpetuate any particular picture of the world. Bultmann proposed that the best way of interpreting the N.T. language was by means of existentialist philosophy, especially that of Martin Heidegger (1889-), because this philosophy itself was but a secularized form of a Christian understanding of man and, moreover, was the most adequate contemporary philosophy. Bultmann's proposals created a storm in theological circles. Some theologians rejected it outright, others accepted it, and still others believed his analysis to be correct but argued that Heidegger's philosophy was not the best vehicle for the type of interpretation required. (See Biblical Criticism; Existentialism; Faith; Hermeneutics; Historicity of Human Existence; Justification; *Kerygma*; Liberal Protestantism; Myth; Neo-Reformed Theology; Soteriology; Word of God.)

Deontological is a word used to characterize an ethic constructed solely on moral obligation and duty in contrast to an ethic founded on consequences or ends. D. systems are preoccupied with the right, teleological systems with the good. A D. theological ethic stresses the law as an expression of the will of God. A teleological ethic stresses the law as a pattern for the fulfillment of human life. Although divergent in tendency, most teleological systems seldom are able to ignore the right, just as most D systems cannot divorce the right from the good. (See Covenant; Ethics, Christian; Ethics, Contextual; Eudaimonism; Heteronomy; Justice; Law and Gospel; Natural Law; Sanctification.)

Depravity, Total, is the term used to characterize the Prot. Reformers' view of man under the power of ORIGINAL SIN. The view is frequently misunderstood. It does not mean that man is totally bad; rather it means that there is nothing in man that has not been infected by the power of sin. Since FAITH constitutes the true harmony and integrity of all human faculties, sin is a disharmony that affects the total being of man. (See Image of God; Original Righteousness; *Similitudo Dei*; Sin, Original.)

Descent into Hell (Hades). In the so-called Apostles' Creed there is the phrase "he descended into HELL," which is a translation of the Latin phrase *descendit ad inferna*. This phrase does not occur in the Old Roman Symbol from which the Apostles' Creed was probably developed, nor is it to be found before the 4th century. It is not clear what the noun *inferna* refers to, since it may be translated "place of departed SPIRITS" or "hell," these by no means being identical in traditional R.C. and E.O. belief. Nor are the passages in the N.T. clear which are invoked to support the belief (Matt. 27:52 f.; Rom. 10:6-8; Eph. 4:8-10; I Pet. 3:18-20). There have, therefore, been numerous interpretations of the phrase. Some R.C. theologians argue that between his death and resurrection, Christ descended into the outermost fringes of hell (*limbus patrum*), where the SOULS of the just who had died before his advent reposed, and brought them back to heaven. Others extend the benefits of his descent to PURGATORY. E.O. teaching is that Christ descended into HADES, the place of all departed spirits, and redeemed some. Luther (1483-1546) gave various interpretations of the phrase during his career, although in his sermons he usually condescended to popular imagery and pictured Christ descending into the citadel of SATAN and conquering him and his legions. Calvin (1509-64) departed markedly from traditional belief and interpreted the phrase to mean that Christ "suffered in his soul the dreadful torments of a person condemned and irretrievably lost. . . ." Most Prot. confessions of faith leave the matter undecided. (See Hades; Hell; Immortality; Intermediate State; Limbo; Paradise; Sheol; Soul.)

Determinism is the view that all events whatsoever are to be understood as the necessary outcome of certain causes and so may be regarded as instances of laws. This belief has been stated in many ways and for many different kinds of reasons. Sometimes it has been advanced on metaphysical grounds, i.e., as an implication of MATERIALISM or of spiritualistic PANTHEISM. Sometimes it has been advocated for theological reasons, namely that GOD foreknows and foreordains all that comes to pass. In more recent times, it has been claimed that D. is a presupposition of science, since scientific explanations presuppose that all events can be explained in terms of cause-effect relations capable of formulation in laws. The doctrine has been attacked on the same diverse grounds. Some metaphysicians have maintained that there are SUBSTANCES which are characterized by a genuine spontaneity or freedom. Some theologians have argued that God's omnipotent power is not incompatible with genuinely independent secondary causes. And many recent philosophers of science have insisted that science only presupposes statistical regularities (laws) which in themselves say nothing about the necessary causation of single events.

The problem of D. has been most discussed in THEOLOGY in relation to the problem of the FREEDOM OF THE WILL. Furthermore, theological discussion of this is made more complex than corresponding philosophical discussion by the interjection of two factors secular philosophers are not concerned with, the relation of God's power, knowledge, and providential action to human action, and the problem of sin and GRACE. (See Foreknowledge; Freedom of the Will; Omniscience; Omnipotence; Perfection, Theological; Predestination; Synergism.)

Deus Absconditus means "the hidden god," a term harking back to the verse "Truly, thou art a God who hidest thyself. . . ." (Isa. 45:15). It was a favorite term of Luther's (1483-1546), who argued that speculative attempts to ascertain the nature of GOD always turned God into an object or a "naked majesty" that struck terror into man's heart and, therefore, drove him away from the revealed God (*deus revelatus*) in Christ, who is always the gracious god "for us." (See Conscience; Grace; *Theologica Crucis*.)

Deus Revelatus. See *Deus Absconditus*.

Devil. See Satan.

Dialectical is an adjective applied to reasoning and has had different meanings throughout the history of thought. Originally, dialectic simply meant "conversation" and so quite loosely describes the dramatic method used in Plato's (c.427-347 B.C.) early dialogues. These conversations usually had a pattern of logical development, however, and it is to this pattern that the term D. is often more narrowly applied. In medieval THEOLOGY, the D. method took the form of stating an opinion from some authority and then giving a counter-opinion by another and, finally, providing a solution that reconciled the two contradictions. In modern philosophy, the term is associated with the philosophical logic of Hegel (1770-1831), who argued that it is the very nature of reason to posit a thesis that generates an antithesis that, in turn, leads to a synthesis reconciling both thesis and antithesis. Hegel believed that this logic was a clue to the nature of reality itself, and his application of this logic to history was very influential for the D. materialism of Karl Marx (1818-83), who professed to see the same laws at work in the economic affairs of men. The term D. was taken up by the neo-Reformed theologians, largely under the influence of Kierkegaard (1813-55). It was characteristic of the latter to think always in relation to two apparent opposites, like freedom and necessity, and to characterize one in terms of the other. Dialectic was thus closely related to PARADOX. The underlying presupposition of his D. method was that human experience is so complex that it cannot be discussed without continually keeping the apparent contradictions and tensions in it before the mind. Reinhold Niebuhr (1892-), for example, argues that man is both free and limited and these two aspects of his selfhood are so related that one can only discuss man's limits in the light of his freedom and his freedom in the light of his limits, hence, dialectically. (See Existentialism; Neo-Reformed Theology; Paradox.)

Dialectical Theology. See Neo-Reformed Theology.

Dispensationalism is a type of religious thought that divides God's dealings with the world into certain "times" or "dispensations," each characterized by unique duties and responsibilities. The COVENANT with Moses, for example, is regarded as inaugurating one dispensation while the covenant made through Christ another. Some fundamentalist groups have divided history into an elaborate system of dispensations of innocence, of CONSCIENCE, of civil government, of promise, of law, of GRACE, and of the kingdom. The name is derived from an English word once used to translate the Greek word *oikonomia*, which only appears four times in the N.T. and only once with temporal connotations. (See Covenant; Covenantal Theology; *Heilsgeschichte*; Millennialism.)

Docetism. A term derived from the Greek word meaning "to seem" and applied to those christological theories of the early part of the 3rd century in which the humanity and suffering of Jesus Christ were regarded as only apparent (seeming) and not real. It is now broadly and sometimes pejoratively used to describe those views which emphasize the divinity of Christ by minimizing, where they do not deny, his human limitations. (See Accommodation; Apollinarianism; Christology; *Homoousion*; Hypostatic Union.)

Dogma is derived from the Greek word meaning "that which seems good" and was used in antiquity to refer to such things as the decrees of kings and principles regarded as axiomatic by the various philosophic schools. D. is now applied somewhat generally to those official beliefs of a group thought to be so fundamental that to deny them is warrant for expulsion or excommunication from that body. Thus, one may speak loosely of the D. of Marxism as well as the D. of the Christian CHURCH.

In its more technical theological sense, however, D. is applied to those doctrines explicitly formulated by the church and held to be normative for its members by the duly constituted authorities. In this sense, D. is narrower in range than doctrine or teachings, since not all doctrines have a dogmatic status. It follows that what a group regards as D. is dependent on what it regards to be the legitimate authority of the church. R.C.s regard all the pronouncements and creeds of all the councils up to the latest Second Vatican Council as having dogmatic status, together with the *ex cathedra* pronouncements of the Pope on FAITH and morals, which are defined as infallibly inspired. The E.O. and Anglican churches, however, only regard seven councils as genuinely ECUMENICAL and do not accept the authority of the Pope. Prot.s accept only four councils as genuinely representative of the whole church and, thus, when they use the word D. at all, restrict it to the doctrine of the TRINITY and the christological formulations that came from those four councils. It is interesting to note in this connection that Prot. denominations usually do not speak of their own official theological statements as D.s but as confessions of faith.

For several reasons, the idea of D. itself has been the subject of much discussion among Prot. theologians in the last generation: (1) the necessity of coming to grips with the doctrines and traditions of the various churches (including Roman Catholicism) because of the new interest in mutual understanding and, possibly, reunion; (2) the elaborate historical justification of the claim by the great historian Adolf von Harnack (1851-1930) that the central D.s of the church were really determined by the Greek speculative spirit and are alien to the Biblical point of view; (3) the argument by some Prot. theologians (Bultmann, Tillich, the Niebuhrs) that the "D." of JUSTIFICATION by faith alone means, paradoxically, the end of D. in the technical sense of the word, since it is an implication of the PROTESTANT PRINCIPLE that every material theological statement is a highly relative product of its times and shot through with human error. Although the details of Harnack's historical claim no longer go unchallenged, it is clear that he merely provided a case illustration of this last theological objection to D. The real problem of D. is the problem of infallibility and how it can be conceived within a church that insists on the Protestant Principle. (See Church; Ecumenical; Faith; Justification; Orthodoxy; Protestant Principle; Symbolics.)

Dogmatics. See Theology.

Donum Superadditum is a technical term that plays an important role in R.C. teaching concerning man's nature and his sin. It refers to the supernatural gifts given to Adam over and above his essential human nature and that were then lost when he sinned. (See Image of God; Sanctification; *Similitudo Dei*; Sin, Original.)

Dyophysitism. From the Greek words meaning two natures, this term was used by the monophysites to characterize the belief of the orthodox party (defenders of the creed of Chalcedon) that there were two natures coexisting in the one PERSON Jesus Christ. (See Christology; Monophysitism.)

Dyothelitism. From the Greek words meaning two wills, this term designates those who hold that in Jesus Christ there were two distinct wills, one divine and one human, united in perfect harmony. This doctrine was made DOGMA at the Sixth Ecumenical Council at Constantinople in 680-681. (See Christology; Monothelitism.)

E

Ebionite is a term derived from the Hebrew word meaning "the poor" and originally referred to a sect of Jewish Christians in the 1st century of the Christian era. They apparently emphasized the religious significance of the LAW, rejected Paul's teachings, and generally regarded Jesus as an inspired prophet rather than the divine WORD OF GOD. For this reason, the term is sometimes used loosely as an adjective to qualify any CHRISTOLOGY that minimizes the divinity of Christ. (See Adoptianism; Christology.)

Economic Trinity. See Trinity, Economic.

Ecstasy literally means "standing outside of oneself" and has traditionally been applied to an extraordinary psychic or spiritual state which has often seized prophets and mystics. E., so viewed, has usually been characterized by the suspension of normal physical functions. In Western Christendom, E. has been regarded as one of the normal stages in the mystical way, that is, as the result or accompaniment of a direct intuition of the deity. Paul Tillich (1886-) has attempted to purge the concept of its esoteric connotations and to restore it as a valid theological concept. For him, E. is the subjective side of REVELATION in which reason is driven beyond the limits of the subject-object relation and experiences the mystery of the ground of BEING and meaning. Driven to its limits, reason experiences the shock of finitude or NON-BEING, but this shock is at the same time overcome in the elevating sense of the divine presence. (See Beatific Vision; Holy.)

Ecumenical is derived from the Greek word *oikoumene*, which originally meant "the whole inhabited world." Doubtless because of this association, the ancient CHURCH councils, which were attended by representatives from all over the Roman Empire, were called E. councils. Since the decisions of these councils were believed to represent a consensus among all the churches, the creeds they formulated are often called E. creeds. Since the SCHISM between the East and West, most non-Roman communions insist there have been no E. councils after the Second Council of Nicaea in 787, and, hence, limit the total number of them to seven. R.C.s, on the other hand, regard any council as E. if duly called by the Pope and if its decisions are ratified and promulgated by that See. These decisions are then regarded as infallible. Excluding the Second Vatican Council, R.C.s acknowledge twenty E. councils.

In modern times, the word E. has taken on a related but quite specific meaning. It refers to the movement to unite all those churches who call themselves Christian. The extent of the desired unity is a matter of some discussion. The foci of this discussion have tended to be what is called faith and order, the former referring to doctrine, the latter to church organization or polity. Without depreciating this concern with faith and order, others have emphasized the importance of seeing unity within the whole context of the mission of the church. (See Apostolicity; Church; Dogma; *Ekklesia*; *Koinonia*; Laity; Schism; Notes of the Church.)

Efficacious Grace. See Grace, Efficacious.

Einmaligkeit is a German word for the quality of absolute uniqueness, that which happens only once. It is frequently used to indicate the uniqueness of God's REVELATION in Jesus Christ or of some aspect of the event itself, such as the resurrection. It usually is intended to exclude the view that Jesus Christ is only an illustration of some universal truth that might have been apprehended by human reason.

Ekklesia is the Greek word used in the N.T. to designate the CHURCH, where E. means the people of GOD called into community by the preaching of the Gospel of Jesus Christ, the forgiveness of sins, BAPTISM, and the indwelling of the Holy Spirit. The term has several shades of meaning. Sometimes it refers (1) to the eschatological community awaiting the final consummation and sometimes (2) to the local congregation in a specific city and sometimes (3) to the whole church wherever it may be, of which the local congregation is but an embodiment. In contemporary ECUMENICAL discussions, the word has become very popular, partially because it is not so easily misunderstood as the word "church" frequently is. (See Church; *Koinonia*; Laity.)

Election comes from the Greek word meaning "choice" and traditionally has been used to refer to the decision whereby GOD chooses some and not others to be the agency of his will. In so far as Christian theologians have distinguished between the eternal will of God and the temporal expression of that will, E. is but a manifestation of the ETERNAL DECREES.

The definition of E. given above deliberately cloaks a fateful ambiguity. Does E. refer to the particular means by which God brings about a more general end, or does E. refer to the end itself? More specifically, does God elect Israel to be the bearer of his graciousness and mercy to all men, or is the E. of Israel the end in itself? If the former, then to be the "Chosen People" may, from a human point of view, be an unwelcome burden or curse, since it entails a special mission and responsibilities. If the latter, then to be the "Chosen People" is a designation for special blessings from which the non-elect are excluded.

There is some evidence of both views in the O.T. and, hence, there exists an unsolved problem. On the one hand, the very fact that Israel is "the Elect" means that Israel enjoys the special favor of God. Yet, on the other hand, it was a fact that Israel had forsaken the COVENANT (the divine E.), and a righteous God, therefore, would surely punish—perhaps even forsake—Israel for this. But if Israel was "the Chosen People" how could God do this? The notion of a "righteous remnant" became the forlorn attempt to solve this when appeals were not made to an apocalyptic end of history.

A similar problem existed within Christendom from the earliest days, as St. Paul's tortured attempts to deal with the problem in his Epistle to the Romans reveal. It was especially complicated when E. was identified with salvation. If someone who claimed to be elected lapsed, it could always be said that he never really was elected. The doctrine was further complicated by the classical idea of God who was in no way affected by the world and who was the sole cause of everything that happened. E. then became identified with PREDESTINATION, the view that from all ETERNITY, and without respect to any other consideration than his own arbitrary will, God eternally elected some and not others to be saved. With this a host of somewhat artificial problems arose: If a man really had FAITH (was elected) could he ever lapse again? What are the evidences of E.?

In our own time, Karl Barth (1886-), more than any other theologian, has challenged this identification of E. and predestination. He argues that the error arose because theologians have not taken the REVELATION in Christ with utmost seriousness. Jesus Christ is the one who is elected to reveal that God elects to be for and with every man unconditionally. In the E. of Jesus Christ, Barth insists, God has intended the E. of all men. He has taken rejection and death upon himself. Barth has been accused of UNIVERSALISM, but he denies that he has drawn any such inference. He claims that the theologian has no other purpose than to interpret the WORD OF GOD, and the Word of God is that God elects to be with men. (See Decrees, Eternal; Grace; Predestination; Revelation; Word of God.)

Elohim is the most common Hebraic designation of deity used in the O.T. Since the word has a plural ending and may also be used simply to denote "gods," some Biblical scholars think the O.T. usage reflects a polytheistic background. This is denied by others who claim that the plural form was often employed by the Hebrews to indicate majesty.

Emanation. In certain philosophies and theologies, E. is used to signify the process by which finite beings are derived or flow from the SUBSTANCE of the one divine reality. In so far as the realm of finite being is derived from the very being of the infinite, E. is to be contrasted with CREATION out of nothing. A central analogy that has often been used to illustrate E. has been that of fire and its sparks. The fire is the one ultimate being that casts the "creaturely" sparks out of its very being. These creaturely sparks are essentially divine,· although they have a kind of independence. The idea of E. played an important role in certain forms of GNOSTICISM and in neo-Platonism, both of which profoundly influenced early Christianity. In neo-Platonism especially, the finite order represents a hierarchy or series of degrees of E.s, SOUL, for example, being higher than matter. Christian theologians have always regarded the theory of E. with suspicion, because it verges on PANTHEISM and seems incompatible with the idea of creation out of nothing. (See Creation; Creationism; Filiation; Generation; Gnosticism; God; Immanence; Panentheism; Pantheism; Procession; Soul; Theism; Transcendence.)

Empiricism is a philosophical term designating the view that all knowledge is ultimately derived from experience. E. is to be contrasted with RATIONALISM, which holds that the mind may arrive at substantial knowledge of the world by reason alone and without appeal to experience.

The influence of the empiricist tradition on Christian THEOLOGY is too complex to permit a brief summary statement. This complexity is partially due to the fact that the word "experience" itself has been variously understood. In general, however, it may be said that one classical theological position has been to accept E. in philosophy but to regard theological propositions as revealed, hence as expressions of FAITH rather than of knowledge. Within this position, theologians have differed as to how far experience yields any significant knowledge that might aid theology, some claiming that one may prove at least the existence of GOD, others denying that one can do so (see Natural Theology; Proofs for the Existence of God). It was not until the modern period that some Christian theologians attempted to construct a thorough-going empirical theology. This attempt for the most part was a phenomenon within LIBERAL PROTESTANTISM. Two general types of empirical theology may be distinguished:

(1) where theological propositions are alleged to be statements about or inferences from religious experience of some sort (which is said to be one form of experience as such); (2) where theological propositions are but inferences drawn from the "facts" of all public experience (order, harmony, moral obligation, the correlation between mind and reality), and where no special appeal is made to religious experience. (See Liberal Protestantism; Metaphysics; Naturalism; Natural Theology; Philosophy of Religion; Proofs for the Existence of God; Rationalism; Theism.)

Enhypostasis is a technical term for a theory concerning the relation between the divine and human natures in Jesus Christ. Rejecting ANHYPOSTASIS (the impersonal humanity of Jesus) as a self-contradictory idea, the advocates of E. hold that there is no independent human personality of Jesus but that he became fully personal with the INCARNATION. The theory has been defended in modern times by H. M. Relton and is based on the premise that no man is fully a PERSON unless he is united with GOD, and that Jesus, by virtue of his perfect union, can be regarded as a perfect man. The term was proposed by Leontius of Byzantium (d. 543), as a compromise to the proposals of the monophysites, on the one hand, and the dyophysites, on the other. (See *Anhypostasis*; Apollinarianism; Christology; Dyophysitism; Hypostatic Union; *Logos*; Monophysitism; Person.)

Epistemology comes from the Greek words *episteme* (knowledge) and *logos* (discourse) and is applied to that part of philosophy concerned with the extraordinary number of issues surrounding the origins and nature of human cognition and knowledge. Since Plato (*c.*427-347 B.C.) first distinguished knowledge from belief and opinion and argued that all genuine knowledge was the apprehension of certain eternal structures (forms) by the intellect, philosophers have asked what constitutes knowledge, what is presupposed when one says "I know," and whether knowledge is derived from sense experience or is a product of pure reason or a synthesis of both. In more recent times, E. has increasingly been preoccupied with scientific knowledge and the language of many of the sciences, mathematics. What are scientific "laws"? How are they ascertained? To what degree are they certain? Do they presuppose the "uniformity of nature"? Why is it possible to have certainty in mathematics and geometry but not in history, or chemistry, or biology? These broad questions raise, in turn, a host of related issues.

The epistemological questions and answers of almost all of the various philosophers have influenced THEOLOGY, positively or negatively, because theology has always had an intimate relation to Western philosophy. This has been true since the earliest theologians relied heavily upon the E. of Plato. The problem of "revealed" vis-à-vis "natural" knowledge has been paramount from the beginning and continues to be in most theological systems, although the form of the problem has changed radically with the rise of the sciences in modern times. If all knowledge requires verification and science is knowledge *par excellence* because of its use of the verification principle, in what sense is theology knowledge? And if theology has no mode of verification, how is it to be distinguished from elaborate conjecture or belief? Are there reasonable conjectures? If so, what are the criteria? Theologians have sought with varying degrees of success to cope with these questions that go to the heart of their enterprise. Sometimes they have simply asserted that REVELATION is its own criterion; sometimes they have appealed to a special type of religious intuition; sometimes they have looked upon value judgments as illustrative of FAITH; and sometimes they have pointed out that theological judgments are similar to metaphysical judgments which, it is alleged, have their own particular kind of testability. (See Analogy, Way of; Apologetics; Being; Empiricism; God; Metaphysics; Natural Revelation; Natural Theology; Proofs for the Existence of God; Rationalism; Revelation; Theism.)

Eschatology literally means "discourse about the last things" and refers to that part of Christian doctrine concerned with the final end of man. Traditionally, it has encompassed such matters as the second coming of Christ (PAROUSIA), the RESURRECTION OF THE DEAD, the IMMORTALITY of the SOUL, the FINAL JUDGMENT, and heaven and HELL. In Roman Cathol-

icism, E. also includes the CHURCH's teachings about PURGA-
TORY, LIMBO, and the BEATIFIC VISION.

The E. of the N.T. is intelligible only against the
background of O.T. and Jewish apocalypticism. In general,
the O.T. hope is centered around the restoration of the
COVENANT with Israel, through which it is believed GOD
will restore his reign over the entire world. For the most
part, the O.T. writings about the Day of Yahweh are marked
by restraint, and, so far as depictions of time and details
are concerned, the emphasis falls on God's judgment of
Israel and the hope for renewal. Toward the end of the O.T.
period, however, the hopes of Israel came increasingly to be
expressed in the fantastic imagery of apocalypticism: the
terrors and woes preceding the coming of the Messiah, the
convulsions of nature, the frightful battle between angelic
hosts and the legions of SATAN, the establishment of a temporal reign of the righteous, the resurrection of the dead,
the final judgment, the punishment of the wicked, and the
creation of a new heaven and earth.

The preaching of Jesus presupposes this widespread popular belief, and it may even have determined the framework
of his own message. But within this framework he seems
to have stressed the present sovereignty of God, God's demand
for repentance, God's graciousness, and the love command-
ment. Furthermore, Jesus rejected any speculation concerning
the last days. The earliest Christian community, however, saw
in Jesus' death and resurrection the beginning of the "end
of the age," and they gathered together expectantly in the
hope of the second coming and the resurrection. Traces of
this earliest hope are found scattered throughout the Gospels
and the letters of Paul. The continued delay of the *parousia*
constituted a crisis of belief for the early church, and it was
resolved only by the creative insights of Paul and the author
of the Fourth Gospel who, with differing emphases, shifted
the locus of FAITH from a future hope to present communion with the Holy Spirit and life in the Body of Christ.

The history of Christian thought reveals an extraordinary
diversity of content and emphasis so far as E. is concerned.
In certain periods, the expectation of an immediate end has
dominated life and thought and there have been elaborate

speculations concerning the end. In other periods, the idea has played little role at all. In R.C. and Prot. ORTHODOXY, the doctrine has largely taken the form of teaching the main outlines of the destiny of the soul. The Prot. Reformers, for the most part, were reluctant to engage in speculation concerning the last times or the destiny of the soul and, like Calvin (1509-64), deplored the tendency to "leave not a corner of heaven unexplored." They contented themselves with the thought that we can only see through a glass darkly.

E. in LIBERAL PROTESTANTISM for the most part took the form of theories of progress and of the immortality of the soul. The Biblical idea of resurrection was regarded as but a SYMBOL for the latter and the idea of the KINGDOM OF GOD a symbol for the former. The neo-Reformed theologians rebelled against this reduction of the Biblical ideas to the hopes of Western civilized society. On the other hand, even though these neo-Reformed theologians wished to honor the intention of the Bible, they could not accept the symbols of resurrection and the Kingdom of God literally. Furthermore, they were not altogether comfortable about the fact that Jesus' own preaching seemed to be so influenced by 1st century thought forms. Neo-Reformed theologians sought solutions to this kind of problem of interpretation in many directions.

In his later writings, Karl Barth (1886-) has argued that the symbols of the resurrection and second coming must be taken with deadly seriousness. Rudolf Bultmann (1884-) and Paul Tillich (1886-), on the other hand, argue that these are mythological ideas which require interpretation or DEMYTHOLOGIZATION. Reinhold Niebuhr (1892-) regards the ideas as highly symbolic forms of expressing confidence in the ultimate meaning of history. (See Annihilationism; Apocalyptic Literature; *Apocatastasis*; Beatific Vision; Chiliasm; Demythologization; Hell; Immortality; Judgment, Final; Kingdom of God; Limbo; Millennialism; *Parousia*; Resurrection of the Dead.)

Eschatology, Realized. See Kingdom of God.

Essence is the term used to signify the nature of anything, what defines it as belonging to a particular class. E. may be contrasted with EXISTENCE, on the one hand, and ACCIDENT, on the other. If existence refers to the concrete ACTUALITY of something, i.e., that there is a man named Peter, and accidents refer to the individual peculiarities of that being, i.e., that Peter has blue eyes and is short-tempered, E. refers to the characteristics Peter must exemplify in order properly to be called a man. The concept has played an important role in classical philosophy. The aim of all thought, both Plato (c.427-347 B.C.) and Aristotle (384-322 B.C.) insisted, was to apprehend the eternal structures (E.s) of reality. Furthermore, a rational ethic presupposed the concept of E., for unless one knows what the distinctive nature of man is, one can hardly prescribe what he should do in order to fulfill his nature. Traditional THEOLOGY was based on the same formal distinctions. The essential structures of reality were said to be grounded in the eternal mind of GOD, the LOGOS. The distinctive nature of man was believed to be his possession of a rational SOUL that could worship God. Finally, God was defined as that being in which E. and existence coincide, i.e., his E. is to exist. Some forms of EXISTENTIALISM, especially that of Jean-Paul Sartre (1905-), have been marked by a wholesale assault on the preoccupation with E. in the Western tradition; hence the slogan "existence precedes essence." To some extent this criticism has influenced contemporary Prot. theology, although not greatly. Most religious existentialists simply redefine the nature of man; they do not deny that he has one. (See Accidents; Actuality; Being; Contingent; Existence; Existentialism; *Logos*; Metaphysics; Necessary Being; Ontological Argument; Substance; Universals.)

Eternal Life. See Immortality; Resurrection of the Dead.

Eternity has had two distinct but related meanings in Christian THEOLOGY: (1) as a general concept for a mode of EXISTENCE not subject to time; (2) as a peculiar attribute of GOD alone. The former meaning dominates discussions of IMMORTALITY; the latter is more strictly theological. So far as (1) is concerned, E. has been regarded either as timelessness or as endless duration. In Greek thought time and change were inseparable correlates, hence E. was not endless duration, which might involve change, but a type of existence in which there was no change. This view had a profound influence on Christianity, especially the idea of the final vision of God in which the believer participates in God's own timeless love for himself (see Beatific Vision). This view has been sharply challenged in modern times as being foreign to Biblical thought, especially by the N.T. scholar Oscar Cullmann (1902-), who insists that the Bible thinks of E. as endless duration.

The problem of E. has long been bound up with the strictly theological problem of God's mode of existence and his relation to the world of time. The most impressive and influential attempt to think through the problem in ancient times was that of Augustine (354-430), who argued that time came into being with CREATION and that God creates time. Since time is a function of change, God's consciousness, it was argued, embraces past, present, and future in one synoptic and comprehensive vision. The problem with Augustine's view, which is more or less the traditional Christian view, is that it is difficult to speak of God's knowledge of the future without implying DETERMINISM, and it is no accident that determinism frequently creeps into this position. Furthermore, it is difficult to do justice to the Biblical language of God's acts in time.

The classical Augustinian view has been severely criticized in modern times from quite divergent points of view. It has been rejected by the German philosopher Hegel (1770-1831), by some religious existentialists like Nicholas Berdyaev (1874-1948), and by process philosophers like Alfred N. Whitehead (1861-1947) and Charles Hartshorne (1897-), and, theologically, by those who regard it as unbiblical and speculative. Karl Barth's (1886-) theology may be understood as the most impressive modern Prot. attempt to present an alternative view to the classical conception of God's E. (See *Actus Purus*; Attributes of God; Being; Creation; Foreknowledge; God; Impassibility; Omniscience; Perfection, Theological; Personalism; Predestination; Theism.)

Ethics, Christian, is a term loosely applied to a number of related though distinct things: moral codes, divine com-

mandments, systematic inquiries into the philosophical presuppositions of moral codes, the construction of a theory
of value, the application of Christian moral principles to
practical problems. Ever since the Greek philosophic spirit
and Hebraic historical religion united to form the distinctive
ethos of Western Christendom, C.E. has been, for the most
part, systematic and critical reflection on the moral judgments
of those who share a certain perspective, the key to which
is the life of Jesus of Nazareth. Within this very general
framework, however, there has been an extraordinary diversity
of emphasis, style, and content, such a diversity that it is
impossible to provide an exhaustive classification of the types
of C.E. in so brief an article. Some commentators have distinguished two basic types, the axiological or TELEOLOGICAL
and the DEONTOLOGICAL, the former being concerned with
the definition of the good, the latter with the problem of the
right or duty. But these types necessarily overlap, since the
delineation of man's good necessarily implies duties, just as
duties ultimately presuppose some understanding of the good.
Nevertheless, there is some validity in the distinction, because
each is marked by a kind of different ethos and style. Within
these two types there are subtypes, depending on how one
specifies the good or the right. Some axiological theories, for
example, define the end of man as the BEATIFIC VISION, while
others define it in terms of life with other men in the KINGDOM
OF GOD, which, in turn, may be variously understood. Each
of these will lead to differing emphases and problems. One
of the most impressive Christian teleological ethics was constructed by Thomas Aquinas (c.1225-74), an ethic which still
stamps the character of Roman Catholicism. His ethic was
built on the idea that man had two ends, a natural and a
supernatural one. Each end has its appropriate principles and
VIRTUES and its corresponding means of realization. The
principles of each are applicable to all moral problems in
some way or other and it is the business of CASUISTRY to work
this out. The ethics of the Reformers, on the other hand,
were determined by the polarity of LAW AND GOSPEL, which
led them to reflect continually on the Ten Commandments
and the concrete responsibilities of the Christian man in his
earthly VOCATION. Still other Christian ethicists have been

primarily concerned with CHRISTIAN PERFECTION or with the purity of the Christian community. One of the profoundest revolutions in Prot. ethical theory occurred with the rise of the SOCIAL GOSPEL, its criticism of moralistic individualism, and its demands and program for social JUSTICE. This movement, together with the challenge of Marxism and the collapse of the unity of the Western world through world war, has stimulated both R.C. and Prot. ethicists to profound reflection on social problems as well as on the basic principles of love and justice. Some of the most penetrating ethical and social criticism of the last two decades has come from such Christian philosophers and theologians as Emil Brunner (1889-), Jacques Maritain (1882-), H. Richard Niebuhr (1894-1962), Reinhold Niebuhr (1892-), and Paul Tillich (1886-). In more CATHOLIC churches, C.E. is called MORAL THEOLOGY. (See *Agape* and *Eros*; Casuistry; Conscience; Culture, Theology of; Decalogue; Deontology; Ethics, Contextual; Ethics, Social; Eudaimonism; Law and Gospel; Moral Theology; Natural Law; Perfection, Christian; Sanctification; Sin, Actual; Sin, Original; Social Gospel; Virtue; Vocation.)

Ethics, Contextual refers to the view that depreciates the reliance on ethical principles and norms alleged to be binding in every situation and appeals rather to a sympathetic understanding and judgment of the specific context in which action is required. This type of contextualism is particularly to be found in some contemporary Prot. ethicists, especially those influenced by EXISTENTIALISM, and is usually associated with the position of Dietrich Bonhoeffer (1906-45), a Prot. theologian executed by Hitler, whose posthumously published writings have been very influential. Contextualists generally argue that norms and principles more often than not are used as an escape from the difficult burden of making a lonely and free judgment about every situation; they provide, therefore, an escape from responsibility. The uniqueness of the situation and the uniqueness of one's own requirements and potentialities are such that they require a unique decision no norm or law can anticipate. Christian contextualists frequently insist that love is the only binding obligation but that love cannot be regarded as a principle in the usual sense of the word. (See *Agape* and *Eros*; Casuistry; Conscience; Deontology; Ethics, Christian; Law and Gospel; Natural Law; Perfection, Christian; Sanctification; Vocation.)

Ethics, Social is that part of CHRISTIAN ETHICS concerned with man's social relationships judged by standards implicit in the Christian FAITH. In this general sense, S.E. has been a perennial concern of Christian theologians from the very beginnings of the Christian CHURCH, for they have reflected on such matters as marriage and divorce, sexuality, the family, economic life, war, slavery, the function of courts, work and VOCATION, the theater, the aims of the state, etc. Traditionally, the normative principles believed to govern these spheres were derived from the NATURAL LAW, a law also believed to be embodied in the Ten Commandments. Because of this long tradition, an enormous and rich literature of the social teachings of the church exists. In the 19th and 20th centuries, there was an increasing conviction that traditional natural law theory was unable to deal with the complexities and injustices of the new industrial order, especially the conflicts between labor and capital. The proponents of the SOCIAL GOSPEL turned to the new social sciences for their analyses, and turned to various political ideologies, like democratic socialism, for their vision of what the future order should be. Informing it all was a profound sense of the dignity of the individual. The neo-Reformed theologians were critical of what they believed to be the naïve theological assumptions underlying the Social Gospel but they were no less concerned with S.E. The writings of Karl Barth (1886-), Emil Brunner (1889-), H. Richard Niebuhr (1894-1962), Reinhold Niebuhr (1892-), and Paul Tillich (1886-) deal extensively with problems concerning the economic and political order, race, war, social JUSTICE, marriage and the family, and even art. (See *Agape* and *Eros*; Casuistry; Conscience; Culture, Theology of; Decalogue; Ethics, Christian; Ethics, Contextual; Liberal Protestantism; Natural Law; Perfection, Christian; Sanctification; Sin, Actual; Sin, Original; Social Gospel; Vocation.)

Eucharist is a proper noun derived from the Greek word meaning "to give thanks," and refers to the SACRAMENT of the Lord's Supper or Holy Communion. While it does not appear as a proper noun in the N.T., it was so used very shortly thereafter. Until modern times, the E. has always been the central element in the drama of Christian worship and as a practice, therefore, unites almost all Christendom, the Quakers and the Salvation Army being the notable exceptions. The interpretation of it, however, has often been a matter of controversy and has separated Prot. from R.C. as well as Prot. from Prot.

The gradual development of the theory and practice of the E. is far too complex to relate here. By the time of the Prot. Reformation, however, the main elements in R.C. belief and practice were these: (1) the elements of bread and wine are miraculously changed into the SUBSTANCE of the body and blood of Jesus Christ after the words of consecration said by the priest (the DOGMA of TRANSUBSTANTIATION); (2) the MIRACLE can only be performed by a duly ordained priest; (3) the Mass itself is to be understood as a propitiatory sacrifice for the sins of the living and the dead. Closely associated with these elements was the practice of the adoration or worship of the E. and the withdrawal of the cup from the laity.

Although the Reformers were in disagreement among themselves concerning how Christ may be said to be present in the E., they were united in rejecting all of the elements mentioned above. This rejection followed quite logically from their basic convictions concerning the nature of FAITH and GRACE. Holding that faith was a whole-hearted confidence in the graciousness of God, they basically could not accept the view that the Mass was a propitiatory sacrifice, or that the reality of Christ's presence was dependent on a priestly act, or that grace was an infused substance. Calvin's (1509-64) view is quite typical when he writes that the sacrament "is added as a seal, not to give efficacy to the promise of God, as if it wanted validity in itself, but only to confirm it to us."

The Reformers' various views on the E. reflect their peculiar historical situations. Zwingli's (1484-1531) concern was to repudiate the R.C. conception of the Mass as a sacrifice and the notion of the bodily presence of Christ. He stressed, therefore, the symbolic nature of the E. Luther (1483-1546), on the other hand, was alarmed at the alleged excesses of the views of Carlstadt (c.1480-1541), a contemporary rebel against Roman Catholicism, as well as the "symbolic" view of Zwingli. He stressed, therefore, the real presence of Christ in the E. The theological point at issue (though obscured by personal jealousies and politics) was the mode of Christ's presence in the E., and this, in turn, reflected differences over some of the fine points of CHRIS-TOLOGY. Calvin's position is often regarded as the mediating one: Christ, he believed, is mysteriously present in power in the E. but the elements are not miraculously changed nor is the notion of a priestly miracle appropriate.

There has been a renewed interest in the E. as embodying in a dramatic way the entire Gospel, an interest not a little stimulated by the drive toward reunion among the Prot. churches, on the one hand, and the new openness of Roman Catholicism, on the other. New possibilities of understanding have been opened up, although it is still a tragic fact that the central rite of Christianity remains a matter of dispute in Christendom. (See Church; Consubstantiation; *Ex Opere Operato*; Faith; Grace; Habit; Infusion; Real Presence; Sacrament; Transubstantiation.)

Eudaimonism comes from the Greek word *eudaimonia*, which means literally "the well-being of the daemon" or SOUL, and refers to those ethical theories that make the aim of all right action the health or well-being of the agent. Since what constitutes health or well-being is itself a matter of dispute, there are a variety of eudaimonistic ethical theories. Ancient Christian writers naturally believed that the true health of the soul consists in the love of GOD and, to this extent, advocated a Christian E. This tendency has been sharply criticized by some contemporary Prot. theologians, especially the Swedish Lutherans Anders Nygren (1890-) and Gustaf Aulen (1879-). (See *Agape* and *Eros*; Deontological; Ethics, Christian; Law and Gospel; Perfection, Christian; Sanctification.)

Evil. See Theodicy.

Exegesis refers to the process of interpreting a text. It is to be distinguished from translation, on the one hand, and from inquiry into the principles of interpretation (HERMENEUTICS), on the other, although they are all closely related. Since Christian THEOLOGY is based on the conviction that the Bible contains the REVELATION of GOD, E. has always been of special theological importance. Theologians have sought to clarify obscurities and apparent contradictions in the text so that the meaning of it might become clear. The first systematic exegete was Origen of Alexandria (c.185-c.254). Aware of the obscurities in and moral offensiveness of some of the O.T., he interpreted the text on the Platonic premise that nothing is to be believed that is unworthy of God. He then distinguished several levels of meaning: (1) the plain or literal, which constitutes the great bulk of historical material; (2) the moral, which is sometimes illustrated by the historical and sometimes is itself the subject matter; (3) the allegorical or spiritual, which has to do with the divine truths which are often hidden beneath the husks of apparently absurd or offensive passages. In general, these three types of E., with differing emphases and modifications, were practiced by theologians until the Reformation.

The difficulty with ALLEGORICAL INTERPRETATION is that it enables the theologian to use Scripture simply to illustrate the DOGMAS of the CHURCH. But the Reformers believed the dogmas of the church should be judged by the Scriptures. They sensed the dangers in allegorical E. and rejected it. Luther's (1483-1546) basic principle was that all Scripture, taken in its plain sense, should be judged by the GOSPEL of Christ. By this he did not mean that all Scripture was to be made to conform to Christ but that if, on plain reading, it did not conform (as he thought the books of James and Revelation did not) it was not Scripture or the WORD OF GOD. With the rejection of allegorical interpretation, however, all the old difficulties with which allegory was designed to cope (absurdity, contradiction, moral offense) reappeared and were aggravated by the later Prot. view of the literal inerrancy of the Bible. The rise of BIBLICAL CRITICISM, therefore, constituted a crisis for Prot. E. LIBERAL PROTESTANTISM sought to meet it by accepting the critical method, by reading the texts in terms of their historical context, and by finding the religious value of them to be in the development from primitive religion to the ethical monotheism of the prophets and Jesus. NEO-REFORMED THEOLOGY, without rejecting historical criticism or the plain sense, believed that liberal Protestantism had not seen the true theological intention of the Biblical authors—to witness to the acts of God in history. Criticisms of this mode of E. have recently arisen and the issue is far from settled. (See Accommodation; Allegorical Interpretation; Biblical Criticism; Biblicism; Demythologization; Form Criticism; Fundamentalism; Gnosticism; Hermeneutics; Inspiration of the Bible; Myth; *Religionsgeschichtliche Schule*; Word of God.)

Existence. In classical THEOLOGY, E. is usually contrasted with ESSENCE and refers to the ACTUALITY in time and space of any subject, in contrast to its mere possibility or potentiality. For example, after having defined the essential characteristics of a thing (what it is), to assert its E. is to say *that* there is such a thing so defined. In EXISTENTIALISM, however, the word E. is given a somewhat different meaning. It refers to the peculiar and unique way in which human beings live their lives and, hence, incorporates aspects of both E. and essence as formulated in classical philosophy and theology. Since the distinctive nature of human E. is choice or freedom, and freedom, in turn, cannot be defined as a thing, Jean-Paul Sartre (1905-) has argued that "man has no essence" or that "E. precedes essence." Other so-called existentialists, for example Martin Heidegger (1889-) and Karl Jaspers (1883-), have had no interest in elaborating Sartre's formula. Their aim, rather, is to understand the nature of reality (or BEING) by grasping the peculiar mode of E. that is human, hence their concern with certain phenomena that are clues to the understanding of human E.: ANXIETY, melancholy, guilt, despair, choice. (See Actuality; Alienation; Anxiety; Authentic Existence; Being; Essence; Metaphysics; Necessary Being; Non-Being.)

Existential is an adjective frequently and often loosely used in contemporary theological and religious literature to signify something that is of ultimate significance for one's being; for example, an E. truth. (See Existentialism.)

Existentialism is the name of a philosophical movement that emerged shortly before the Second World War in Germany, spread to France and America, and reached its zenith in the late forties and fifties. Quite diverse so far as its specific teachings are concerned, it is united more by its common concerns, motifs, and emphases. The two most influential German exponents of it are Martin Heidegger (1889-), whose *Sein und Zeit (Being and Time)* appeared in 1927, and Karl Jaspers (1883-), the second volume of whose *Philosophie* appeared in 1932. The most famous French existentialist is Jean-Paul Sartre (1905-). There are a number of other lesser known but formidable writers in the movement as well. All of the most important figures, however, were indebted to the writings of Sören Kierkegaard (1813-55), a once-neglected Danish author whose works were not discovered and translated into German until early in this century and into English until still later.

Although no general description of E. exactly fits any one exponent of it—indeed, Heidegger claims not to be an existentialist—the movement may be characterized roughly as follows. It begins with the conviction that Western philosophy since the Greeks has been preoccupied with the idea of ESSENCE, the general and universal features of anything, rather than with concrete, individual, human EXISTENCE, the former being counted more real (because unchanging) than the latter. Consequently, Western philosophy has been intellectualistic and rationalistic. It has not only been irrelevant so far as illuminating life is concerned but has actually obscured the truth about human existence. The fundamental categories of classical philosophy (SOUL, VIRTUE, SUBSTANCE, ACCIDENTS, essence, existence) are all impersonal and fail to do justice to the basic character of human life as change, consciousness, process, movement, passion, and decision. In short, they fail to indicate the historical nature of human existence. This rejection of the emphasis of classical philosophy accounts for two otherwise apparently contradictory tendencies in E.: (1) the attack on abstract thought and intellectual detachment, hence the writings of novels, essays, poetry, and plays by existentialists who wish to get their readers involved; (2) the highly abstruse development of new categories that aim to do justice to the unique character of human existence.

The search for new categories to describe human existence (*Dasein*) is most characteristic of Heidegger's philosophy, and he shares with the others the emphasis on the radical freedom of man. Man is a being who can lose or win himself. He does not acquire authentic selfhood "naturally" (essentially) the way one acquires teeth and a beard. He can lose himself by surrendering his freedom to an ideology, an orthodoxy, or a set of moral values, and he can win himself only by authentic and often lonely decision and resolution in the face of the concrete situations he faces. The character of man's being can best be explored through such basic human phenomena as ANXIETY, concern, CONSCIENCE, one's feeling of shame before others, and guilt, to mention a few. These phenomena are not just psychological "accidents" but reflect the basic nature of man as a temporal, embodied consciousness thrown into a world he did not make and which threatens him with death. E., in short, emphasizes the crucial importance of decision, the moment, temporality and death for a philosophic understanding of man.

E. had a profound impact on the so-called neo-Reformed theologians, the early Karl Barth (1886-), Rudolf Bultmann (1884-), Friedrich Gogarten (1887-), Emil Brunner (1889-), Paul Tillich (1886-), and Reinhold Niebuhr (1892-), as well as on some R.C. philosophers and theologians, Gabriel Marcel (1889-) and Karl Rahner (1904-). Although these theologians have quite diverse positions, they share in common the existentialist attack on the language of substance and soul as a way of talking about man and, hence, are able to interpret FAITH in different terms. The self, they argue, is a unity of radical freedom and limitedness, and faith is the acceptance of this paradoxical unity. But faith is not the possession of a creed or a doctrine, nor is it belief; it is, rather, the decision to be oneself as *this* PERSON in *this* situation, a decision that must be made again and again. This decision is made possible by the gracious and unconditioned acceptance of man by GOD which enables man to have the courage to be himself. This faith is made possible through the proclamation and acceptance of the GOSPEL in which God himself confronts man with his word of acceptance. Existential theologians try to interpret the Scripture in this manner, to show that in and under the mythological concepts and ideas is an understanding of human life that is a viable possibility for modern man. (See Anxiety; Authentic Existence; Being; Conscience; Demythologization; Existence; Existential; Historicity of Human Existence; I-Thou; Phenomenology; Self-Understanding.)

Existenziell is a technical term in the writings of Martin Heidegger (1889-) and Rudolf Bultmann (1884-) and denotes specifically a particular and concrete act of existing in contrast to *existenzial*, which denotes a universal pattern or structure that is embodied in some particular or concrete act. In so far as existentialist THEOLOGY is concerned with an analysis of the universal structures of man's EXISTENCE (*Existenzialien*), it presupposes the concrete and specific (E.) acts of definite men. (See Existentialism.)

Ex Opere Operato is the Latin term frequently used to describe the R.C. view that GRACE is conferred through the sacramental act itself (*opus operatum*) if the requisite conditions are present. The idea is not, as frequently interpreted, that the SACRAMENTS are effective whether the recipient receives them worthily or not; on the contrary, R.C. teaching is that if no intention is present the sacrament is not efficacious. The intention, however, need only be a virtual one, i.e., the act must be consciously intended even if it is done distractedly and unreflectively. In this sense, the sacraments confer grace in the nature of the case as soon as the minimal conditions are fulfilled. Prot.s reject the view, insisting rather that the sacraments are intended for FAITH, and without faith are only empty signs. (See Faith; Grace; Sacrament.)

Expiation is the making right by means of some act or offering for the offense or injury done to some PERSON. It is thus closely related to ATONEMENT, PROPITIATION, and sacrifice. According to the theory of the atonement dominant in Western Christendom since Anselm (1033-1109), Jesus Christ made E. for the sins of man by virtue of his substitutionary death on the cross. How the believer takes advantage of this is a matter of difference among Prot.s and R.C.s. (See Atonement; Propitiation; Redemption; Satisfaction; Soteriology.)

F

Faith. In the history of Christian thought, two general tendencies concerning the concept of F. may be observed: (1) F. is regarded more nearly as belief or as mental assent (*assensus*) to some truth, whether about the nature of GOD (supernatural truth) or about the past (historical truth). (2) F. is understood to be the basic orientation of the total PERSON that may include belief but is best described as trust (FIDUCIA), confidence, or loyalty. Advocates of the first more intellectualistic model tend to regard F. as but the first step toward salvation, one that requires the additional steps (VIRTUES) of hope and CHARITY in order to be complete. Advocates of the second more voluntaristic model see all actions and thoughts of man as but expressions of his basic orientation and, therefore, regard F. alone as constituting the decisive and proper relationship to God. The basic disagreements between Prot. and R.C. as well as among the Prot.s themselves may be explained to a great extent in terms of these two differing conceptions of F.

On the whole, the theologians of the early CHURCH tended to regard F. intellectualistically—as the acceptance of tradition or as the apprehension of certain eternal and divine truths. This is not to say that they conceived the entire Christian life in these terms. On the contrary, it was just because they did not think F. could be identified with salvation that they found it necessary to supplement F. with mystical experience or, as in the case of Clement of Alexandria (*c*.150-*c*.215), with a higher mode of intellectual intuition or *gnosis*. St. Augustine

(354-430) modified profoundly this view in the light of his own emphasis on the will, but even he sometimes regarded F. as but the initial step leading to the highest stage, the love of God.

The most impressive theological system based on the more intellectualistic model of F. was constructed by Thomas Aquinas (c.1225-74), and his teachings on this matter inform the basic doctrine of Roman Catholicism. According to the authoritative statements of Roman Catholicism, F. is to be regarded as an intellectual act of approving assent to certain supernatural truths or DOGMAS because of their divine authority. Although it is argued that the will moves the intellect (and to that extent it is wrong to say that Thomas regards F. as merely an intellectual act), the element of trust or confidence (*fiducia*) is directed to the divine authority, and, therefore, is not said to constitute the act of F. itself but, rather, is a motive anterior to it. For this reason, the R.C. can develop the idea of IMPLICIT FAITH (*fides implicita*), that is, a readiness on the part of the intellectually unsophisticated or ignorant to assent to supernatural truths on authority even though those truths are not known or understood. R.C. doctrine rejects explicitly the idea that F. alone unites a man perfectly to God, because F. requires supplementation by the other two supernatural virtues of hope and charity.

Luther (1483-1546) rejected the limitation of F. to assent and regarded it as the response of the total person in trust to the graciousness of God as it was revealed in Jesus Christ. Since F. was regarded as total and trustful reliance on God's faithfulness, it includes hope and charity. F. is the basic inclination of the heart or will. It followed that the object of F. was not supernatural truth but God himself, his trustworthiness. Thus, Luther frequently contrasted believing a doctrine of the INCARNATION with trusting in the benefits of Christ's coming. Although Luther himself accepted orthodox doctrine, the logic of his position led to the view that doctrine was but an attempt to express F., and not itself the object of F. This, in turn, led to the more radical conclusion drawn by later Prot.s that orthodox doctrine was but a relative and historically conditioned attempt to give utterance to F. in the mercy of God. Since orthodox formulations are relative to one era, they might, in other epochs, stand in the way of a true understanding and F. Calvin's (1509-64) view was similar to Luther's, although it appears more intellectualistic by virtue of Calvin's emphasis on F. as knowledge (*cognitio*). But an inspection of Calvin's use of the word "knowledge" discloses that he means not a knowledge about God's metaphysical nature (his ESSENCE) but a knowledge of God's benevolence and "what is agreeable to his nature."

In subsequent debate with R.C. theologians over the problem of authority, the Prot. Scholastics of the 16th and 17th centuries once more identified F. with assent to certain historical truths and doctrines, although they added that it was also necessary to have confidence that these truths apply specifically to the one affirming them. The accent, however, fell on right belief, and it was against this accent that many groups of Prot.s, Pietists, and Evangelicals rebelled. All stressed the priority of "heart" religion over doctrine.

The impact of science, the corresponding doubts concerning the literal accuracy of the Bible (see Biblical Criticism), as well as the lack of confidence in metaphysical speculation, were the reasons for a new emphasis on Luther's distinction between believing doctrines and trusting in Christ's benefits. This distinction was so sharply drawn that it was possible to emphasize religious experience at the expense of believing orthodox Christian doctrine. Schleiermacher (1768-1834), for example, argued that doctrines were neither objects of F. nor speculative inferences from REVELATION but were simply the religious feelings set forward in speech. Albrecht Ritschl (1822-89) regarded any identification of F. and belief as the essence of Roman Catholicism. Wilhelm Herrmann (1846-1922) sarcastically said that the only difference between Prot. ORTHODOXY and Roman Catholicism was that the latter required one to believe both the Bible and the tradition while the former required only belief in the Bible. It was, therefore, "one-half" Catholicism.

Although the neo-Reformed theologians rejected LIBERAL PROTESTANTISM in many of its aspects, they did not return to the intellectualistic model of F. Almost all of them regarded F.'s object as God's graciousness, not some doctrine about it. Instead of emphasizing feeling or religious experience, however, they used such terms as "encounter," "disclosure," and "EXISTENTIAL truth." Doctrines were regarded as relative attempts to make intelligible what is implied in the encounter with God in Christ. The most impressive exception to this understanding is the THEOLOGY of Karl Barth (1886-), who argues that objective knowledge is given in revelation, although he rejects the R.C. explication of the matter. (See Assurance; Christology; Dogma; *Fides Qua Creditur*; Grace; Heresy; I-Thou; Justification; *Kerygma*; Law and Gospel; Neo-Reformed Theology; Objectification; Revelation; Soteriology; Word of God.)

Faith, Explicit (*fides explicita*) refers, in R.C. and Prot. Scholastic THEOLOGY, to a self-conscious assent to a truth which is apprehended clearly enough to distinguish it from other truths although all that is involved in it may not be perfectly intelligible. It stands in contrast to *fides implicita*. (See Faith.)

Faith, Implicit (*fides implicita*) refers to an assent to the truths that the CHURCH believes even though one has no knowledge of what those truths are which the church believes. It is assent to the divine authority of the church and, implicitly, to what it teaches. (See Faith.)

Faith, Infused (*fides infusa*) is, according to R.C. doctrine, that supernatural VIRTUE by which the intellect is disposed to assent to supernatural truth. (See Faith.)

Fallenness is a technical term in the philosophy of Martin Heidegger (1889-), which has had some influence on contemporary THEOLOGY, both R.C. and Prot. F. is one of the structures of human EXISTENCE and is the loss of self that occurs when one becomes absorbed with others and forgets one's own unique possibilities and individuality. By losing oneself in the anonymous crowd and by letting it determine one's judgments, one becomes estranged from oneself and others. Thus F. manifests itself in a restless curiosity about everything, in trivial gossip, and in evasive speech that conceals the ANXIETY one feels in the face of one's own death; but one decides nothing. Because F. is regarded by Heidegger as a structure of human existence, some theologians have seen it as a philosophical corroboration of the doctrine of ORIGINAL SIN. (See Authentic Existence; Existentialism; Sin, Original.)

Fides Qua Creditur is the "faithing" of the believer, i.e., the subjective act of assent or trust, the act of FAITH itself. It stands in contrast to *fides quae creditur*, the faith that is believed, i.e., the body of doctrine which the believer holds to be true.

Fides Historica is the assent to certain truths about past history.

Fideism is derived from the basic Latin root meaning FAITH, and refers generally to the doctrine that Christian assertions are matters of blind belief and cannot be known or demonstrated to be true. (See Faith; Revelation; Word of God.)

Fiducia means confidence or trust and has been regarded by Prot. theologians as constituting the principal part of FAITH. (See Faith; Grace; Revelation.)

Filiation is a technical term often used by theologians when clarifying the respective relationships among the three PERSONS of the TRINITY. It is used especially of the relationship of the Eternal Son or LOGOS to the Father, in contrast to the relationship of the Holy Spirit to the Father and Son. The Son is "begotten" or "actively generated" in contrast to the Holy Spirit, who "proceeds" by "passive spiration." The Son, therefore, has the special characteristic (hypostatical characteristic) of F. (See *Filioque*; Generation; *Logos*; Modalism; Monarchianism; *Perichoresis*; Person; Procession; Trinity.)

Filioque means literally "and from the Son" and refers to the phrase added to the Nicaea-Constantinopolitan creed by the Western part of Christendom so that it reads "And [I believe] in the Holy Ghost, the Lord and Giver of Life, who proceeds from the Father *and from the Son. . . .*" It was not in the original form of the creed but was added at the Council of

Toledo in A.D. 589. Its use offended the theologians of the Greek church and it ultimately led to a SCHISM between the two branches of Christendom in the 11th century. The Eastern church protested that the doctrine was not to be found in Scripture and that the decision to add the F. clause to the creed was not made by an ECUMENICAL council. Western theologians defended it on Trinitarian grounds and it remains in the Western form of the creed. (See *Logos*; Person; Procession; Spirit–Holy Spirit; Trinity.)

Final Perseverance. See Perseverance.

Foreknowledge is that mode of knowledge theologians have attributed to GOD, it being argued that God knows past, present, and future in one simple and eternal act of cognition. The problem is especially complicated if one says that God not only foreknows but foreordains all events. If F. was simply an expression of the unique and perfect mode of cognition of God, then F. might be interpreted in such a fashion as not to prejudice the freedom of the creatures. But if God's F. is a way of saying that God knows the future because he determines all the antecedent conditions (foreordains and wills them), then it is difficult to know what meaning can be attributed to freedom, and one is committed to DETERMINISM. Duns Scotus (*c.*1264-1308) and Calvin (1509-64) did not hesitate to draw this latter conclusion. William of Occam (*c.*1300-*c.*1349) ingeniously argued that, although it is reasonable on philosophical grounds to say that God knows only the future indeterminately (since future events are more or less indeterminate), one must believe on theological grounds that God foreordains the future. Most contemporary Prot. theologians have tended to emphasize the radical nature of man's freedom, on the one hand, and renounced all attempts to characterize the nature of God's knowledge on the other, thereby avoiding dealing with the problem. Some philosophers of religion, however, have taken up Occam's philosophical suggestion and argued that the future is genuinely indeterminate, even for God. They claim that perfect knowledge, the unique mode of God's knowing, can only mean knowing the actual as actual, the necessary as necessary, the indeterminate as indeterminate, and the possible as possible. (See Attributes of God; Decrees, Eternal; Election; Freedom of the Will; God; Neo-Reformed Theology; Omniscience; Panentheism; Perfection, Theological; Personalism; Predestination; Process Philosophy; Theism.)

Foreordination. See Predestination.

Form Criticism (*Formgeschichte*) is a special method of analysis and interpretation of preliterary or oral traditions. It is based on the conviction that ancient writers frequently collected, arranged, and edited materials (stories, legends, wise sayings, MIRACLE stories, etc.) already circulating in the culture in which the writer lived. Studies of the ancient literature of Israel, Persia, India, and Greece have shown that these units of material possessed distinct characteristics, and that it is possible, therefore, to distinguish an epigram or wise saying (*gnome*) from a special saying attributed to a particular person (*chria*), or a short illustrative story (*paradigm*) from a legend or an etiological MYTH. By noting how these forms persisted or were slightly changed in transmission, the form critics believe they can establish certain patterns of development. F.C. was first applied with great success to the O.T. and, then, to the N.T. The N.T. scholars especially associated with F.C. are Karl L. Schmidt (1891-1956), Rudolf Bultmann (1884-) and Martin Dibelius (1883-1947). By means of F.C. they attempted to establish the earliest and most trustworthy traditions about Jesus of Nazareth. (See Biblical Criticism; Hermeneutics; Inspiration of the Bible; Myth; *Religionsgeschichtliche Schule*; Synoptic Problem.)

Freedom of the Will. Those called libertarians, who defend the F.O.T.W., are more united by what they deny than by what they affirm. What they deny is that human actions are necessitated. What they affirm, however, cannot be so easily summarized, because it depends so heavily on the definitions of such crucial words as "will," "motive," "character," "freedom," all of which, in turn, are intelligible only in terms of larger contexts of thought. Some libertarians have insisted upon a complete and unconditioned power of choice, a position that others maintain makes any idea of human responsibility unintelligible. Others have argued for a power of choice consistent with one's character and the motives which "flow from" that character, a position which, in turn, requires a satisfactory explanation for the formation of character and the strength of motives. Still others have argued that freedom is to be defined as a lack of compulsion, a definition not inconsistent with believing that all action can be described in terms of laws. Still others have insisted that freedom and necessity cannot be intellectually reconciled; both are phenomena experienced by men and the contradiction simply must be endured.

The philosophical problem of freedom is further complicated in THEOLOGY by the ideas of GOD'S PROVIDENCE, OMNISCIENCE, and OMNIPOTENCE, as well as the ideas of sin and GRACE. The idea of God's providence, especially when joined with the ideas of foreknowledge and PREDESTINATION, raises acute questions concerning the independence of the will. If all human events can be foreseen, or if all actions are but expressions of one infinite action, in what sense is human decision really free? Or if, since the fall of Adam, it is impossible for man to will the good, in what sense is choice real and significant? These issues have led to theological controversy again and again in the history of the CHURCH. The earliest and most determinative of these was between Augustine (354-430) and Pelagius (fl. 400-420?) in the 5th century (see Pelagianism). Augustine argued that, although Adam possessed both the ability not to sin (*posse non peccare*) and the ability to sin (*posse peccare*) before his fall, he lost the former by exercising the latter. This original freedom of man, he believed, could only be restored by an act of divine grace. This, however, raises the question whether man has the ability to accept or reject grace and with that question the problem of freedom returns. Augustine quite consistently argued that grace is irresistible and prevenient, that is, that an act of God is itself required to enable the will to accept grace and that this grace is irresistible to those whom God wills to give it. A similar though not identical position was held by Luther (1483-1546) and Calvin (1509-64). This problem is complicated, however, by the notion of predestination, which is but one aspect of foreordination, because if God decrees from all ETERNITY what will happen and who will be saved, in what sense is it meaningful to speak even of Adam's freedom to choose before the fall? Is not one driven to say that even this choice was determined? Unable to accept this consequence, there have been a number of theologians who have insisted on man's freedom to a greater or lesser degree: Pelagius, Molina (1535-1600), Arminius (1560-1609), Wesley (1703-91), and others. Usually these defenders of free will have also attacked or reinterpreted the doctrine of predestination.

Two modern intellectual movements have profoundly influenced contemporary Prot. theology: depth philosophy (especially Freudianism) and EXISTENTIALISM. The former is deterministic in character, and has frequently been used to illumine the phenomena of the bondage of the will. The latter is libertarian and, in the case of Jean-Paul Sartre (1905-), has been marked by a rigorous criticism of Freud's DETERMINISM. Theologians use this philosophy to illumine the nature of human existence as decision. On the whole it may be said that the problem is not yet satisfactorily resolved. (See Anxiety; Arminianism; Election; God; Grace; Omniscience; Omnipotence; Pelagianism; Synergism.)

Fundamentalism is a name that was attached to the viewpoint of those who, shortly after the turn of the century, resisted all liberal attempts to modify orthodox Prot. belief or to question the infallibility of the Bible in any respect. The name is derived from a series of tracts published between 1912-14 entitled *The Fundamentals* that aimed at defining and defending the essentials of Prot. doctrine. The most important of the fundamental doctrines were (1) the INSPIRATION and infallibility of the Bible, (2) the doctrine of the TRINITY, (3) the VIRGIN BIRTH and deity of Christ, (4) the substitutionary theory of the ATONEMENT, (5) the bodily resurrection, ASCENSION, and second coming of Christ (PAROUSIA).

Since most of these beliefs have been part of ORTHODOXY, historians have seen the uniqueness of F. to consist in its violent opposition to all beliefs that seem opposed to some teaching of the Bible. In the twenties and thirties this opposition was focused particularly on any theory of man's origins, especially evolution, that seemed incompatible with the account in Genesis. Consequently, F. tended to be identified with blind opposition to all critical inquiry.

Because of this identification, certain conservative theologians who share the above-described beliefs but who think they can be defended in a rational manner have tended to shirk the name "fundamentalist" and call themselves instead "evangelical conservatives." They generally oppose the spirit of ecumenism and any THEOLOGY, including NEO-REFORMED THEOLOGY, which does not regard the Bible as the absolute and infallible rule of FAITH and practice. (See Biblical Criticism; Inspiration of the Bible; Liberal Protestantism; Neo-Reformed Theology; Protestant Principle; Revelation; Word of God.)

G

Generation is the traditional, technical term used by theologians to explicate the phrase "only begotten" and to describe the relationship by which the eternal Son, or LOGOS, or second PERSON of the TRINITY is related to the Father. It is said to be that act in which the *Logos* has eternally communicated to it the ESSENCE of the Father. It is further understood to be a necessary and not a willed or voluntary act of G. (See Filiation; *Filioque*; *Logos*; Person; Procession; Trinity.)

Geschichte. See *Historie.*

Glossolalia means literally "speaking in tongues" and refers to an ecstatic spiritual state that manifests itself in unintelligible utterances. It was a phenomenon in the early CHURCH and is deliberately cultivated in certain pentecostal and other groups that regard it as a direct manifestation of the Holy Spirit. The apostle Paul warns against its excesses in his first letter to the church at Corinth (I Cor. 12-14). (See Ecstasy.)

Gnosticism is the name given by historians of religion to an extraordinarily variegated type of religious thought and practice that was widespread in the Graeco-Roman world in the first centuries of the Christian era. In almost all of its forms, it was regarded as a dangerous threat to Christianity, although early Christians sometimes borrowed its SYMBOLS and terms to express their FAITH. There are a number of scholarly theories accounting for the origins of G., but most agree that it is a loose confluence of many diverse streams of thought emanating from pre-Christian mystery religions in Egypt, Syria, and Babylon. Although a confluence, the mythologies and beliefs of the various streams had certain common motifs. A central one was the conviction that salvation was to be had by the deliverance of the SPIRIT from its imprisonment in the world, a deliverance accomplished by means of a secret knowledge or *gnosis*. The basic motif found expression in elaborate and complex mythologies concerning how the spirit came to be imprisoned and how its deliverance was to be accomplished. Not uncommon was the MYTH of a divine deliverer who comes from the kingdom of light in a disguise, slips through the network of the evil powers of darkness who stand guard over the enslaved world, releases the stupefied and captive spirits of light, and provides them with the secret knowledge and password that will enable them to return to their eternal home. Certain gnostics naturally interpreted Christianity in these terms and the theologies of two of them, Valentinus (fl. 138-158) and Basilides (fl. 130-140) were very influential. The dangers that the early more orthodox Christians saw in G. were its pessimistic denial of the goodness of CREATION, its depreciation of bodily life, and its denial of the real humanity of Jesus. (See *Religionsgeschichtliche Schule.*)

God is, in Christian THEOLOGY, both a proper name and an abstract noun for deity. This twofold meaning reflects a fundamental problem within theology that manifests itself at many levels, the problem of relating the God who may be named and addressed in prayer to the absolute and underlying power of the universe called deity. This problem is particularly acute when this underlying power is thought to be either absolutely incomprehensible or an unchangeable, infinite, impassible, omniscient, and omnipotent being. For in both cases, the question is how the FAITH that comes to expression in the personal symbols can be reconciled with the belief that is reflected in the SYMBOL of the incomprehensible One of mystical piety or the impassible, omniscient, omnipotent ABSOLUTE of abstract theology and philosophy. This, in turn, leads to a dilemma: if the personal symbols are taken seriously, Christianity seems to degenerate into ANTHROPOMORPHISM; if, on the other hand, the symbols of absoluteness are definitive, the nerve of Biblical religion seems to be cut.

The earliest Christian theologians attempted to interpret the Christian faith in terms of Greek philosophic categories. In the Greek philosophic tradition there were actually two basic models for interpreting the nature of deity and its relation to the world. On the one hand, the deity might be conceived as the supreme and ineffable principle of truth, beauty, and goodness, the One about which nothing could be legitimately said but which was the timeless origin of all things. On the other hand, the deity might be conceived of as a sovereign SOUL or *demiurge* who molds and fashions the world in the light of ultimate principles or forms. Ironically, it was the former idea which seemed most adequate to the early Christian theologians, with the possible exception of Origen (*c*.185-*c*.254). God, therefore, was conceived as the utterly transcendent, timeless, changeless absolute which, like Plato's Form of the Good, was "beyond BEING in dignity and power," so that very little could be predicated of it. The attributes of this One were largely negatively defined. "He" was absolutely simple (containing no complexity or distinctions, except those of the TRINITY), immutable (in no sense capable of change), eternal (in no sense subject to time), ubiquitous or omnipresent (in no sense subject to space), infinite (in no sense limited), omnipotent (in no sense limited in power) and uncaused (possessing ASEITY).

The definition of God in these terms inevitably requires that the personal symbols of Biblical religion be regarded as but poetic metaphors, useful for piety, perhaps, but meaningless for theoretical understanding. The tension between piety and understanding can be seen in a medieval theological classic, St. Anselm's (1033-1109) *Proslogion* (Chap. 8):

"But how art thou compassionate, and, at the same time, passionless? For if thou art passionless, thou dost not feel sympathy, thy heart is not wretched from sympathy for the wretched; but this it is to be compassionate. But if thou art not compassionate, whence cometh so great consolation to the wretched? . . .

"Truly, thou art so in terms of our experience, but thou art not so in terms of thine own. For, when thou beholdest us in our wretchedness, we experience the effect of compassion, but thou dost not experience the feeling. Therefore, thou art both compassionate, because thou dost save the wretched, and spare those who sin against thee; and not compassionate, because thou art affected by no sympathy for wretchedness."

A related problem arises in discussion about the knowledge of God. If God is the absolute and changeless one, how can such a being even be known, not to say talked about? This matter is more complex than appears at first sight, because it is not the case that those who insist on the absoluteness of God also insist on his unknowability, as one might expect. Nor is it true that those who tend to cling to the personal symbols insist that God is knowable. On the contrary, those who have regarded God as the absolute, changeless First Cause have traditionally insisted that the EXISTENCE of such a cause may be established by reason, while those who have regarded God as a personal subject have tended to insist that personal subjects are just the kind of beings that must reveal themselves if they are to be known. Luther (1483-1546), for example, poured scorn on the "naked absolute" of NATURAL THEOLOGY and insisted that faith must cling to the REVELATION of the merciful God in Christ Jesus. Many neo-Reformed theologians argue in this same fashion.

The situation is made still more complex because some theologians who otherwise seem committed to personal symbols frequently use language and concepts that presuppose the classical absolutist conception. They equate the knowledge of God with the knowledge of God's forgiveness while at the same time they so define God that it is difficult to see how the language of forgiveness has any meaning at all. Secular philosophers are particularly critical of this tendency on the part of many theologians. In this respect, one might say that the crucial problem of contemporary theology is how to talk about God so that the personal and concrete symbols may be seen not only to be intelligible but appropriate without sacrificing the language of absoluteness and perfection. (See *Actus Purus*; Analogy, Way of; Attributes of God; Being; Creation; *Deus Absconditus*; Faith; Natural Theology; Omniscience; Omnipotence; Panentheism; Perfection, Theological; Proofs for the Existence of God; Theism; Theodicy; Transcendence; Trinity.)

Gospel. See Law and Gospel.

Grace is perhaps the most crucial concept in Christian THEOLOGY because it refers to the free and unmerited act through which GOD restores his estranged creatures to himself. Although all Christian churches accept this formal definition, they disagree as to how this unmerited act is to be conceived, what estrangement means, and how it is overcome. But this is to say that the concept of G. itself is intimately related to all of the other crucial concepts in a theological perspective, just as they, in turn, are determined by the idea of G. One can better understand the concept by attending to some of the major disagreements between the two branches of Western Christendom, R. C. and Prot.

The R.C. concept of G. is finally based on the conviction that salvation is nothing less than the divinization of the SOUL, the enjoyment throughout ETERNITY of the beatitude God himself enjoys. To achieve this end, it is necessary that the soul be elevated to a higher order of BEING. An INFUSION of supernatural powers and VIRTUES is required, the exercise of which will MERIT for man the splendor of the final BEATIFIC VISION; SANCTIFYING G. is that elevating, supernatural power. Adam and Eve possessed it before the fall but lost it with that aboriginal calamity, although they did not lose their natural powers of reason and will (see Sin, Original). RE-DEMPTION is the restoration of that supernatural power and the virtues it infuses, and it is made possible by the SATIS-FACTION made to God's JUSTICE by Jesus Christ and the participation of the believer in his mystical body, the CHURCH, through which the lost sanctifying G. is once more given.

Over the centuries, R.C. theologians have created a host of fine theological distinctions to deal with the questions and issues that naturally arose concerning this scheme. Is the first movement of the will toward FAITH an effect of G. or simply a free, autonomous human act? If it is an effect of G., then are those that are not so prompted by G. abandoned intentionally by God? If they are abandoned, in what sense are they really responsible for not being saved? ACTUAL G. and SANCTIFYING G., PREVENIENT G. and subsequent G., SUFFICIENT G. and EFFICACIOUS G.—these and numerous other concepts, which many Prot. theologians seem unaware of, enabled the R.C. to order and defend his beliefs with great subtlety. These distinctions, however, all rest on the view that G. is a supernatural power that, without destroying the FREEDOM OF THE WILL, infuses the supernatural virtues of faith, hope, and CHARITY into the soul, virtues that are rewarded with the final vision for which life is destined. It follows also that G. may be given and received in degrees, and that the successful use of what one has merits an increase in G.

Luther (1483-1546) only gradually realized that his conception of JUSTIFICATION by faith alone was irreconcilable with the basic R.C. premise. Prot. theologians commonly say that the difference between Luther and Rome was that G., for the latter, was an impersonal SUBSTANCE or medicine while, for the former, it was the attribute of God, his graciousness. This is somewhat misleading. It would be better to say that G., for Luther, is what God is. It is God resolving to be for man, to be present to him despite his rebelliousness. G. is not a divine attitude that could as easily be replaced by another one, like wrath. It is, rather, God acting out of his deepest being. On the other hand, Luther and the other Reformers insisted that God's turning to man was a free act and in no way merited. This gratuitous character of G. was especially stressed by noting that man had lost the IMAGE OF GOD by virtue of his sin. Luther rejected the R.C. distinction between the natural and supernatural endowments of man and argued, therefore, that man had even destroyed his free will (see Image of God). The result was an inevitable acceptance of PREDESTINATION and the rejection of the idea of merit. But the important aspect of Luther's teaching was that G. was primarily the forgiveness of sins that removed the barrier of personal communion between God and man. This teaching was ultimately irreconcilable with the R.C. idea of G. as an infused power imparting certain virtues to the soul. For if G. denotes God's forgiveness, then there are no degrees of G. Either one is forgiven or one is not. One may make distinctions among the effects or gifts of G., but one cannot divide G. itself. Also, the notion of G.-given virtues meriting further G. was unacceptable, just as the notion of a G. for special occasions (actual G.) no longer seemed intelligible. Furthermore, the notion of a prevenient actual G. leading to justification implied, thought Luther, that there could be G. that was not itself justifying. This was an unacceptable idea to him. Finally, Luther's conception necessarily involves the rejection of the SACRAMENT as the instrumental cause of G. The preaching of the WORD OF GOD is the "cause" of faith and it need not be limited to the sacraments.

The subsequent development of Protestantism, apart from Prot. SCHOLASTICISM, may be partially interpreted as the unfolding of the logic of these views of G. modified by the impact of science and BIBLICAL CRITICISM. LIBERAL PROTESTANTISM thought it necessary to give up the ideas of a historical fall, original sin, and a vicarious ATONEMENT as well as the idea of a radical forgiveness of sins that seemed to be their correlate. Nevertheless, the basic Prot. idea that G. could only be understood in personal terms lived on in the liberal emphasis on the love of God and the rejection of the idea of infused G. But if CREATION and fall were not believed to be historical events and God is regarded as essentially merciful, then why is G. necessarily and exclusively linked to the one event of Jesus of Nazareth? The liberal Prot. could

110

see no reason for stressing the exclusiveness of G. in Jesus of Nazareth and, therefore, he increasingly interpreted Christ as the highest example or illustration of G.

The so-called neo-orthodox or neo-Reformed theologians reacted against the theology of liberal Protestantism, especially its conception of man and its SOTERIOLOGY. Although the neo-Reformed theologians believed it impossible to return to the belief in a literal historical PARADISE and fall, they did believe that the MYTH of original sin contained more truth than the liberal idea of inevitable progress and man's inherent goodness. Consequently, the idea of G. became crucial for the new theology. The problem was how to conceive of this G. and its relation to nature. Neo-Reformed theologians differed on this point. Some reserved the word G. for God's personal presence in certain historical events, of which the Bible is the record. G. is thus radically different from the creative powers of nature. Others, like Paul Tillich (1886-), tended to think of G. as the power of being that preserves all being from nothingness and that is peculiarly transparent in certain ecstatic events called REVELATIONS. Tillich, then, makes a distinction between G. in creation, G. in salvation, and providential G., which combines elements of each. Tillich's view once more suggests degrees of G. Nevertheless, all forms of neo-Reformed theology reject the R.C. view of the sacraments as the instrumental cause of G. and, therefore, the idea of G. as an infused substance. (See *Agape* and *Eros*; Christology; Church; Election; Faith; Habit; Spirit–Holy Spirit; Image of God; Justification; Law and Gospel; *Ordo Salutis*; Revelation; Righteousness of God; Sacrament; Sanctification; Soteriology; Word of God.)

Grace, Actual, is, according to R.C. teaching, a passing or temporal help or power given by GOD to enable the SOUL to perform some particular act. It is usually contrasted with SANCTIFYING OR HABITUAL G.

Grace, Cooperating. In classical THEOLOGY, C.G. is that by which GOD concurs or cooperates with a man already converted to strengthen him in FAITH.

Grace, Efficacious, is, according to R.C. teaching, that G. that is inevitably followed by the effect for which it is intended and is one form of ACTUAL G. It is usually contrasted with SUFFICIENT G.

Grace, Irresistible, is the G. that cannot be resisted by the will of man.

Grace, Prevenient, is, according to R.C. teaching, the supernatural power that quickens and assists the will to have FAITH. In Protestantism, it is often used more generally to refer to the G. preceding man's decision but is not always identified with a specific quickening power.

Grace, Sanctifying or Habitual, is, according to R.C. teaching, a supernatural but permanent quality infused into the SOUL that imparts to that soul the power of performing actions that are supernatural in character. The three infused powers or VIRTUES or HABITS are FAITH, hope, and CHARITY. S.G. is sometimes called habitual G. In Protestantism, S.G. refers to the gift of the Holy Spirit which renews the PERSON and strengthens him in love for GOD and the neighbor.

Grace, Sufficient, is, according to R.C. teaching, a form of ACTUAL G., which, though sufficient to do what it is intended for, is not efficacious because of the resistance of the recipient. According to some R.C. teaching, all men have sufficient G. to lead them to FAITH.

H

Habit. In MORAL THEOLOGY, especially R.C., a H. is a disposition to act in a particular way and may, therefore, be regarded as good (a VIRTUE) or bad (a vice). According to R.C. teaching, H.s may be said to be infused or acquired.

Infused H.s are the gifts of SANCTIFYING GRACE and are supernatural. Acquired H.s are the result of repeated acts and training. If they tend toward the realization of man's proper nature they lead to the natural and cardinal virtues. (See Anthropology; Ethics, Christian; Faith; Grace; Infusion; Merit; Perfection, Christian; Sacrament; Sanctification; Sin, Actual; Sin, Original; Sins, Mortal and Venial; Virtue.)

Hades means generally "place of departed spirits" and was used in the Septuagint to translate the Hebrew word SHEOL. Since in the subsequent theologies of both Judaism and Christianity the departed spirits were assigned differing places depending on their earthly behavior, the word fell into disuse in favor of the more particular names "heaven," "HELL," PURGATORY, and "LIMBO" (*limbus patrum, limbus infantium*). The Latin phrase *descendit ad inferna* (or *ad infernos*) may be translated "descended into H." H. was probably not understood by the early Greek CHURCHES to refer to hell in the narrow sense but to a more general place of departed spirits or a provisional state of heaven. (See Descent into Hell; Eschatology; Hell; Immortality; Intermediate State; Limbo; Purgatory; Resurrection of the Dead; Sheol; Soul.)

Heilsgeschichte comes from the combination of two German words that, taken together, mean "salvation history." In the context of THEOLOGY, H. refers to the revelatory and saving acts of GOD whereby he has sought to save the world and to which the O.T. and N.T. primarily bear witness. This H. begins with the CREATION of the world and the various ancient COVENANTS foreshadowing the great covenant with Israel and culminating in the life, death, and RESURRECTION of Jesus Christ, which itself points forward to the final saving act, the PAROUSIA, that will bring an end and culmination to history itself.

The idea, though not the German word, played an important role in early Christian theology, especially in the writings of Irenaeus (*c*.130-*c*.200) and Augustine (354-430), for it provided the basis for a distinctive philosophy of history. If the Greeks tended to think of history as meaningless, and the Romans tended to see it only in terms of their own civilization, the Christian theologians above argued that history had a meaning but one that could not be identified with any human civilization. Largely lost as a dominant conception in medieval theology, the idea of H. has been important in Protestantism almost from the beginning. It underlies both COVENANTAL THEOLOGY and DISPENSATION-ALISM, important movements in the 17th and 19th centuries respectively. With the interest in the philosophy of history, on the one hand, and Biblical theology, on the other, the idea of H. once again became a central concern of Prot. theology in the 20th century. It particularly recommended itself to some theologians because it called attention to the fact that Christianity is a religion inextricably bound up with historical events rather than a PHILOSOPHY OF RELIGION, a mysticism, or a religion at whose center stand certain timeless truths. Furthermore, the object of this religion is a personal God who acts, rather than an absolute principle or an unmoved mover. It followed, it was alleged, that theology is not the systematic organization of doctrine extracted from a textbook (the Bible) but a recital of God's "history with man."

Although salvation history seems to be the plain meaning of Scripture, it does not lack criticism from other Prot. theologians who also understand themselves to be Biblical in spirit. These critics argue, first of all, that H. suggests a kind of naïve supernaturalism in which certain events are attributed to the agency of God and others not, and, moreover, this agency is conceived in almost anthropomorphic terms. Secondly, the idea of H. implies that FAITH is primarily an assent to certain historical reports (*fides historica*) or to a philosophy of history. But this not only involves a sacrifice of the intellect (see Heteronomy) but is contrary to the central intention of the Gospel, which is to bring men into an encounter with God in the present moment. What good does it do me, it is asked, to believe that God acted 2,000 years ago in Palestine? H. theologians reply that the purpose of the idea is to make us confident of the present activity of God. The critics reply that no amount of preaching about the past will aid a man to find a real God in the present. (See Covenantal Theology;

Election; Faith; Grace; I-Thou; *Kerygma*; Providence; Word of God.)

Hell. In traditional Christian THEOLOGY, both R.C. and Prot., H. has been regarded as the state of utter and irrevocable damnation to which the unregenerate SOUL is condemned after death. The question of whether this precise doctrine is taught in the Bible is a matter of some dispute, partly because it is doubtful whether the Bible knows anything about an immortal soul and partly because there are passages in the N.T. (I Cor. 15:24-29; I Pet. 4:6; Rom. 11:28-32, 14:9-12; Phil. 2:9; I Tim. 2:4) which, if they do not actually contradict such an idea, at least raise some questions about the traditional interpretation. It can scarcely be doubted, however, that Jesus warns of an "unquenchable fire of 'Gehenna'" (Mark 9:43-48) and that the ideas of a future judgment and separation of the righteous and unrighteous are prevalent throughout the N.T.

Although there were Christian theologians in early times who, like Origen (*c*.185-*c*.254), argued that H. was not a final, irrevocable state, this view was ultimately rejected, and Scholastic theologians, both Prot. and R.C., have not hesitated humorlessly to develop relatively detailed descriptions of the sufferings of the damned. Their sufferings fall, it is alleged, into two categories: the privative, or *poena damni*, and the positive, or *poena sensus*, the former being the forfeiture of the divine presence, the latter including the inner tortures of despair and anguish and the external torments by demons, fire, etc. R.C.s believe there are other intermediary states between H. and heaven, PURGATORY and the two forms of LIMBO, but Protestants have rejected this further subdivision.

The doctrine of H. as an irrevocable state has been attacked from both within and without the CHURCH. Nicholas Berdyaev (1874-1948), echoing the philosopher Nietzsche (1844-1900), believed it is a horrible idea and a manifestation of resentment. Theological criticisms, on the whole, are based on the conviction that the idea is fundamentally alien to the basic christological affirmation that GOD wills that all shall be saved (I Tim. 2:14) and forever seeks the lost. Some theologians, therefore, have advocated ANNIHILATIONISM or UNIVERSALISM or the idea of a "second chance." Most contemporary theologians have remarkably little to say about the doctrine. For the most part they point out that it expresses the important notion that the decision of FAITH is one in which the entire self is at stake and that, so long as a man is free to choose, he may himself reject God's presence. But they refuse to develop any doctrine of the matter. The most powerful objections to the entire idea of damnation are those of Karl Barth (1886-), who argues that the church has only one word to preach, the ELECTION of man in Jesus Christ. (See Annihilationism; *Apocatastasis*; Beatific Vision; Conditional Immortality; Election; Grace; Hades; Immortality; Intermediate State; Judgment, Final; Limbo; Purgatory; Resurrection of the Dead; Sheol.)

Henotheism. The worship of a single god without the express denial of other supernatural beings (or deities).

Heresy in its loose sense refers to the conscious and willful rejection of any doctrine or belief held to be normative by the authorities of a group or an institution. Roman Catholicism defines a heretic as any baptized PERSON who, wishing to call himself a Christian, denies the truth of any DOGMA revealed to the CHURCH. It also distinguishes between "formal" and "material" H., the former being a deliberate and defiant denial of some truth, the latter being an uninformed and ignorant rejection of it. Only the former is a sin and deserves excommunication. H. is to be distinguished from APOSTASY and SCHISM. Until the 19th century, Prot.s generally regarded H. as the willful rejection of any truth taught in the Bible. Although many Prot. bodies had drawn up confessions or statements of FAITH, these were not regarded as binding on the CONSCIENCE, except in so far as they were believed to be expressions of Biblical truth. With the rise of BIBLICAL CRITICISM, then, defining H. also became a problem. Schleiermacher (1768-1834) tried to establish an "essence of Christianity" and to interpret H. as some distortion of it. Not accepting this, Karl Barth (1886-) has interpreted H. as the willful and arbitrary abstraction of one element from the whole of doctrine and the placing of it with equal weight beside the christological center. The question of H. is obviously closely linked with the question of truth, on the one hand, and communal discipline, on the other, and, therefore, raises the fundamental question of authority. (See Anathema; Apostasy; Blasphemy; Dogma; Faith; Schism.)

Hermeneutics is the inquiry concerned with the presuppositions and rules of the interpretation of some form of human expression, usually a written text, although it could also be an artistic expression of some kind. The presuppositions of H. have been the subject of lively philosophical debate, although there have been certain general areas of consensus; for example, that an interpreter of a text must be a master of the language and grammar in which the text was written and possess a knowledge of the historical context out of which the document comes and which it reflects. Some philosophers have also insisted that the interpreter must have a basic sympathy with the author or his thought. Others have insisted that what the interpreter primarily requires is a prior understanding of the fundamental issues with which the text is concerned; for example, an interpreter of a musical text must have some sense of the nature, means, and limits of a specific musical form of expression, just as an interpreter of a legal document must have some prior conception of the problems of jurisprudence. Over and beyond these questions, philosophers have debated whether it is really possible to understand human expressions from cultures radically different from the interpreter's own, or whether an interpreter can discern the personal motivations of an author of a text, or whether an interpreter can understand a text with which he basically disagrees. These questions are obviously relevant to the interpretation and understanding of Scripture. Does Scripture, for example, require a special method of interpretation or does it simply demand the methods common to the interpretation of any text? Are there Christian principles of interpretation? Is it possible to understand Scripture sympathetically and still not be a Christian? Because Prot. THEOLOGY since the Reformation has been preoccupied with the authority of Scripture, it is clear why the problems of H. appear again and again in

Protestantism. Quite recently, existentialist philosophers like Martin Heidegger (1889-) have written of a H. of EXISTENCE, the argument being that since man's being is historical, it requires historical interpretation. (See Accommodation; Allegorical Interpretation; Demythologization; Exegesis; Biblical Criticism; Historicity of Human Existence; Myth; Revelation; Word of God.)

Heteronomy is derived from the Greek words *heteros* (other) and *nomos* (law). It means generally a law imposed on one from without and so a law one would not impose on oneself were one free. It received a somewhat technical meaning in the moral philosophy of Immanuel Kant (1724-1804) which has influenced Prot. moral theory considerably. It refers to any alleged duty or principle of moral action that does not arise from one's own rational will. Paul Tillich (1886-) uses the term analogously, although he has extended its use so that it plays an important role in his philosophy of culture in general and in his THEOLOGY in particular. Anything (law, truth, moral principle, doctrine, artistic expression, culture) is heteronomous if it is alien to the inherent and essential structures of BEING (the LOGOS of reality). Tillich contrasts H. with autonomy, which is the rejection of any law or principle except the one which comes from one's own (autonomous) nature, and theonomy, which is a principle or law that fulfills the law of one's own being by uniting it with the ground and source of all being. For example, the law of love is not a heteronomous demand imposed by an arbitrary GOD, but is the law of man's deepest nature and, therefore, expresses the law of being-itself. (See Being; Culture, Theology of; *Logos*.)

Higher Criticism. See Biblical Criticism.

Historical Jesus is a somewhat ambiguous term with wide currency in modern Prot. THEOLOGY since the title of Albert Schweitzer's (1875-) very influential book, *Von Reimarus zu Wrede*, was rendered in English as *The Quest of the Historical Jesus* (1910). The term H.J. refers to the picture of Jesus as reconstructed solely by means of modern critical historical methods. The term is somewhat ambiguous because it may mean the actual Jesus or what can now be known about the actual Jesus. These are not necessarily the same, for, as we commonly realize, what can be presently known about something is not necessarily what was really the case. This difference as far as Jesus is concerned has especially loomed large in the past few decades, for some N.T. scholars have argued that, while it cannot be doubted that Jesus lived and had an extraordinary influence on his disciples, what those same disciples left as records for us do not permit us to establish much about the course of Jesus' life (apart from his brief ministry) or what he thought about himself. Albert Schweitzer unwittingly contributed to this skepticism about the possibility of painting a reliable picture of Jesus because he showed how most of the historians of the 19th century painted a picture of Jesus that was nothing more than a projection of their own liberal ideals. Schweitzer argued that Jesus could only be understood as a child of his times, a wild prophet. Theologians and others read Schweitzer's book and concluded that this modernization of Jesus, as well as Schweitzer's portrait, was possible only because so little good historical evidence was preserved in the Gospels. This conclusion was strengthened by FORM CRITICISM, which showed how much of the chronological framework of the Gospels was really an invention of later writers and didn't belong to the earliest oral traditions. Many modern N.T. scholars are unhappy with this skepticism and have called for a "new quest of the H.J.," one based on sounder methods and showing that the essential portrait of Jesus in the Gospels is correct.

Historicism is a name given to that view which regards any PERSON, event, culture, institution, or philosophy as capable of being explained solely in terms of its historical antecedents. It emerged in the 19th century, although its roots go back to the work of Johann Herder (1744-1803) in the 18th. In some sense, H. is a presupposition of all historical inquiry, since that inquiry presupposes that any historical event or idea must be understood primarily in terms of its own context and time. But the doctrine assumed metaphysical proportions

119

when all of history was regarded by the philosopher Hegel (1770-1831) as the inevitable and logical unfolding or development of the Absolute Idea. If strictly held, H. raises profound questions concerning the possibility of freedom and the nature of value, not to mention the possibility of knowledge, for if everything is simply the product of historical causation then it is difficult to understand what one means by freedom or knowledge. H. is, therefore, frequently identified with relativism. H. became a theological problem when it was claimed that Christianity, too, must be explained as an expression of the historical forces making for Western culture and had, therefore, no claim to absolute significance. Ernst Troeltsch (1865-1923), a German philosopher and theologian, is frequently identified with this type of H.

Historicity of Human Existence. The traditional idea of the SOUL as an enduring SUBSTANCE with ACCIDENTS has been attacked from a number of different but related philosophical perspectives in the last century. EXISTENTIALISM and PROCESS PHILOSOPHY, particularly, have insisted that the self is always in the process of becoming and that human decision is the decisive factor in determining what character the self will have in any given instant. The self, in this sense, can only be understood in terms of its decisions, its historicity. This is the meaning of the otherwise curious assertion "Man has no nature, he only has a history" (Ortega y Gasset). Behind the existentialist criticism of the idea of the self as a substance lies the *Lebensphilosophie* (philosophy of life) of Wilhelm Dilthey (1833-1911). The self, Dilthey argued, is a peculiar synthesis of thought, will, and feeling which is only intelligible in terms of its immediate lived relationships. Since these are conditioned by one's culture, a self can only be understood, he thought, in terms of its historical environment. R. G. Collingwood (1889-1943), a British philosopher, also has argued that the distinctive characteristic of man is his thought processes and that all thought can only be understood in terms of its historical context. History is the rethinking of past thought. This general type of criticism and interpretation of the self has had a profound influence on the conception of the aims and purposes of historiography as well as philosophical ANTHROPOLOGY. The aim of the historian, it is argued, is not simply to record past "facts" but to understand the past by reliving the thoughts and intentions of its actors, to explain why they acted as they did. In philosophical anthropology, this position has led to an emphasis on the historical nature of the self and all the related problems such an emphasis raises. (See Anthropology; Existence; Existentialism; Freedom of the Will; Hermeneutics; Historicism; Process Philosophy; *Religionsgeschichtliche Schule*; Soul; Substance.)

Historie is a seldom-used German word meaning "history" which has been given a quite technical meaning in some contemporary Prot. theological discussion concerning the relationship between objective historical facts and Christian FAITH. H. means that which is public and verifiable according to generally accepted standards of history writing (historiography). So understood, it is to be contrasted with *Geschichte*, another German word which also must be translated into English as "history" but which refers to the *significance* of a historical fact and so cannot be made public or verifiable by historical canons. The distinction is required because the one English word "history" obscures the two meanings: fact and significance. In this way, a theologian may say that God's action in Jesus Christ is historical (in *Geschichte*) without being historical (in H.), in the sense of being publicly verifiable by the methods of secular historiography. That there was a man named Jesus is H.; that he was the REVELATION of GOD is *Geschichte*. Without such a distinction, a theologian would be forced to say either that God's act is not historical (because what is historical may be the object of historical research) or that it is historical but not open to inspection. (See Historical Jesus; Revelation; Word of God.)

Holy. In the Bible, "H." and its cognates are used with a wide though related range of meanings. Primarily, holiness is predicated of GOD and denotes his awful majesty and purity. He is the "high and lofty one, who inhabits eternity, whose name is H." Derivatively, PERSONS and things may be called H. in so far as they participate in the holiness of God. In the Book of Leviticus men are commanded to be H. because God is H., and it is understood that this includes being just, truthful and merciful. So, too, in so far as the moral commandments are fused with ceremonial ones, objects like the temple, the altar, the Holy of Holies can also be called H. Holiness has traditionally been regarded as one of the NOTES OF THE CHURCH.

Like the term PERFECTION, H. has been traditionally used to designate the uniqueness of God's mode of being in contrast to that of the creatures. So understood, holiness is not one attribute among others but a quality of all of them. As Gustaf Aulen (1879-) points out, holiness is the "background of the conception of God." The term has received considerable attention and popularity in the last few decades following the publication in 1917 of Rudolf Otto's (1869-1937) *The Idea of the Holy*. Convinced that a unique kind of apprehension underlies the religious consciousness, Otto used the category H. to designate it. Religious consciousness is marked by an overwhelming feeling of creatureliness and awe in the presence of the power of life and BEING. Although the H. points in part to conceptualizable qualities, like moral goodness, the experience of the H., Otto believed, basically was non-rational. It is an ecstatic feeling of the "wholly other." Otto used such terms as *mysterium tremendum et fascinans* and the *numinous* to characterize the "object" of this feeling, and the terms *sensus numinus* to refer to the human "faculty" that perceives the H. Otto himself constructed a philosophical theory of religious consciousness on the basis of this analysis of the experience of the H. but it has been less influential than the analysis itself. (See Ecstasy; I-Thou; Revelation.)

Holy Spirit. See Spirit–Holy Spirit.

Homoousion means "of one and the same nature" and is used in the Nicene Creed (325) to describe the relationship of the eternal Son or LOGOS to the Father in the godhead. Since the Arians had insisted that the *Logos* is subordinate and not of the same divine nature, the orthodox party at Nicaea had H. inserted into the creed in order to make clear how far the Arians departed from the CATHOLIC confession. The strictest Arians could not accept the term and would not sign. Unfortunately, the term lent itself to a monarchian or non-Trinitarian interpretation and, after Nicaea, there were many who were unhappy with it, and would have preferred *homoiousion* ("like the Father in all essential respects"). Through the efforts of Athanasius (*c*.295-373), however, the Nicene formula was so interpreted as to be acceptable, and it was reaffirmed at the First Council of Constantinople in 381. (See Arianism; Christology; *Hypostasis*; *Logos*; Person; Monarchianism; Subordinationism; Trinity; Wisdom.)

Hypostasis is a Greek term that played an important role in the controversies out of which the doctrine of the TRINITY emerged. Before its meaning became fixed, it seems to have been capable of three interpretations: (1) that which defines something as belonging to a class, hence, essential being (*ousia*); (2) that which stands under a given set of properties; (3) a particular embodiment of certain qualities, hence, "individual being." This ambiguity of meaning was not only a source of confusion to Greek-speaking theologians but raised further problems for the Latins, who could not be sure whether to translate the term "H." as *substantia* or *persona*. Gradually, its meaning became fixed as "individual being" and so roughly equivalent to the Latin *persona*. The term *ousia* was rendered as SUBSTANCE (*substantia*). This enabled Latin and Greek theologians to agree on the formula "three *hypostases* in one *ousia*" or "three persons in one substance." (See Person; Substance; Trinity.)

Hypostatic Union. The technical term for the union of the divine and human natures in the one being Jesus Christ. It is usually contrasted with the idea of a moral union of two wills (the divine and human) in Jesus. Orthodox doctrine affirms the H.U. and rejects a moral union. (See Christology; *Logos*; Word of God.)

I

I-Thou. A term made famous by the Jewish philosopher Martin Buber (1878-) in his poem-book *I and Thou*, first published in German in 1923. He distinguished between two basic attitudes or postures men could assume toward the beings and things in the world, that of openness, receptivity, and engagement, or that of objectivity, detachment, and disinterestedness. The two postures are represented symbolically by two primary words, "I-Thou" and "I-It." By hyphenating these words, Buber dramatized his insight that the "I" of the "I-Thou" relationship was a different "I" than the "I" of the "I-It" relationship. "The primary word 'I-Thou' can only be spoken with the whole being. The primary word 'I-It' can never be spoken with the whole being."

Two common misunderstandings of Buber require these observations. (1) Buber did not intend to divide the world into two types of beings, PERSONS (Thous) and things (Its). Rather, the two primary words signify two kinds of attitudes men can assume toward any person or thing. One can, Buber noted, be seized by something in nature (a tree) or an artistic expression and so stand in an I-Thou relationship to it. One "encounters" it rather than viewing it in a utilitarian fashion. (2) Buber did not suggest the I-It relationship is evil. The realm of disinterested knowing is also necessary for man. It is only when man lives as though this I-It realm is the only one and uses it to escape from the realm of I-Thou that it becomes evil.

Man only finds AUTHENTIC EXISTENCE in the realm of I-Thou, and this realm is uniquely to be found in human relationships. On the basis of this insight, Buber formulated an ethic of responsibility, dialogue, and communication. Furthermore, this relation between man and man provides the analogy for man's relation to the "eternal Thou," which is, however, only encountered in and through the I-Thou relationships of this world. Thus, the I-Thou relationship with the "eternal Thou" is one that includes all others.

Buber's thought has had a profound influence on some Prot. theologians, especially Karl Heim (1874-1958), Friedrich Gogarten (1887-), Emil Brunner (1889-), H. Richard Niebuhr (1894-1962), Reinhold Niebuhr (1892-) and, to some extent, Paul Tillich (1886-) and Karl Barth (1886-). (See Authentic Existence; Ecstasy; Existentialism; Faith; *Fiducia*; Historicity of Human Existence; *Koinonia*; Neo-Reformed Theology; Objectification; Soul; Transcendence.)

Image of God (*imago dei*) is the likeness to GOD in which, according to Gen. 1:26 f., God originally created man. It has been suggested by some O.T. scholars that these verses express a primitive belief that man's likeness to God consists in his bodily form and not in his possession of SPIRIT, as in modern thought, because elsewhere in the O.T. God is regarded not as a spirit but as one who can be seen (Num. 12:8). However that may be, since the 1st century B.C., the I.G. has been taken to refer to an original spiritual possession of some sort that was lost in the fall, and this meaning, albeit in various forms, has persisted in the history of Christian thought. In the N.T. the idea is already connected with the scheme of salvation: Christ is called the I.G. (II Cor. 4:4; Col. 1:15), and the true believer is one being renewed in that likeness by the Holy Spirit.

The concept has played an important role in R.C. and Prot. discussions concerning the nature and extent of ORIGINAL SIN. R.C. THEOLOGY makes a distinction between certain supernatural gifts given to Adam in addition to his natural human ones and those gifts truly essential to his EXISTENCE as man. The former are composed of the supernatural endowments of SANCTIFYING GRACE, which gives JUSTICE, and the preternatural gifts of IMMORTALITY and integrity. The preternatural gifts do not belong to man by nature, yet they do not, like grace, put man in the supernatural order of being. When Adam fell, according to R.C. teaching, he lost his supernatural endowments (the SIMILITUDO DEI) and his preternatural gifts, but his human nature (*imago dei*) remained intact. To be sure, his human nature was "wounded," since man was left vulnerable to CONCUPISCENCE, but the wound was not so deep as to permit one to say that man's essential powers of reason and free will (his I.G.) were destroyed.

The Prot. Reformers rejected this distinction. They believed that it was based on a bad EXEGESIS of Gen. 1:26 f. (see *Similitudo Dei*). They also believed it suggested that the fall did not involve the loss of something essential to human existence and, hence, that sin was not to be regarded as a distortion of the human ESSENCE. Luther (1483-1546) argued that man had lost the I.G. in everything but name only, and this involved the loss of FREEDOM OF THE WILL. Calvin (1509-64) regarded the I.G. as a kind of integrity possessed by Adam whereby the passions were governed by the reason and his nature was a harmoniously ordered whole. This integrity was not annihilated or effaced but was "so corrupted that whatever remains is but horrible deformity" (See Depravity, Total). In general, the Lutheran tradition emphasized the loss of the I.G. while the Calvinist tradition regarded it as corrupted but not lost. R.C. theologians considered the Prot. view anti-humanistic and destructive of natural morality. Prot.s, on the other hand, regarded the R.C. view as implying that sin did not go to the root of human existence. Prot. Scholastic theologians tried to systematize the Reformers' views but did so in such a way that their own views appeared to offer only a verbal alternative to those of their R.C. counterparts. Reformed theologians, for example, argued that since sin is not a part of man's essence (i.e., technically, an ACCIDENT) man's ORIGINAL RIGHTEOUSNESS must also be regarded as not belonging to that essence. Lutheran dogmatists argued that although the I.G. was natural to Adam it was not constitutive.

The idea of the I.G. was especially pleasing to LIBERAL PROTESTANTISM as a SYMBOL of man's kinship with the divine and of his IMMORTALITY, even though the idea of original sin and the loss of the I.G. was distasteful. This position was rigorously attacked by the neo-Reformed theologians, who, in general, returned to the views of the Reformers, although they were not uncritical of them. Reinhold Niebuhr (1892-), for example, argues that the Reformers were correct in rejecting the notion of lost supernatural gifts but were wrong when they claimed that the I.G. was totally lost. Niebuhr tried to do justice to the idea of a remnant of man's essential nature (I.G.) without falling into either error.

The doctrine of the I.G. has sometimes been used as a basis upon which to insist on a purely natural knowledge of God without benefit of special REVELATION. Within this framework, there occurred a very heated debate between Emil Brunner (1889-) and Karl Barth (1886-) in the thirties. Brunner argued that although the content of the I.G. was destroyed, the form of it remains and that this constitutes a "point of contact" between God and man. Barth rejected the distinction and claimed that the I.G. was an "eschatological" concept and in no sense the basis for a natural knowledge of God. (See Anthropology; Faith; Freedom of the Will; Grace; Natural Revelation; Natural Theology; Original Righteousness; Sin, Original; Soul.)

Immaculate Conception refers to the R.C. belief that the Virgin Mary was preserved free from the stain of ORIGINAL SIN from the first moment of her conception "by a unique GRACE and privilege of the omnipotent GOD and in consideration of the MERITS of Jesus Christ, the Saviour of the human race." Prot.s generally reject the belief, and it was even vigorously debated among R.C.s until 1854, when Pope Pius IX taught it in the bull *Ineffabilis Deus*. Although no ECUMENICAL council has positively declared it to be a R.C. DOGMA it is generally regarded as such because of the bull mentioned above and because the Council of Trent (1545-63) explicitly exempted Mary from its statement on the original sin of man. (See Sin, Original.)

Immanence is that technical term used to denote the nearness or presence or indwelling of GOD in the CREATION. It is usually contrasted with TRANSCENDENCE. Traditionally, Christian THEOLOGY has asserted both the I. and transcendence of God and, hence, rejected DEISM, on the one hand, and PANTHEISM, on the other. So far as God is regarded as immanent, he is believed to be sustaining and preserving creation generally and, more particularly, energizing the wills and SOULS of the believers. So far as God is regarded as transcendent, his

127

activity and power is believed not to be exhausted by the world. Transcendence suggests the independence or freedom of God to be immanent. It is commonly said that LIBERAL PROTESTANTISM emphasized the I. of God while NEO-REFORMED THEOLOGY stressed his transcendence. (See Being; Creation; Deism; God; Grace; Infusion; Inspiration; Liberal Protestantism; Omnipresence; Panentheism; Pantheism; Providence; Sanctification; Spirit—Holy Spirit; Synergism; Theism; Transcendence.)

Immensity is one of the traditional ATTRIBUTES OF GOD and refers to that property whereby the divine ESSENCE is not limited or circumscribed or bound by any place but penetrates and fills all places. (See Omnipresence; Ubiquity.)

Immortality usually refers to some sort of EXISTENCE of the human personality after death. More narrowly, however, it refers to the continued existence of the SOUL. Although this distinction between soul and personality is not usually made either in popular religious belief or in later Christian THEOLOGY, it is an important one, because in Greek philosophy, upon which early Christian theologians were very dependent, I. was attributed only to the rational part of the soul and by no means referred to a concrete, personal existence. Furthermore, I. was but one aspect of the more general Greek idea of the essential divinity of the soul. The soul, it was believed, not only continues to exist after physical death but enjoyed an existence previous to its earthly embodied career (see Pre-existence of Souls). This belief in the divinity of the soul was incompatible with three Christian beliefs, all of which reflect the O.T. background: (1) the belief in CREATION; (2) the rejection of any soul-body dualism in which the soul is regarded as imprisoned in the body; and (3) the hope for a RESURRECTION OF THE DEAD, which implies an affirmation of a full and real personal existence. Subsequent Christian doctrine attempted to reconcile the Greek and the Hebraic ways of thinking. Generally, it was argued (1) that each individual soul was created; (2) that the soul goes immediately to some INTERMEDIATE STATE after death, where it awaits the FINAL JUDGMENT; (3) that the soul is rejoined to the body at the final judgment and is assigned some permanent existence depending upon the sentence of the eternal judge. Classically, Prot.s differed from R.C.s only in their views of the intermediate state of the soul. LIBERAL PROTESTANTISM generally discarded the idea of the resurrection of the body and, hence, any idea of an intermediate state, although there were differences concerning such matters as eternal punishment or HELL. The neo-Reformed theologians, on the whole, regarded this liberal view as unbiblical, and they reaffirmed what they believed to be a more authentic Christian view, the resurrection of the body. They interpreted this, however, as a SYMBOL expressing the convictions (1) that man is a unity of SPIRIT and nature (body) and that the soul cannot be separated from the body; (2) that man's earthly life does not exhaust its meaning and that God will complete and fulfill this existence "beyond history"; (3) that I. is not an inherent right or property of man but a divine act of re-creation. (See Annihilationism; *Apocatastasis*; Conditional Immortality; Eschatology; Hell; Immortality; Intermediate State; Judgment, Final; Limbo; Pre-existence of Souls; Purgatory; Resurrection of the Dead; Soul.)

Impassibility means not capable of being affected or acted upon and has been attributed to GOD alone in classical THEISM and Christian ORTHODOXY. The presupposition of this attribution is the Greek idea that passibility involves potentiality, and potentiality, change. Change, in turn, is less perfect than the changeless. It follows that God, being perfect, is not affected by anything and is immutable. He is pure ACTUALITY (ACTUS PURUS).

Since Biblical and Hebraic thought is marked throughout by the conviction that God is a loving, compassionate being who acts, the attribution of I. has always constituted something of a problem for classical theologians (see God). In more recent times, the idea of the divine I. has been attacked by many philosophers of religion, like Miguel de Unamuno (1864-1936), Nicholas Berdyaev (1874-1948), F. R. Tennant (1866-1957), Charles Hartshorne (1897-), to mention a few, as well as by such theologians as Karl Barth (1886-), Emil Brunner (1889-), Gustaf Aulen (1879-), and Reinhold

Niebuhr (1892-). (See Actuality; *Actus Purus*; Aseity; Attributes of God; Being; *Causa Sui*; God; Panentheism; Perfection, Theological; Theism.)

Impersonal Humanity of Christ. See *Anhypostasis*.

Imputation is a legal term meaning "to reckon as" and refers to a type of judgment in which the quality of one PERSON is ascribed to another. For example, one man's guilt may, under certain conditions, be imputed to another. The term played an important role in traditional Prot. THEOLOGY, it being held that GOD (1) imputed Adam's sin and guilt to succeeding generations and (2) imputed Christ's righteousness to those who have FAITH. The latter was especially important in controversies over the R.C. conception of MERIT. The Reformers held that man is declared to be righteous in God's sight not because of any righteousness of man's own but because God, on account of Christ's sacrifice, chooses to reckon man as righteous. R.C. theologians opposed this doctrine, insisting that SANCTIFYING GRACE confers a real righteousness of man's own that merits reward. Although many contemporary Prot. theologians now hesitate to use the language of I. because of its legalistic connotations, they tend to regard it as an attempt to safeguard the insight that God unconditionally accepts those who are estranged from him without regard to their moral purity. (See Atonement; Faith; Grace; Justification; Merit; Righteousness of God; Satisfaction; *Simil Iustus et Peccator*; Sin, Original; Soteriology.)

Incarnation is the "becoming flesh" of the divine LOGOS in Jesus Christ. (See Christology; Hypostatic Union; *Kenosis*; *Logos*; Revelation; Soteriology.)

Infralapsarianism. See Predestination.

Infusion is the technical term used mostly by R.C. theologians to describe the process by which supernatural GRACE is given to (infused into) the SOUL. The term is generally rejected by Prot. theologians in so far as it implies that grace is

regarded as a supernatural SUBSTANCE rather than the divine
favor or graciousness of GOD. (See Eucharist; Faith; *Fiducia*;
Grace; Habit; Justification; Sacrament; Sanctification.)

Inspiration in THEOLOGY has traditionally meant to be directly
under the influence of the SPIRIT of GOD so that what one
says or does has a special sanction or warrant. So understood,
I. is a fairly broad notion and not necessarily limited to those
whose actions are reported in the Bible or who have written
it. In this view, many prophets and teachers whose names
have been lost to posterity may have been inspired. The idea
of I., however, has been closely related to the problem of
infallibility and authority in the history of Christendom
because many religious prophets of one kind and another have
claimed to have been inspired. In Protestantism, I. gradually
came to be identified with the writing of the Bible (see Inspiration of the Bible) and in R.C. with both the Bible and
the REVELATION alleged to be contained in tradition. In
Protestantism, whether one is inspired is to be judged by his
consistency with Scripture. In Roman Catholicism it is the
function of the vested authority of the CHURCH to declare
what has been inspired. In certain Christian groups and sects,
I. is not so confined and is associated with charismatic and
mystical experiences that may have no doctrinal importance.
(See Inspiration of the Bible.)

Inspiration of the Bible. It was believed by both Christians
and Jews that the O.T. was written under the special influence
of the SPIRIT of GOD and that it possessed, therefore, a
peculiar authority for FAITH and practice. This concept was
naturally extended to the writings of the N.T. by the Christians, although the specific term "INSPIRATION" was rarely
used in this connection until the 15th century. So long as the
Bible and the institutional CHURCH were regarded as bearing
witness to one monolithic truth, it was not necessary to
develop an elaborate doctrine of the I.B. But when the
Reformers pitted Bible against church DOGMA, it was clear
that both Prot.s and R.C.s would have to formulate more
carefully their views on this matter. Luther's (1483-1546)
views on the I.B. appear, in retrospect, to be quite radi-

cal. Convinced that the sole content of REVELATION is man's JUSTIFICATION in Christ, Luther identified the inspiration of the Holy Spirit with the proper witness to Christ (the WORD OF GOD). This Word, then, became an inner standard (canon) by which the various writings of the Bible were themselves to be judged. This "canon within the canon" enabled Luther to be quite critical of much within the Bible. To cite some examples, he observed that: (1) the prophets were quite often in error; (2) the Book of Kings is more reliable than the Book of Chronicles; (3) Esther probably should have been left out of the Bible; (4) not all of the Synoptic Gospels are of equal value; (5) the Epistle of Hebrews erred in denying the possibility of a second repentance; (6) the author of the Book of James "mangles Scripture"; (7) the Book of Revelation reveals nothing. Calvin (1509-64) also distinguished between the Word and the words of Scripture but not in such a way that the former stood as a criterion for the latter. He argued that although God had spoken to the fathers in diverse ways and this had been transmitted orally, the Holy Spirit had now moved others to record it. Thus, the written record constitutes the infallible oracles of God that are necessary for the maintenance of true doctrine. Calvin's tradition was taken one step further and Luther's completely forgotten in the Prot. SCHOLASTICISM of the late 16th and 17th centuries. Both Lutheran and Reformed theologians insisted that every word of the Bible was supernaturally inspired, not only as to style but even as to punctuation. They combined, then, the doctrine of the plenary I.B. (all of the Bible is inspired and is infallible) with the doctrine of verbal inspiration (the words themselves were dictated by the Holy Spirit).

R.C. dogma is that the Bible is supernaturally inspired but is less specific concerning the mode of inspiration and the degree and type of infallibility (i.e., whether the historical accounts are as infallible as those texts pertaining to faith and morals). In 1870, the Vatican Council decided that the canonical books "contained revelation without any mixture of error," but left open whether revelation may be distinguished from other types of statements that also occur in Scripture. Pope Leo XIII (1810-1903) in his *Providentissimus Dei* enunciated, to be sure, a far stronger view when he wrote, "It is absolutely wrong and forbidden, either to narrow inspiration to certain parts of Holy Scripture, or to admit that the sacred writer has erred"; but encyclicals are not dogma, and this statement is interpreted quite liberally by some modern R.C. Biblical scholars. BIBLICAL CRITICISM practically destroyed belief in verbal inspiration and put an unbearable intellectual strain on the belief in plenary inspiration. All but fundamentalist theologians were willing to concede that there were errors of fact and contradictions in the Bible. But they, like the Prot. Scholastics, felt that, once it was conceded that an author had erred, the whole document was to be distrusted. Their position hardened in the face of the liberal Prot. position that the Bible was a purely human act of creation by religious geniuses. Neo-Reformed theologians tried, on the one hand, to preserve the authority of the Bible and, on the other hand, to accept the results of Biblical criticism. In general, they found in Luther's theory of the I.B. a viable alternative. The Bible is a witness to the Word of God in Jesus Christ and thus contains the GOSPEL, but this in no way entails, it is alleged, the infallibility of all of the texts. The Word is true, but the witness is, like all human witness, a relative one. (See Biblical Criticism; Demythologization; Exegesis; Form Criticism; Hermeneutics; *Kerygma*; Miracle; Modernism; Myth; Protestant Principle; *Religionsgeschichtliche Schule*; Revelation; Synoptic Problem; Word of God.)

Intermediate State refers to the state of the SOUL between the time of physical death and the FINAL JUDGMENT. By means of this idea, traditional Christian THEOLOGY tried to reconcile the ideas of the IMMORTALITY of the soul and the resurrection of the body. Theologians have differed widely over the nature of this state, debating whether or not the soul is conscious, may reform, or undergoes purification. (See Annihilationism; Eschatology; Hell; Immortality; Judgment, Final; Judgment, Particular; Purgatory; Resurrection of the Dead; Soul.)

J

Jesus Christ. See Christology.

Judgment, Final, Sometimes called the general or last judgment, it refers to that judgment whereby, according to traditional Christian teaching, the final destiny of the PERSON is decided after the RESURRECTION OF THE DEAD. (See Eschatology; Hell; Immortality; Millennialism; Resurrection of the Dead; Soul.)

Judgment, Particular, refers to that judgment made with respect to each individual SOUL immediately upon the death of its body and before the FINAL JUDGMENT on the "last day." Such an idea occurs in R.C. THEOLOGY as well as in Prot. ORTHODOXY, the only difference being that in R.C. theology the soul may be sent to PURGATORY instead of to heaven or HELL, while traditionally there are only the latter two alternatives in Protestantism. (See Eschatology; Hell; Immortality; Intermediate State; Judgment, Final; Purgatory; Resurrection of the Dead; Soul.)

Justice has been used in three closely related ways in the history of Christian THEOLOGY: (1) as a term for the nature of GOD; (2) as a term for the integrity or righteousness of man lost by virtue of his sin; (3) as a term for the proper relationship which should obtain between man and man in his social life. In its first meaning, the term played a decisive part in the SOTERIOLOGY of Martin Luther (1483-1546) and in Reformation theology generally. In its second meaning, the term has played an important role in Christian ANTHROPOLOGY (see Image of God; Original Righteousness; Sin, Original). In its third meaning, the term has been crucial in CHRISTIAN ETHICS. In R.C. MORAL THEOLOGY, J. is defined as that VIRTUE that disposes a man to give every other man those rights belonging to him. St. Thomas (*c.*1225-74) regarded J. as one of the cardinal virtues. He accepted the Aristotelian distinction between general and particular J., the former having to do with the common good, the latter having to do with private good, which was further subdivided into communative and distributive J. Underlying such definitions is the theory of NATURAL LAW. The Prot. Reformers, though not Aristotelian, also accepted the idea of natural law and believed it to be embodied in the Ten Commandments, which they regarded as containing the requirements for Christian life as well as for civil J. LIBERAL PROTESTANTISM was especially concerned with the requirements of social J. (see Social Gospel) as were the neo-Reformed theologians, although the latter were critical of the liberal tendency to identify social J. with the KINGDOM OF GOD. These neo-Reformed theologians have been particularly concerned with the relationship between love (AGAPE) and J. Some, like Emil Brunner (1889-), tend to distinguish quite sharply between love and J., relegating love to purely face-to-face relationships and J. to those duties required by one's VOCATION or office. Others, like Reinhold Niebuhr (1892-), interpret love as a kind of perfect ideal which, though never realizable, drives one to seek a kind of relative J. in the complex and imperfect social relationships characterizing human existence. Still others, like Paul Tillich (1886-), interpret J. as an inherent pattern of BEING which is indissolubly connected with power and love, all of which are grounded in being-itself, (See *Agape* and *Eros*; Decalogue; Ethics, Christian; Ethics, Contextual; Ethics, Social; God; Image of God; Justification; Law and Gospel; Natural Law; Original Righteousness; Righteousness of God; Sin, Original; Social Gospel.)

Justification comes from the Latin *justificatio*, which, with its cognates, was used in the Latin Vulgate to render the Greek *dikaisosis*, which, with its cognates, was used by Paul in his N.T. letters to signify that act by which GOD brings man back into proper relationship with him. How that act is to be understood was the main point of contention between the Prot. Reformers and the R.C. theologians. For the R.C., J. literally means the making just of the sinner, i.e., it involves the INFUSION of supernatural GRACE that blots out sin, regenerates the SOUL and makes it worthy of the creator who fashioned it. This is accomplished by the preparation of the soul by the gifts of ACTUAL GRACE and then the impartation of SANCTIFYING GRACE through the SACRAMENT of BAPTISM. For the Reformers, J. was regarded not as the infusion of a renovating grace that makes the soul objectively worthy of forgiveness; rather, J. is the act of divine forgiveness whereby, because of the sacrifice of Christ, an unworthy man no longer has his guilt reckoned against him. Accepting that pardon by FAITH, the unworthy man is renewed in his heart. Calvin (1509-64) once perceptively noted that there was no controversy between himself and the "sounder schoolmen" concerning the beginnings of J., but that the R.C. believed "that a man, once having been reconciled through faith in Christ, is accounted righteous with God on account of his good works, the MERIT of which is the cause of his acceptance," whereas he, Calvin, held that faith and faith alone is reckoned as righteousness.

R.C. theologians tend to regard the Prot. view as a purely legalistic and forensic one, because J. seems to be simply the act of remitting punishment and involves no transformation of the justified PERSON. Prot.s, on the other hand, tend to regard the R.C. view as based on the idea of merit and a magical view of the sacraments. To some extent, both criticisms are caricatures and justifiable only to the extent that a few theologians in both groups have sometimes written in extreme ways. Both Reformed and Lutheran theologians, for example, have written as though J. is solely a juridical act that involves no interior change in man, and some R.C.s, on the other hand, have written as though J. were a reward for the merit of cooperating with actual grace. Both Luther (1483-1546) and Calvin, however, argued that J. was not only the forgiveness of sins but involved the gift of the Holy Spirit and a new righteousness. In fact, they often talked about it in language that suggests something like infusion. But both of the Reformers were also careful to add that the transformation of the believer is not the condition of J., nor is it so complete that the Christian life is not a continual cry for forgiveness.

On the other hand, some R.C.s insist that what they call merit is itself a gift of God and that J. is entirely gratuitous.

Nevertheless, there is an important difference in emphasis between the two views. Luther and Calvin believed the R.C. so views grace that it does not always include God's unconditional acceptance of the sinner, thus shifting the emphasis from the preaching of the GOSPEL and faith to the taking of the sacraments with their supernatural power. The R.C., on the other hand, believes that the Prot. view leads to ANTINOMIANISM, vitiates the JUSTICE of God, who ordained human life so that good works merit salvation, and destroys the intrinsic importance of the sacraments.

Contemporary neo-Reformed theologians tend to see the real difference between these two views to consist in the conception of God's righteousness. Luther, by identifying the RIGHTEOUSNESS OF GOD with his mercy, was expressing the conviction that God brings men into communion with himself by accepting them as persons who do not need to establish some worthiness of their own first. It is this radical acceptance that enables man to overcome the despair over his guilt. The R.C., on the other hand, argues that God's righteousness is his justice, that first requires a man to become worthy by the reception of supernatural grace in the sacraments. (See Baptism; Eucharist; *Ex Opere Operato*; Faith; Grace; Infusion; Justice; Righteousness of God; Sacrament; Sanctification; Word of God.)

K

Kairos is a Greek word frequently appearing in the N.T. which has a variety of meanings all associated with time. It may mean a fixed and definite time, a season, or when a thing comes to pass. Until very recently, it was widely regarded as meaning "fulfilled time" or "just the right time" and so was contrasted with the Greek word *"chronos,"* which also means "time," but which is alleged to be more specifically connected with measurable or clock time. On the basis of this distinction it was pointed out that the N.T. recognized that certain times have a unique and specific qualitative character or significance. Paul Tillich (1886-) made special use of this distinction in his philosophy of history in order to indicate those unique epochs or times that constitute turning points and demand a particular response. The coming of Jesus Christ is a K. in this unique sense. It points to the fact that all events are *kairoi* (the plural) in which the eternal judges and transforms the temporal. It has recently been argued, however, that although this philosophy of history may be correct, it cannot be based on the linguistic usage of the two words in the N.T., where *chronos* and K. are used interchangeably. (See Eternity.)

Kenosis is derived from the Greek word meaning "to empty," a form of which is used by Paul in Phil. 2:7, where he writes that the heavenly Christ "emptied himself, taking the form of a servant, being born in the likeness of men." K. has, therefore, come to be associated with a particular theory of the INCARNATION, the kenotic theory. In this view, the divine LOGOS or second PERSON of the TRINITY is said to have laid aside (emptied himself of) his divine attributes of OMNIPOTENCE, OMNISCIENCE, and OMNIPRESENCE and assumed all the limitations of human EXISTENCE. Although it is problematical whether this view is to be found in ancient Christian thought, it enjoyed something of a vogue in the 19th century, especially in Lutheran and English THEOLOGY. It was believed that the kenotic theory avoids DOCETISM and permits the application of the full range of human predicates to Jesus, including limitation in knowledge. (See Christology; *Logos.*)

Kerygma is a noun derived from the Greek verb meaning "to proclaim" and has become almost a technical term in contemporary Prot. THEOLOGY, although as shall become evident, it is somewhat ambiguous. In the N.T., the abundant use of three words indicate the distinctive response of the early Christian community to the life and death of Jesus of

Nazareth: *katangellein* (to declare), *kerussein* (to proclaim), and *euangelizesthai* (to proclaim the good news). The content of this proclamation was that the age of fulfillment promised by the prophets had come, that it had reached its climax in the life, death, and RESURRECTION OF CHRIST. It called for repentance and promised the Holy Spirit to those who repented. The noun K., then, assumed a twofold meaning: it could refer to the content of the proclamation or the act of proclamation itself.

The term K. has come to have a central place in contemporary Protestantism for several reasons. In the first place, BIBLICAL CRITICISM, it is believed, especially FORM CRITICISM, has shown how much of the N.T. has been shaped by the K. The Gospel accounts are not objective historical reports but proclamations of the divine significance of Jesus. Because this is so, it has been further argued, it is fruitless to try to go behind this preaching for a factual picture of Jesus. The attempt, therefore, to base Christianity on such a factual picture, as liberal theology tried to do, reflects a misunderstanding of the N.T. message itself. In the second place, the fact that the K. is basically an appeal to the listener to give up his former SELF-UNDERSTANDING and to accept himself as a justified sinner, has especially recommended itself to those theologians impressed by EXISTENTIALISM, because it makes clear that the K. is basically not a teaching or a DOGMA addressed to the intellect but a call to a new life. It does not solicit assent to facts but a decision of FAITH. Since this is the case, Rudolf Bultmann (1884-) and others have insisted that the K. must be continually reinterpreted so that it does not become frozen into a doctrine a man must believe even if he has to sacrifice his intellect.

Both of these lines of reasoning carry with them certain problems. If the K. is defined solely in terms of its content about the death and resurrection of Jesus, then is it historically correct to say that Jesus preached the K.? Bultmann says it is not correct, since he believes it is clear that Jesus did not preach about his own death and resurrection. Does that mean, then, that Jesus preached one thing and Paul and the early CHURCH another? If so, is there any continuity between Jesus' message and the K. of the church? Since a radical discontinuity raises serious question, several of Bultmann's students have suggested that the real content of Jesus' message about the graciousness of GOD was the same as that of the early church, although the form of it was different. To establish this, however, assumes that one can go behind the K. of the church and establish a firm historical portrait of Jesus. Secondly, it broadens the concept of K. to mean the inner content of Jesus' message (God's graciousness) and does not limit it to the explicit preaching about Jesus' death and resurrection. If the K. refers to Jesus' own teaching and preaching, however, why and how did the preacher become the one preached about? These are some of the current issues surrounding the term K.

Kingdom of God is a SYMBOL that has had an extraordinarily rich and varied history in Christendom. Special attention has been paid to it because it played such an important role in the teachings of Jesus and because it is so bound up, therefore, with one's view of his unique role and function. In its Greek form, the term probably means the more active "the reigning of GOD" rather than the more static "kingdom of God." Beyond this, however, N.T. scholars are divided as to the meaning and use of the symbol in the preaching of Jesus. Did Jesus expect the supernatural coming of God that would bring history to an end in the near future? Or did he regard himself as in some sense already bringing the sovereignty of God so that he could speak of the K.O.G. in the present tense? Or does the truth lie somewhere between these two views? Albert Schweitzer (1875-) believed that Jesus looked for the immediate and supernatural end of the world in his lifetime, and Schweitzer made much of those utterances attributed to Jesus—there are about four—in which this seems clearly to be the meaning. Those who, like C. H. Dodd (1884-), emphasize that Jesus spoke as if the K.O.G. were realized in his own life and death ("realized eschatology"), point to the many passages in which Jesus said, in effect, "if it is by the finger of God that I cast out demons, then the K.O.G. *has come upon you*" (Luke 11:20). They explain away the futuristic references as reflecting the beliefs of the early

CHURCH, not of Jesus. There are still others who argue that the truth lies between these views: Jesus regarded his mission as the sign of the in-breaking of God's redemptive rule, but he looked to the end of history for the final culmination and victory of this rule.

It seems clear that how one interprets this issue depends on the meaning he gives to the phrase K.O.G. and this, in turn, reflects a more fundamental decision concerning the PERSON and work of Christ and his relationship to the K.O.G. Those Christians who have wanted to say that God's rule is realized when men are obedient to him have tended to say that Jesus Christ was the "coming of the kingdom" and that to be "in Christ" is to be "in the K.O.G." This understanding lies behind Augustine's (354-430) identification of the K.O.G. with the elect, an identification that too easily slipped over into the identification of the K.O.G. with the church in medieval times. Those Christians, however, who tend to equate the K.O.G. with God's sovereignty and then conceive of that sovereignty, as Calvin (1509-64) did, in terms of God's OMNIPOTENCE, will tend to see the K.O.G. both as present and as the final culmination of world history. Those Christians, however, who attribute real independence and freedom to the creatures and who can only conceive of the K.O.G. as the total overcoming of all evil will regard the K.O.G. as a wholly future reality. This may be accompanied by an extreme pessimism about this world together with the hope for an immediate end to it, or it may serve to heighten one's sense of obligation for the present and may be accompanied by a hope that looks to the distant future. If one argues that Jesus himself reveals how God reigns, then it is not so much a case of deciding what the phrase means and then of accommodating the interpretation of Christ to it as of giving the term its meaning by reference to the work of Christ. Theologians who have thought in this way have tended to argue that Jesus Christ's life and death disclose that God's sovereignty and power are those of suffering love and that this is why Jesus may be said to bring them and yet why, from a human standpoint, history seems to be ambiguous. The future references are then interpreted as an expression of the confidence that this sovereignty of God's love is the final meaning of history. (See Chiliasm; Christology; Eschatology; Millennialism; *Parousia*; Providence; Theodicy.)

Knowledge. See Epistemology; Natural Theology; Revelation.

Koinonia is a word frequently used in the N.T. to refer to the peculiar kind of communion Christians have with GOD and with one another in Christ. Paul frequently uses it when writing of Christians who share in God's GRACE, the Gospel, or the promise of the Holy Spirit. It points to a unique form of communion made possible by the RIGHTEOUSNESS OF GOD as revealed in Christ. It is also used of the community which Christians should have with one another, one marked by mutual sympathy and concern, i.e., AGAPE. The word is frequently used in contemporary theological literature to refer to the kind of community that should characterize the churches instead of the undisciplined occasional gathering of individuals for worship, on the one hand, or a kind of superficial friendliness characteristic of the fraternity or lodge meeting, on the other. (See Church; *Ekklesia*; Laity.)

L

Laity is derived from the Greek word *laos*, meaning "people." L. has traditionally been used to distinguish the ordinary believer from the clergy, a distinction particularly sharp in all those churches commonly calling themselves CATHOLIC, although only less so in some branches of Protestantism. This distinction has been attacked by some younger theologians and priests in both Protestantism and Roman Catholicism. They argue that the true function of the ecclesiastical offices in the CHURCH is to promote knowledge and piety among the whole people (*laos*) of God. They deny, however, that THEOLOGY or church discipline is the peculiar work of the clergy alone. Consequently, the term L. is increasingly used as a rallying cry by these theologians. (See Church; *Ekklesia*; *Koinonia*.)

Last Judgment. See Judgment, Final.

Last Things. See Eschatology.

Law and Gospel are two closely related terms that have played an important role in Christian THEOLOGY, especially in that theology inspired by the writings of the apostle Paul. In his letters, Paul contrasts JUSTIFICATION by means of the works of the Law with justification by FAITH in the Gospel (literally "good news") of Jesus Christ. By the Law Paul means (1) the cultic ritual and moral commandments of the O.T. and (2) the eternal will of God for human life that is known even to the Gentile. The intent of this Law is to bring man to grateful trust in the Creator and to responsibility for the world. But in his ANXIETY to secure his own life, man does not see the true intent of the Law but uses it as a means of establishing himself righteous in his own eyes. Thus the Law, which was intended to bring man to a relationship of sonship, becomes the basis for PRIDE and boasting. Paul understands the Gospel to consist in the judgments (1) that man cannot win life by means of the external works of the Law, (2) that GOD is gracious and accepts man despite man's unacceptability. Faith is obedience to this Gospel, and in obeying it, one fulfills the true intent of the Law.

The Reformers, especially Luther (1483-1546), made this Pauline distinction the basis for their theology. Luther said that the distinction between L. and G. "contains the sum of all Christian doctrine." By the Law, Luther meant the total claim of God on human life, the "Thou shalt," whether it appears in the Mosaic law or the NATURAL LAW, or even in the Sermon on the Mount. The demand of this Law is perfect love. Just because it demands such love, Luther believed it impossible for sinful man to fulfill it. Therefore, it only intensifies man's sin and despair instead of bringing him into fellowship with God. Law exposes sin but cannot cure it. By the Gospel, Luther means the message that God has revealed himself in Christ not as a tyrant or lawgiver, but as an infinitely compassionate saviour. With this in mind, Luther speaks quite critically of the Law as an enemy of faith. On the other hand, since, as we have seen, he regards the inner meaning of the law to be love, and this presupposes a gracious God, it is not easy for him to place L.A.G. in such sharp contrast. Therefore, Luther often speaks of L.A.G. as but two sides of one coin, the Law being a demand and the Gospel a gift, but both having the same content. Only in so far as the Law tempts man to trust in works is it disparaged, which is to say, it requires interpretation in the light of the Gospel. Luther sometimes distinguishes two uses of the Law, a civil and a spiritual one. The civil use of the Law refers to its ability to specify generally what society requires for peace and order. The spiritual use of the Law is to convince man of his sinfulness so that, despairing of himself, he may cling to the mercy of God in Christ. Calvin (1509-64), more than Luther, stressed the positive function of the Law as a guide to the Christian life, but this is a matter of degree and not of kind. (See Decalogue; Faith; Grace; Justification; *Kerygma*; Natural Law; Righteousness of God; Sanctification; Word of God.)

Lex Naturalis. See Natural Law.

Liberal Protestantism is a somewhat loose designation for a wide range of religious thought unified less by specific doctrines than by a temper of mind and certain common motifs. It originated in the 19th century and achieved its zenith in this country in the decades preceding the Second World War. It was characterized by (1) an eagerness to discard old orthodox forms if they were judged to be irrational in the light of modern knowledge or irrelevant to what was regarded as the central core of religious experience; (2) a confidence in the power of man's reason when guided by experience; (3) a belief in freedom; (4) a belief in the social nature of human EXISTENCE; (5) a FAITH in the benevolence of GOD and the goodness of CREATION. Consequently, L.P. enthusiastically endorsed critical scholarship (especially BIBLICAL

CRITICISM), confident that it could only benefit faith, and tried to establish points of contact with science, philosophy, and all forms of human reasoning. The father of the movement is generally acknowledged to have been the German theologian Friedrich Schleiermacher (1768-1834). His basic thesis was that the heart of the Christian religion consists in a certain quality and structure of the religious affections of which theological statements are but the verbal expression. It follows that all doctrines must be shown to be directly related to the religious self-consciousness, a principle that involves a rather radical transformation of such orthodox doctrines as creation, ORIGINAL SIN, and the divinity of Christ, to mention a few. Although critical of Schleiermacher, Albrecht Ritschl (1822-89) manifested the same kind of drive for the relevant and the essential. He argued that Christian THEOLOGY should be freed from all metaphysical speculation and should be seen as an attempt to express judgments of value, especially of the saving significance of Jesus of Nazareth. More personalistic and ethical in emphasis than Schleiermacher, Ritschl explicitly rejected the orthodox doctrines of original sin, Christ's ATONEMENT, and eternal damnation. He stressed the moral perfection of Christ and his REVELATION of the divine love. It was characteristic of Ritschl to reject the attributes of God's holiness and wrath and to equate God with love.

At the turn of the century, L.P., especially in America, was characterized generally by an emphasis on the fatherhood of God, the supreme moral and religious example of Jesus, the essential goodness of man and his infinite capabilities of growth in reason and freedom, the duty of doing something to correct all those conditions—whether ignorance or social injustice—that stultified the being of man (see Social Gospel). Once ORTHODOXY was widely regarded as a hindrance to reason and experience it was inevitable that a wide spectrum of religious belief would develop, ranging from the most extreme, judged by traditional standards, to the moderate. There were those liberal theologians, like Henry N. Wieman (1884-), who were, in effect, religious naturalists, rejecting all beliefs that could not be verified in human experience. God was but a name for that creative dimension in human experience which strives for the realization of the good. On the other hand, the great majority of liberal Prot.s were evangelical liberals who did not break so radically with traditional Christianity. They emphasized the moral and religious perfection of Christ and held him up as an example of faith and morals as well as a revelation of the gracious fatherhood of God. These evangelicals differed from their orthodox counterparts by reason of their toleration of and openness to various doctrinal beliefs, their impatience with literalism of all forms, and their general rejection of the orthodox understanding of man and the theories of atonement that arose from that understanding. (See Biblical Criticism; Immortality; Modernism; Personalism; Religious *a Priori*; Social Gospel; Soul.)

Limbo is, according to R.C. THEOLOGY, that place where the SOULS of unbaptized infants go. Not having received SANCTIFYING GRACE and so dying in ORIGINAL SIN, these infants, on the one hand, do not suffer the pains of HELL but, on the other hand, they are excluded from the perfect joy of the BEATIFIC VISION. Unable to accept the more rigorous judgment of Augustine (354-430) that unbaptized infants are consigned to eternal damnation, many R.C. theologians have taught that these infants do not grieve but have a purely natural happiness. This infants' limbo (*limbus infantium*) is to be distinguished from the "limbo of the fathers" (*limbus patrum*), where the saints of the old COVENANT repose and to which Christ is believed to have descended between his death and resurrection. (See *Apocatastasis*; Beatific Vision; Descent into Hell; Hell; Immortality; Intermediate State; Purgatory; Soul.)

Loci Theologici means literally "theological topics" in Latin and was a name commonly given to systems of doctrine by early Lutheran theologians.

Logos is the Greek word for discourse or reason. In the 2nd and 3rd centuries of the Christian era, it became the name for the mind or reason of GOD, which perfectly mirrors or expresses his being and which was completely embodied in the man Jesus of Nazareth. This idea probably represents the weaving together of several more ancient strands of thought: (1) the Greek idea of the divine Mind (*nous*) which informs all things and constitutes the harmony and structure of the universe; (2) the Jewish conception of the pre-existent and eternal WISDOM which contains the Law as the perfect pattern and archetype of human existence; (3) the Near Eastern idea of a pre-existent heavenly man who represents the embodiment of all human perfection. The degree to which the author of the Fourth Gospel and St. Paul were dependent on any one or all of these strands of thought is a matter of debate, but it is true that they interpreted the life of Jesus as the disclosure of a pre-existent, eternal pattern that expresses the wisdom of God.

The apologetic theologians of the early CHURCH found the L. terminology to be a perfect device for expressing the relationship of Christ to God as well as for providing a point of contact with the philosophic and religious views to be found outside of the church and its tradition. The L. was the mind or reason of the incomprehensible divine source (*Monas*), hence, the perfect expression and mirror of God's being. The L. is the son, the image, of the Father, coeternal yet subordinate in the sense that the L. is the image of the incomprehensible *Monas* rather than the *Monas* being an image of the L. This L., moreover, is the source of all truth, wherever it be found, whether in Moses or in Plato. Consequently, a L. theologian, like Clement (*c.*150-*c.*215) of Alexandria did not have to depreciate Greek philosophy but, on the contrary, could say that when Plato witnessed to truth, beauty, and goodness, he had been inspired by the same L. that was perfectly embodied in Jesus Christ.

Two somewhat divergent tendencies were discernible among those who employed the L. idea. The characteristic tendency of the Alexandrian school was to emphasize the utter remoteness and incomprehensibility of the divine source or *Monas* and to subordinate the L. to it. The other tendency was to identify the Father and the L. so closely as to border on MONARCHIANISM, as in Irenaeus (*c.*130-*c.*200). Origen (*c.*185-*c.*254) of Alexandria tried to hold these two tendencies

147

together, although there are passages in his writing that may be interpreted in either of the two ways. Those who emphasized the subordinate nature of the L. gradually drifted into ARIANISM. Those who emphasized the identity of the L. and the Father became monarchians. The struggle between these two emphases gradually led to the formation of the doctrine of the TRINITY. (See Christology; *Homoousion*; Monarchianism; Person; Pre-existence of Christ; Recapitulation; Subordinationism; Trinity; Wisdom; Word of God.)

Lord's Supper. See Eucharist.

Love. See *Agape* and *Eros*.

Lower Criticism. See Biblical Criticism.

M

Materialism as a metaphysical theory is the view that all reality is basically matter in motion and that all human activity can be explained without recourse to mind or SPIRIT except in so far as these, in turn, may be seen as by-products or "secretions" of MATTER. It is commonly confused with NATURALISM. M. is one form of naturalism but not all naturalists are materialists. (See Empiricism; Metaphysics; Naturalism; Panpsychism; Personalism; Process Philosophy.)

Matter. In Aristotelian philosophy, this is a term for that which can undergo transformation or change, which receives form. As such, it is potentiality and is to be contrasted with ACTUALITY and form. The concept plays an important role in the philosophy and THEOLOGY of Thomas Aquinas (*c.*1225-74). In more recent thought, M. has a variety of meanings, ranging from that which occupies space, has mass, weight, impenetrability and is non-mental to that which is organized by the mind in cognition. The meaning must be derived from the context. (See Materialism.)

Merit is a term that has played an important role in R.C. THEOLOGY and has generally been despised by Prot.s According to R.C. teaching, M. is that quality of human actions making them worthy of divine reward. Prot.s have denied that human actions have any such quality and insist that one's status before GOD is defined purely in terms of the divine forgiveness or, as classical Protestantism expressed it, by the IMPUTATION of the M.s of Jesus Christ. To argue otherwise, Prot.s claim, is to legalize the relationship between man and God and to justify self-righteousness. Put simply, the argument is that men are saved by GRACE alone. R.C.s reply, however, that the Prot. argument rests on a misunderstanding. Good (meritorious) works are themselves due to God's grace working in the SOUL. These, in turn, deserve M. or an increase in grace culminating in eternal life. Since the initial grace, which moves man to repent, is not given on the basis of M. but out of compassion, no legalism is involved. The doctrine of M. says that the good works of the justified deserve further reward, not that the beginnings of JUSTIFICATION are due to M. Finally, no absolute claim can be made on God; rather, the basis for the "claim" of the just is simply that God has gratuitously promised to reward their good works. From the foregoing, it is clear that the real issue between Prot.s and R.C.s is not whether there are good works but how justification is related to them, how justification and SANCTIFICATION are related to grace, and how grace is defined and mediated. (See Faith; Grace; Justification; Righteousness of God; Sanctification.)

Metaphysics has traditionally been the rational analysis of the necessary and universal aspects of BEING, of the characteristics any thing must exemplify if it is to exist at all. So understood, it is that enterprise that investigates what "to be" means, what universal and general principles are exemplified in anything that is. The name "M.," which simply means "after the Physics," became accidentally attached to this enterprise because Aristotle's writings on this subject were placed immediately after *The Physics* in the important Andronikas edition (70 B.C.) of Aristotle's works.

Traditionally, most Christian THEOLOGY has been closely allied with M. With the rise of the sciences, however, M. increasingly fell under suspicion, especially when M. was conceived by some not so much as an analysis of the universal structures of EXISTENCE as a speculative inquiry into the nature of things allegedly beyond experience. This suspicion was fortified by the fact of apparently irreconcilable theories concerning the nature of the "real world" and such problems as the relation of the mind to the body, etc. The German philosopher Immanuel Kant (1724-1804) tried to show that the human mind inveterately raises such questions without being able to answer them because of its intrinsic dependence on sense experience. Kant's criticism was widely taken to be devastating to M., and Prot. theologians since that time have been eager to disassociate themselves from M. and reason, appealing rather to REVELATION and FAITH. Most R.C. theologians, on the other hand, simply refused to accept Kant's criticisms. Positivistic philosophers have gone one step further than Kant and argued that if metaphysical statements are unverifiable and, therefore, meaningless (because they have to do with non-experienced realities), so, too, are theological statements. Process philosophers argue that both the Kantian and positivistic criticisms depend on a false definition of M., i.e., an inquiry into objects beyond experience, and do not apply to M. in its original sense, as an analysis of the universal structures of ordinary experience. Paul Tillich (1886-), also, has done a great deal in theology to reawaken interest in M. understood in this original way. He prefers the name ontology for this enterprise, however, because of the bad connotations of the term M. (See Being; Cosmology; Empiricism; Epistemology; Existentialism; God; Natural Theology; Process Philosophy.)

Millennialism refers generally to the belief in a thousand-year period (millennium) in which the KINGDOM OF GOD is to flourish and prosper. Millennialists tend to fall into two camps: (1) those who believe that the millennium will follow the PAROUSIA or "second coming" of Christ (premillennialism); (2) those who believe that the millennium will precede the *parousia* of Christ (postmillennialism). There are many variants of both views. Generally, premillennialists believe that shortly before the second coming the world will be marked by extraordinary tribulation and evil and the appearance of the ANTI-CHRIST. At his coming, Christ will destroy this anti-Christ and believers will be raised from the dead. There will then follow a millennium of peace and order over which Christ will reign with his saints. At the close of this time, SATAN will be loosed and the forces of evil will once again be rampant. The wicked will then be raised, and a FINAL JUDGMENT will take place in which Satan and all evil ones will be consigned to eternal punishment. Postmillennialists generally have taught that the millennium will precede the *parousia* of Christ. There will be a golden age of the reign of the CHURCH on earth that will be followed by a conflict between good and evil and the coming of Christ. (See Anti-Christ; Apocalyptic Literature; Chiliasm; Eschatology; Judgment, Final; *Parousia*; Resurrection of the Dead.)

Miracle. In the N.T., certain events are described as "powerful deeds" (*dynameis*), "wonders" (*terata*), and "signs" (*semeia*). They were, as the words suggest, regarded as manifestations of the power of GOD believed to be uniquely at work in Jesus. As the Greek idea of NATURAL LAW took firm hold of the Christian mind in the first centuries after Christ, these three terms increasingly became merged into the one concept M., which was customarily defined as the direct supernatural activity of God working contrary to the known laws of nature. So understood, M.s were regarded as proofs of the divinity of Christ and the authority of the Bible.

With the rise of the natural sciences in the 17th and 18th centuries and the corresponding picture of nature as a machine operating according to immutable laws, the idea of M. came under sharp attack from outside the CHURCH, although orthodox theologians within continued to insist it was a part of true Christian belief. The great revolution within

Christendom, however, occurred with the rise of LIBERAL PROTESTANTISM and its acceptance of BIBLICAL CRITICISM. For the liberal Prot. did not believe that FAITH needed miraculous proofs. Furthermore, he believed that it was dishonest history to exempt the Bible from the same standards of criticism that had been so successful in the study of other scriptures and ancient documents, which were also replete with M.s. The only conclusion to draw, he thought, was that ancient peoples believed all unusual persons and events were miraculous, and that the authors of the N.T. were no exception. This conclusion was disturbing to the orthodox, and for several decades before the Second World War controversy raged over M.s and Biblical criticism.

Although the neo-Reformed theologians rejected many liberal theological ideas, they accepted Biblical criticism and its presuppositions. The M. stories in the N.T. were interpreted as a primitive way of expressing the significance of Jesus for faith. More recently, some Christian apologists have argued that new developments in science show that the idea of the impossibility of M.s is itself untenable. This is probably true, but it is doubtful, suggest others, whether this has any theological significance. For the question the historian must answer is not "Are M.s impossible?" but "In this particular case, what constitutes the evidence for supernatural intervention?" The new science makes it even harder to decide that the M.s of one's own religion are truly supernatural while those of other religions are not. (See Biblical Criticism; Inspiration of the Bible.)

Modalism is an interpretation of the doctrine of the TRINITY in which the PERSONS of the Trinity are viewed as modes of divine action rather than as eternal and essential distinctions within the divine nature itself. Such a view first flourished in the 3rd century A.D. as a form of MONARCHIANISM. Its proponents insisted on the complete and undivided sovereignty (*monarchia*) of GOD and thereby rejected any distinctions in the being of God, such as Father, Son, and Holy Spirit. Sabellius (early 3rd century) appears to have argued that God is one individual being and that the terms Father, Son, and Holy Spirit are simply names applied to the different forms (modes) of action of that one being and, therefore, do not refer to eternal and intrinsic distinctions within the godhead. (See Trinity.)

Modernism is a term used to denote a quite definite movement within Roman Catholicism in the first decade of this century and also, more loosely, a type of thought current in American Protestantism in the late twenties and the thirties. In Roman Catholicism, M. is identified with the religious philosophy of a group of men—A. F. Loisy (1857-1940), L. Laberthonnière (1860-1932), E. Le Roy (1870-1954), G. Tyrrell (1861-1909)—who aimed to synthesize the dogmas of Roman Catholicism with the "truths of modernity." Such a synthesis involved the full acceptance of BIBLICAL CRITICISM as well as the reinterpretation of DOGMA. Basic to this reinterpretation was a highly sophisticated theory of truth that owed much to PRAGMATISM and resembles some modern EXISTENTIALISM. In this view, the real cannot be known or talked about in abstract propositions. Reality can only be grasped intuitively through moral action. Religious FAITH, therefore, is not the giving of intellectual assent to propositional truth on divine authority but is a deep, inward, moral appropriation of the divine SPIRIT. A dogma, argued Le Roy, performs the negative function of guarding against error without being able to perform the positive function of stating precisely what is true. Its real positive function, then, is practical or moral; it states a "rule of conduct," an obligation to act in a certain way. To believe, for example, that "Christ is risen" is not to believe in the resuscitation of a corpse, Le Roy insisted, but to live as if Christ were our contemporary. In 1907, the teachings of M. were condemned by Pope Pius X.

M. is often loosely applied to the views of certain American Prot. thinkers—Harry E. Fosdick (1878-), Shailer Mathews (1863-1941), H. N. Wieman (1884-)—who interpreted the Bible and religion along evolutionary or developmental lines. So understood, M. is frequently contrasted with FUNDAMENTALISM. The concern of these modernists was to reconcile science and religion, and they did so by rejecting supernaturalism and by interpreting the idea of GOD as a creative force that preserves and maximizes "the total good of all human living." (See Biblical Criticism; Dogma; Existentialism; Faith; Liberal Protestantism; Naturalism; Pragmatism; Revelation; Symbol.)

Monarchianism is a type of thought which flourished in both the eastern and western parts of Christendom in the 3rd century. Stressing the undivided unity and sovereignty (*monarchia*) of the godhead, it generally rejected any view which distinguished sharply among Father, Son, and Holy Spirit and especially any view that regarded them as concretely distinguishable individual beings. (See Trinity.)

Monism. The metaphysical theory that there is but one fundamental reality of which all other beings are but attributes or modes, if they can be said to be real at all. (See Acosmism; Being; Pantheism; Theism.)

Monophysitism is a type of christological belief that flourished in the eastern part of Christendom (Palestine, Antioch, and Egypt) after the Council of Chalcedon in 451. Concerned to emphasize the immutable and perfect nature of Jesus Christ, they argued that there was only one dominant nature in him after the INCARNATION and it was divine. This view differs from the Creed of Chalcedon which specified two complete natures in one PERSON. Although some monophysites definitely rejected the Chalcedon Creed, others thought it could easily bear their own interpretation. The movement soon became divided and this, in turn, was complicated by the break between the two parts of the Empire and by tensions between the Roman Bishop (or Pope) and other bishops. M. was finally condemned at the 6th Ecumenical Council in 680-681, although the belief still lives on in three churches: the Coptic, the Jacobite, and, to some extent, the Armenian. (See Christology; Dyophysitism; Hypostatic Union.)

Monothelitism. A type of christological theory proposed in the 7th century by the patriarchs of Constantinople and Alexandria in the hope of unifying the Eastern Empire, which was badly split by the monophysite controversy and threatened by Arab expansion. It was proposed that the acts of

Jesus Christ be viewed as an expression of one divine-human operation (*energia*) instead of two (a human and a divine) cooperating wills. The formula of the monothelites, therefore, was "we confess one will of the Lord Jesus Christ." This formula occasioned new debate, and a Greek monk, Maximus Confessor (*c.*580-662), vigorously defended the doctrine that there were two wills in Christ, one divine and one human, in perfect harmony. At the 6th Ecumenical Council in Constantinople (680-681), the dyothelite (two-wills) doctrine was given dogmatic status: "two natural wills and two natural operations indivisibly, incontrovertibly, inseparably, inconfusedly. . . ." (See Christology; Dyothelitism.)

Moral Theology. The name most often given by CATHOLIC theologians to the application of Christian THEOLOGY to the moral conduct of man. Prot. theologians generally use the term CHRISTIAN ETHICS. (See Casuistry; Ethics, Christian; Law and Gospel; Natural Law; Perfection, Christian; Sanctification; Sin, Actual; Virtue.)

Mortal Sins. See Sins, Mortal and Venial.

Myth. Since this word is used so variously in both contemporary scientific and theological literature, any definition of it will appear to be arbitrary. In common language, the word is used to denote stories that have no basis in fact, but this meaning is too loose for the anthropologist or the philosopher. Their attempts, however, to define and classify M.s in terms of their content have broken down. One cannot say, for example, that all M.s deal with the supernatural, or with sacred origins, or with phenomena in nature. Nor has it proved true that all M.s are imaginative representations of some abstract truth. Since M. is difficult to define in terms of its content, many scholars have sought to define and to classify M.s in terms of their cultural or communal function. Thus, Bronislaw Malinowski, an anthropologist, views M. as a sacred story that expresses and codifies belief, safeguards morality, vouches for the efficacy of ritual, and contains rules for morality. M.s, then, can be contrasted with legends, fairy tales, etc. This conception of M., it should be noted, implies no judgment on the truth of the story; indeed, it is possible in principle to have a true story serve such a function. Critics of this view of M. argue that it tends to see M. as a legitimate expression of man's SPIRIT and, therefore, opens the door to irrationalism. They prefer, on the contrary, to define M. as a story, sacred or not, that is not true or credible. This definition of M. also has certain disadvantages, however. Furthermore, it is too loose to be of much use to the specialists. Still another philosopher, Ernst Cassirer (1874-1945), views M. as a peculiar way of apprehending and talking about the world, a way characteristic of the prescientific mind, and he has attempted to describe its structure in great detail. Discussion surrounding the appropriateness of the term for referring to certain elements in Scripture was precipitated in our time largely by an essay by Rudolf Bultmann (1884-) in 1941, although Reinhold Niebuhr (1892-) had written an essay "The Truth in Myth" half a decade earlier. Bultmann used the term in a very special sense: to refer to the primitive tendency to objectivize powers that in reality are not capable of being so objectified, and he called for an existentialist interpretation that did justice to primitive intuition without falling into literalistic error. (See Analogy, Way of; Biblical Criticism; Demythologization; Exegesis; Form Criticism; Hermeneutics; *Religionsgeschichtliche Schule*; Symbol.)

N

Naturalism means quite generally that view which denies the EXISTENCE of any reality transcending nature. It stands opposed, therefore, to any kind of supernaturalism, if by the latter is meant any deity or being apart from nature. There has always been a naturalistic tradition in Western philosophy but its hallmark in most recent times has been its identification of reality with that which may be investigated by the natural sciences. N. has frequently been identified with MATERIALISM but this identification is not necessary, as can be seen in that form of religious N. advocated by a number of liberal Prot. theologians and philosophers of religion in the past few decades and which was, for a brief time, so influential. Henry Nelson Wieman (1884-   ), for example, argued that even though naturalists believe that all reality is temporal and spatial, N. by no means denies that this reality contains beauty, value, consciousness, mind, and many other things that make reality infinitely rich. GOD is the name, Wieman argued, for that eternal factor in experience which operates to transform man and to drive him to realize his potentialities and highest good. Some religious naturalists call themselves Christians because they believe such a power emanated from Jesus. (See Immanence; Modernism; Panentheism; Pantheism; Theism; Transcendence.)

Natural Law (*lex naturalis*) in Christian THEOLOGY traditionally refers to the inherent and universal structures of human EXISTENCE which can be discerned by the unaided reason and which form the basis for judgments of CONSCIENCE about the good (that which realizes the natural end or goal of a being) and the evil (that which thwarts the natural end or goal of a being) and which, therefore, make it possible to say that the right is the rational. Every human act, therefore, is either in accordance with the N.L. or not. Since it was argued by N.L. theorists that human nature was unchanging, it followed that the N.L. was unchanging. In fact, it was regarded as grounded in the eternal law, which, in turn, is an expression of the divine ESSENCE.

N.L. theory underlies the entire moral philosophy of Thomas Aquinas (*c.*1225-74) and, to a great extent, R.C. ethical teaching. But it is by no means peculiar to Roman Catholicism, and it was accepted, with some important modifications, by Luther (1483-1546) and Calvin (1509-64) as well. St. Thomas argued that since passion and ignorance often lead men astray, GOD provided for men a REVELATION of the N.L. in the Ten Commandments or DECALOGUE, as he also revealed the supernatural law in Christ and the CHURCH. Luther and Calvin also accepted the Decalogue as a revelation of the N.L., although they tended to confine this to the "second table of the commandments" or those having to do with family, marriage, life itself, possessions, VOCATION, and human dignity. More recently, the idea of N.L. has been attacked by Prot. theologians, especially those who advocate a CONTEXTUAL ETHICS or who are impressed by the HISTORICITY OF HUMAN EXISTENCE. (See *Agape* and *Eros*; Casuistry; Conscience; Decalogue; Ethics, Christian; Ethics, Contextual; Historicity of Human Nature; I-Thou; Justice; Law and Gospel; Perfection, Christian; Sanctification; Virtue.)

Natural Revelation. A term sometimes used by theologians to refer to the REVELATION of GOD in CREATION apart from his specific revelation in the events of the O.T. and N.T. So used, it is synonymous with "general revelation." It is often preferred to the term "NATURAL THEOLOGY," which, by virtue of its contrast to "revealed theology," suggests that theological propositions are revealed. The term "revelation" suggests, in contrast, the disclosure of a reality for which one then attempts to find propositions to express what is apprehended in the revelation. So understood, it has been sometimes argued that one may assume N.R. without, thereby, engaging in an independent program of natural theology. One may assume, that is, that God is disclosed in creation although that disclosure may only be properly understood by those who have already been grasped by the special revelation in Jesus Christ. (See Natural Theology; Revelation; Word of God.)

Natural Theology refers to the effort to construct a doctrine of GOD without appeal to FAITH or special REVELATION but on the basis of reason and experience alone. The name is probably derived from M. Terentius Varro, a Roman antiquarian, who distinguished between poetical theology, civic theology, and N.T., the latter being philosophic thought about deity which arises as part of the philosopher's account of nature or reality. So understood, N.T. was not especially contrasted with revealed theology, although it has come to be so contrasted in the history of Christian thought. Plato (*c*.427-347 B.C.) was probably the creator of N.T., for he was the first to set forward a series of arguments for the EXISTENCE of a divine reason at work in the world, to criticize false theological beliefs, and to go even so far as to propose that ATHEISM be treated as a crime against the state. Plato's arguments for the existence of a rational "sovereign soul" were based on the fact of orderly process or motion (*kinesis*) in the world. This process required, he believed, a divine reason, and he criticized all materialistic accounts of the world as well as any view which asserted that the gods were indifferent. Thus, from the beginning N.T. has been characterized by (1) arguments for the existence of God, (2) a polemic against MATERIALISM, (3) reflection on the problem of disorder or evil (see Theodicy).

The earliest Christian theologians were faced with a dilemma so far as N.T. was concerned: if they accepted it, this would seem to make belief in special revelation unnecessary; if, however, they rejected N.T. outright, this would make it impossible to regard all men as responsible and guilty for having rejected the knowledge of God, since all men were not privy to the special revelation.

Besides taking hold of one of the horns of this dilemma, there were other possible solutions to it: (1) one could claim that it was possible in principle to achieve a knowledge of God sufficient for salvation but that since the fall man's reason has been so corrupted that revelation is required; (2) one could claim that reason testifies to the existence and benevolence of a divine being but that there are certain supernatural truths which are, in principle, above reason's ability to establish. The latter solution has, in general, been characteristic of Roman Catholicism, the former of the Reformers and Prot. SCHOLASTICISM.

Thomas Aquinas (*c*.1225-74) argued that it was possible in principle for the philosopher to establish the nature and existence of God, although there were certain truths concerning man's supernatural end that were, in the nature of the case, not capable of being established by reason alone. It is not that knowledge gained solely by the reason is false so much as that it is inadequate so far as one's final blessedness is concerned. Furthermore, although it is possible for the philosopher to establish a number of important truths about God, the majority of men are not capable of highly sophisticated intellectual endeavor and, therefore, a revelation of many of these same truths is necessary. So far as the truths above reason are concerned, reason's proper role is to show that they are not irrational, although it cannot establish their truth.

Luther (1483-1546) and Calvin (1509-64) argued that every man possesses some sense of deity and that God has left innumerable traces of his glory in the created world. Nevertheless, man's sin and stupidity (a favorite word of Calvin's) since the fall are such that God must move men's hearts by an internal and special revelation if they are to know him properly. The deficiency of man's knowledge of God, therefore, is man's own fault. For this reason, neither Luther nor Calvin put any confidence or stock in an independent N.T. that might be used as a support for revealed theology. Their respective followers perpetuated this general attitude, albeit with slightly differing emphases; the Lutheran Scholastics insisting that Scripture was the sole and absolute norm of THEOLOGY vis-à-vis reason, the Calvinists insisting that, although natural knowledge is insufficient for salvation, even fallen reason could establish that God is, that he should be worshiped, that men should live good lives, that the SOUL is immortal, and that rewards and punishments should be commensurate with VIRTUE.

All of these solutions presupposed that philosophy was but the handmaiden of theology and that the truths of the latter were not to be judged by the former, a presupposition the self-evidence of which could be challenged only if one were also willing to challenge the authority of the state. With the breakdown of the close cooperation of CHURCH and state, however, philosophy asserted its independence, and it was inevitable that increasing numbers of philosophers would not only reject the handmaiden status of philosophy but would claim the right (and duty) to subject the claims of revelation to rational scrutiny. The results were diverse, some philosophers claiming that Christianity was merely saying in a different form what rational gentlemen everywhere could derive from reason and common sense (DEISM), and some claiming, more daringly, that certain crucial theological utterances were irrational and ought to be disbelieved. The entire situation in Europe was altered when David Hume (1711-76) argued in a devastating way that the religion of common sense (deism) was based on bad reasoning, that all N.T. was but speculation, and that Christian truth was to be believed, if at all, on blind faith. This might have seemed to be a happy solution for Prot.s—or at least those who had never liked N.T.—except for the fact that the Western world had become aware that there were many kinds of faiths and that, if all were blind, no convincing reason except convention could be given for preferring Christian beliefs to others. The result was a profound skepticism concerning theology as such.

This skepticism was only partially overcome by Immanuel Kant (1724-1804), who argued that the ideas of God, soul, and IMMORTALITY were actually required by virtue of the structure of the human mind and, therefore, were not arbitrary ideas. On the other hand, they could not be made the objects of thought nor could they function in any proofs. These ideas have a legitimate regulative use in organizing and systematizing our theoretical and moral experience, but they cannot themselves be the objects of judgment or experience.

Many impressive attempts were made in the 19th century to show that the Christian creeds were actually symbolic ways of expressing profound philosophic truths that were not threatened by Kant's or Hume's criticisms, but all of these attempts presupposed the norms of reason and, since reasonings were various and philosophers disagreed so radically with one another, philosophical skepticism and relativism were widely prevalent. Some liberal Prot.s, impressed by Hume and Kant, tried to separate theology from philosophy (and from N.T.). They argued that theology was a matter of articulating the insights of religious experience or of organizing one's ultimate judgments of value. Others valiantly tried to develop a N.T. and to overcome the arguments of Hume and Kant.

The problem of N.T. became a matter of discussion among the neo-Reformed theologians when a famous and acrimonious debate occurred between Karl Barth (1886-) and Emil Brunner (1889-) over this matter in the thirties. Barth vigorously rejected the whole idea, and Brunner defended it. The debate had political overtones because Barth believed that the basic issue between the church and National Socialism was whether the church would have absolute and sole fidelity to the revelation in Jesus Christ alone. Barth's position was the basis for the famous Barmen Declaration of the evangelical churches. Barth's christocentrism, however, was not basically shared by the other neo-Reformed theologians like Reinhold Niebuhr (1892-) and Paul Tillich (1886-). Tillich, perhaps more than any other modern theologian, has recast the terms of the debate. He argues that N.T. formulates the basic human questions about God rather than provides proofs or arguments for his existence. Theology's task is (1) to show that these questions presuppose an awareness of finitude and of being-itself and (2) to demonstrate that the Christian SYMBOLS provide an answer to these basic human questions. No one solution to this problem has received wide acceptance, and many younger theologians, influenced by ANALYTIC or PROCESS PHILOSOPHY or EXISTENTIALISM, are seeking new ways of conceiving of the problem. (See Analogy, Way of; Apologetics; Being; Ontological Argument; Proofs for the Existence of God; Revelation; Theodicy.)

Necessary Being is traditionally defined as that being whose ESSENCE it is to exist or which cannot not exist. Classically, theologians have argued that GOD is N.B. Many contemporary philosophers argue that the term is illegitimate, that no being as such is necessary. Necessity, they insist, is properly ascribed only to certain logical propositions. (See Aseity; Being; *Causa Sui*; Contingent; God; Ontological Argument.)

Neo-Reformed Theology refers to a movement that emerged shortly after the First World War in Switzerland, was quickly championed by some of the most creative theological minds of the first half-century, and now dominates the Prot. theological scene in Europe and America. Although common concerns are shared by all those called neo-Reformed, or dialectical, or crisis, or neo-orthodox theologians, each of them is original enough and differs sufficiently from the others to raise the question whether the term N-R.T. has any clear meaning. Each of them is concerned to interpret what Karl Barth (1886-) called "the strange world within the Bible" to modern men, to show its relevance and power for life. All of them believe that the Prot. Reformers saw more clearly than anyone else since Augustine (354-430) the basic themes of that Bible, the TRANSCENDENCE and holiness of GOD, the sinfulness of man, the saving REVELATION of the RIGHTEOUS-NESS OF GOD in Jesus Christ, and the JUSTIFICATION of man by GRACE through FAITH alone. And all of them are critical of the liberal Prot. emphasis on the IMMANENCE of God, the goodness of man, the authority of religious experience, and the gradual coming of the KINGDOM OF GOD on earth, although, on the other hand, they accept the liberal's hard-won victories for BIBLICAL CRITICISM and for the relevance of faith for social action.

The movement is usually regarded as having begun in 1918 with the publication of Karl Barth's commentary on St. Paul's Epistle to the Romans. Not a commentary in the usual sense, it represented an attempt to interpret the thought of St. Paul in a fashion at once faithful to Paul's religious intention and intelligible to the modern reader. Its theme was "God is God," which Barth thought meant three things: (1) that there is an infinite qualitative difference between God and man; (2) that sin is the attempt to obscure this difference, whether by religious experience, mysticism, or moral idealism; (3) that the realization that there is this gap and that it can only be bridged by God and not by man is itself saving faith. Each of these three theses constituted a full-scale assault on LIBERAL PROTESTANTISM and, indeed, the prevailing tendency to interpret Christianity as the highest product of Western culture.

These themes were picked up and developed with distinctive nuances by other young and creative thinkers: in Europe, by Rudolf Bultmann (1884-), Emil Brunner (1889-), Friedrich Gogarten (1887-), Paul Tillich (1886-); in America, by H. Richard Niebuhr (1894-1962) and his brother, Reinhold (1892-). A spirit was afloat, and since this spirit had much in common with that of the Prot. Reformers, it was sometimes characterized as neo-Reformed THEOLOGY. But despite this continuity with the Prot. Reformation, there was also discontinuity; hence the qualification "neo." For it was impossible to ignore the scientific revolution which had occurred or the Biblical criticism which presupposed that revolution. The Reformers lived in a prescientific

163

age and it conditioned their reading of the Bible. The neo-Reformed theologians accepted fully the new science and were quite willing to concede that the WORD OF GOD in Jesus Christ was veiled in an all-too-human form, that the Bible contains MYTHS, legends, and historical errors of all sorts. They were not at all unwilling to regard the VIRGIN BIRTH, MIRACLE, and resurrection stories as primitive ways of expressing the divine significance of Jesus.

Although the neo-Reformed theologians seemed to constitute a common front in the earliest days of the movement, it was inevitable that differences in emphasis and thought would arise, and it is now clear that there are important differences among them. Each of the above-mentioned theologians is a creative thinker in his own right and has made a quite distinctive contribution. Karl Barth's monumental *Church Dogmatics* deserves, many commentators think, to be placed alongside of Calvin's (1509-64) *Institutes* as one of the great systems of Prot. theology. Tillich is known for his unique synthesis of idealism, EXISTENTIALISM, and theology, and his extraordinary ability to bring his thought to bear on all aspects of human culture. Bultmann is one of the great N.T. interpreters of modern times. Reinhold Niebuhr's theological and ethical analyses of economic and political life have altered the thinking of several generations of theological students in America. Brunner, Gogarten, and H. Richard Niebuhr have also been very influential, although in ways less easily characterized.

Nestorianism refers to the christological beliefs of Nestorius, who became Bishop of Constantinople in A.D. 428. Fearing the inroads of APOLLINARIANISM, the view that there was only one fully perfect nature in Christ and that divine, Nestorius opposed the use of the term THEOTOKOS (Mother of God) as an appropriate term for the Mother of Jesus. His reasoning was that Mary was the Mother of the man Jesus only and not of the divine LOGOS. Nestorius was accused of heresy by the unscrupulous but brilliant bishop Cyril of Alexandria, who held that the divine *Logos* was so bound up with complete human nature as to constitute a natural unity (HYPO-

STATIC UNION). Although scholars are uncertain, Nestorius is thought to have believed in a moral rather than a hypostatic union of the two wills in Christ. After a somewhat unseemly and, perhaps, unfair meeting of a council at Ephesus in A.D. 431, Nestorius' views were condemned and he was banished, although he continued to insist on his ORTHODOXY. Certain Eastern bishops agreed with him and formed a Nestorian Church that flourished for centuries and found expression in piety and an impressive THEOLOGY. (See Christology.)

Nominalism refers to a theory of knowledge (EPISTEMOLOGY) which insists that universal concepts or ESSENCES (man, tree, etc.) have no separate and independent reality but are simply names used by the mind to organize individual things with similar characteristics into one class. In the Middle Ages, N. emerged as a reaction to realism, the view that a universal concept is more real than any individual exemplification of it, e.g., the concept "man" is more real than any individual existing man. There were degrees of N., the most extreme being that of William of Occam (c.1300-c.1349), who argued that only individuals exist and that universal concepts are no more than vocal sounds. The controversy over universals played an important part in medieval debates concerning the nature of man and the doctrine of the TRINITY. (See Being; Essence; Existence.)

Non-Being is a term frequently to be found in the writings of philosophical theologians, classical and modern, and is used to refer to the "nothingness" from which finite beings emerge and into which they pass. Classically, finite being is said to be a composite of BEING and N-B. In modern EXISTENTIALISM N-B. is a particularly important concept. Martin Heidegger (1889-), for example, argues that N-B. cannot be thought, it can only be "apprehended" through ANXIETY that perceives the "nothingness" that everywhere underlies human life. Paul Tillich (1886-) defines GOD as that power of being which continually conquers N-B. The REVELATION in Jesus Christ is saving, Tillich believes, because it is the manifestation of

God's participation in and overcoming of the ALIENATION and estrangement (or N-B.) of the world. (See Being; Contingent; Creation; God; Providence.)

Notes of the Church is a technical term sometimes used to signify the defining characteristics of the true CHURCH. Traditionally, there have been four: APOSTOLICITY, catholicity (see Catholic), unity, and holiness. Prot.s have tended to say that the true church exists where the WORD OF GOD is rightly preached and the SACRAMENTS properly administered. (See Church.)

Numinous. See Holy.

O

Objectification. Although this is a technical term found in the writings of some German idealists, especially Hegel (1770-1831), it plays a special role in modern existentialist philosophy and THEOLOGY. The term has a bad connotation because it has to do with the attempt to make objective and manipulatable that which in the nature of the case cannot be, e.g., GOD and the human SPIRIT. Such an idea underlies Martin Buber's (1878-) distinction between I-THOU and I-It (the latter constituting O.) and Rudolf Bultmann's (1884-) demand for a DEMYTHOLOGIZATION of the N.T. For Bultmann, MYTH is an attempt to talk about God in objective, hence inappropriate, terms. (See Analogy, Way of; Existentialism; God; I-Thou; Symbol.)

Omnipotence means the possession of the perfect form of power and is an attribute traditionally predicated of GOD alone. Inspection will reveal that the idea is unclear, and it has, in fact, been a source of considerable controversy and confusion. Does it mean (1) that God can do anything even though it is logically impossible? or (2) that God can do all that his nature permits him to do? or (3) that God can do all that is possible in any given situation? Answers to these questions presuppose, in turn, theories concerning the relationship between logic and reality, not to speak of a concept of the divine freedom. On the whole, classical theologians have, with Thomas Aquinas (c.1225-74), insisted that God can do everything only if the "can" is understood to mean "that which is genuinely possible." In this sense, God is not capable of doing everything that can be said. God cannot, for example, suffer violence, repent, make opposites exist in the same subject at the same time and in the same respect, make a man without a SOUL, make the past not to have been, or create another God. All of these statements are self-contradictory. The question then becomes what we mean when we speak of a perfect mode of power. Karl Barth (1886-) argues that this is the decisive issue, for it is a question of what kind of power God reveals himself to possess. Barth insists that it is not a matter of already knowing what O. is and then of learning through REVELATION that the omnipotent one is our Father; rather, revelation teaches us what power and O. are, in contrast to every preconception. Paul Tillich (1886-), on the other hand, interprets O. to mean the "power of being which resists NON-BEING in all its expressions and which is manifest in the creative process in all its forms." (See Attributes of God; God; Perfection, Theological; Theism.)

Omnipresence is that attribute of GOD whereby he is said to be everywhere present. Traditionally this has meant (1) that God is not localized in time or space, (2) that his creativity and power are at work in everything that is. It is, then, closely related to the idea of God's infinity or, in the language of Prot. SCHOLASTICISM, God's IMMENSITY. The term "UBIQUITY" is often used synonymously. Most theologians have insisted that the term is to be understood qualitatively and not quantitatively, that is, just as ETERNITY does not refer to an unlimited time neither does O. refer to an indefinitely extended space. O. refers, rather, to the creativity of God in everything. Some contemporary Prot. theologians who reject all metaphysical interpretations of the ATTRIBUTES of GOD define O. as the "ability of divine love to maintain itself everywhere unhindered by limitations of space" (Aulen). (See Attributes of God; God; Perfection, Theological; Providence; Theism.)

Omniscience means literally "the knowing of all things" and traditionally has been ascribed to GOD alone. In classical THEISM this has been taken to mean that the divine knows the past, present, and future in one simple, timeless act of cognition. This view necessarily raises innumerable problems, most of which have been debated at great length by theologians. In what sense can God be said to know, since knowledge usually involves being affected by the object one conceives, and God is, by classical definition, impassible? What does it mean to say that God knows the future? If God's knowledge is his ESSENCE, is not what God knows (the world) as necessary as God himself? If there is no distinction between what God knows (his O.) and what he wills (his OMNIPOTENCE) does not God either will evil or not know it? The ways in which theologians have answered these questions are evidence of the extraordinary ingenuity of the human mind.

Most neo-Reformed theologians, in contrast to CATHOLIC and orthodox theologians, regard these kinds of problems as hopelessly speculative and irrelevant and the result of the bad influence of Greek philosophy on Christian THEOLOGY. Emil Brunner (1889-), for example, interprets O. to mean not that God possesses all abstract knowledge but, Biblically, that God is unfailing love, sympathy, and concern. Similarly, Gustaf Aulen (1879-) renders O. as "love's sovereign and penetrating eye." Karl Barth (1886-) treats O. as the WISDOM of God, a perfection of the divine loving. Paul Tillich (1886-) uses the term as a SYMBOL meaning that nothing falls outside the centered unity of the divine life.

There are a few non-catholic philosophers of religion who are interested in the speculative problem but who believe that the classical solution empties the term "knowledge" of all significance when applied to God just because the word "knowledge," if it is to have any meaning, must involve being affected by what one knows. The only solution, it is argued, is to reject the traditional notion of IMPASSIBILITY and to admit that the world does contribute to the richness of God's experience. Alfred N. Whitehead (1861-1947) and Charles Hartshorne (1897-) both explore this alternative. To assert that God is omniscient, they argue, is to say that his knowledge is perfect, which is to say he knows all that it is possible in principle to know—what is actual as actual, probable as probable, possible as possible. Since the future is not actual, it is meaningless either to say that God knows the future or that his knowledge is imperfect because he doesn't know what it is impossible in principle to know. To argue also that if God's experience cannot be enriched because God cannot change merely presupposes the prejudice for changelessness. (See *Actus Purus*; Attributes of God; Being; Foreknowledge; God; Impassibility; Panentheism; Perfection, Theological; Process Philosophy; Theism.)

Ontological Argument is the name for one of the so-called PROOFS FOR THE EXISTENCE OF GOD and is distinguished by its claim to be a genuinely *a priori* argument, that is, one that follows from the meaning of the terms alone. The argument is associated with the name of Anselm of Canterbury (1033-1109), although variants of it are found in the writings of Descartes (1596-1650) and Leibniz (1646-1716). It has recently been argued that there are, in fact, two versions of the argument in both Anselm and Descartes and that the criticisms of Immanuel Kant (1724-1804) and others apply only to one of them. In the first version, Anselm argues that only a fool would say "GOD does not exist," since even the fool must have an idea of God as "that than which nothing greater can be conceived." But since EXISTENCE is a good, the greatest conceivable being must have it, and so God exists necessarily. In the second form of the argument, Anselm writes that God cannot be conceived as not existing since necessary existence is the only mode of existence logically appropriate to the idea of God as perfection. Therefore, either the idea of God is self-contradictory, in which case God could not even conceivably exist, or, granting the consistency of the idea, God exists necessarily.

The first version of the argument is the one usually singled out for rebuttal. The criticism of it is that it treats existence as if it were a predicate, that is, as if it added something to the concept of a thing. But "existence" does not function in our language in this way. After we have defined "horse," to add that one such thing exists does not add anything to the concept "horse" that makes it "greater." To say that a horse exists is a way of saying that there is at least one member of the class of things defined as horses. Therefore, to say that an existing God would be greater than one that existed only in the mind is an illicit way of reasoning.

The second version of the argument is not as easily criticized, because it turns on the point that the idea of perfection involves necessary existence, or better, that contingent existence is a defect so that either the idea of a perfect being is a possible one, in which case such a being necessarily exists, or the idea is an impossible one and a being called God couldn't conceivably exist. The controversial elements in this argument are whether it is logically permissible to talk about necessary existence and whether a consistent idea of God can be formulated. There are those who argue that a consistent idea can be formulated and that necessary existence is a logically permissible concept. There are others who argue that the idea of God is inconsistent and that it is logically incorrect to speak of necessary existence. The challenge that the idea of God is itself fundamentally inconsistent is one that many younger theologians are increasingly interested in. (See Attributes of God; God; Perfection, Theological; Proofs for the Existence of God; Theism.)

Ontologism is the view that it is possible to know GOD directly in this life and not merely by inferences drawn from the created order. Such a view has been championed by some theologians, and was condemned by Pope Pius IX in 1861. O. in its technical form is based on the assumption that true knowledge is knowledge of ESSENCES and that these can only be apprehended with God's aid (the intellectual light) since they are not objectively distinct from God himself. All ideas, then, are but modifications of the idea by which God is apprehended as BEING.

Ontology. See Metaphysics.

Ordo Salutis means "order of salvation" and refers to the pattern of the process by which the individual passes from a state of sin to final REDEMPTION. Such an O.S. necessarily reflects one's THEOLOGY. In R.C. teaching, this O.S. is closely bound up with the sacramental system, beginning with the first movements of GRACE leading one to BAPTISM and the INFUSION of habitual grace. The infused VIRTUES, when properly employed, MERIT further grace, culminating finally in the BEATIFIC VISION of GOD. The Prot. Reformers were not much concerned with any detailed sketch of the O.S., being more impressed by the element of drama and struggle in the Christian life. Their successors, however, elaborated what suggestions they found in their writings. One finds in Lutheran dogmaticians, for example, the following O.S.: the call, illumination, conversion, the ASSURANCE of JUSTIFICATION, REGENERATION, the mystical union with Christ, the new obedience (the reconstituting of the *imago dei*), and final glorification. (See Assurance; Faith; Grace; Justification; Perfection, Christian; Sanctification; Soteriology.)

Original Righteousness. In the classical tradition, *iustitia originalis* refers to the original rectitude Adam enjoyed before the fall. In R.C. THEOLOGY, O.R. refers to the supernatural gifts (*donum supernaturale*), which, strictly speaking, are not a part of man's essential nature but were lost in the fall. According to the Reformers, on the other hand, Adam's O.R. was his likeness to GOD and the harmony of understanding, will, and affections that enabled him to obey the divine LAW both inwardly and externally. (See *Donum Superadditum*; Image of God; Sin, Original.)

Original Sin. See Sin, Original.

Orthodoxy technically refers to "right belief" in contrast to error and HERESY. It may be used more generally to indicate the official and normative teachings of any group, i.e., orthodox Mormonism or orthodox Marxism. It is often used by historians of Christianity as a descriptive adjective, as when it is applied, say, to the party of Athanasius (c.295-373) in the early theological disputes. It is also used as a proper name to refer to those Eastern churches in communion with Constantinople, hence, the Eastern Orthodox churches. (See Dogma; Faith; Heresy.)

P

Panentheism is the view that attempts to reconcile the insights of PANTHEISM, on the one hand, and of DEISM on the other. If pantheism identifies GOD and the world taken as a whole, and deism insists that God and the world are separate entities, P. argues that the world is included in God's being something as cells are included in a larger organism, although the world does not exhaust God's being or creativity. Just as a PERSON is both the sum of all his experiences and parts and yet more than they, so God has all of finite being as part of his being and experience but transcends it. This view necessarily rejects the view of God's complete independence from the world and modifies the classical attributes of IMPASSIBILITY, OMNISCIENCE, and ETERNITY. P. argues that the content of God's experience literally changes, although, abstractly speaking, God will always experience what there is to experience, and in that sense he is omniscient. Since P. holds there are real freedom and spontaneity in the world, it insists that it is impossible, even for God, to know the future; hence, God in some sense is temporal. This position claims to do most justice to both the absolute and the personal SYMBOLS predicated of God. Although elements of this position are to be found throughout the history of Western thought, it has been most systematically elaborated by the philosopher Alfred N. Whitehead (1861-1947), and its religious and theological implications explored by Charles Hartshorne (1897-). (See Attributes of God; Being; Deism; God; Immanence; Impassibility; Omniscience; Panpsychism; Pantheism; Perfection, Theological; Process Philosophy; Theism.)

Panpsychism is the view that all reality is composed of beings that possess consciousness, ranging from the lowest degree of unity, awareness, and purpose to the highest. Some panentheists are panpsychists, but not all panpsychists are panentheists. (See Animism; Matter; Materialism; Panentheism.)

Pantheism is the doctrine that all things and beings are modes, attributes, or appearances of one single reality or BEING; hence nature and GOD are believed to be identical. There are varying types of pantheists, ranging from those that attribute consciousness to nature taken as a whole to those that do not. So, too, various types of piety and ethics are associated with the respective conceptions. Spinoza (1632-77) formulated what is perhaps the most impressive pantheistic system in Western philosophy. He insisted that there could be by definition only one unlimited SUBSTANCE possessing an infinitude of attributes; therefore God and nature are but two names for one identical reality. P. has traditionally been rejected by orthodox Christian theologians because it is alleged to obliterate the distinction between the creator and CREATION with all of the religious consequences following from this. (See Acosmism; Creation; Deism; God; Immanence; Monism; Naturalism; Panentheism; Theism.)

Paraclete. The name used by the author of the Fourth Gospel to signify the spirit of GOD that will strengthen the faithful and guide them into all truth, hence the Holy Spirit. (See Spirit—Holy Spirit.)

Paradise is a term commonly used to signify heaven, although its meaning seems to have shifted somewhat in the history of Western religious thought. In the Septuagint, it is used to designate the Garden of Eden. In later rabbinic thought, however, P. seems to denote that part of HADES where the SOULS of the righteous repose and which may correspond with what R.C.s now call the LIMBO of the Fathers (*limbus*

173

patrum). Jesus' well-known word to the penitent thief in Luke 23:43 may presuppose this late rabbinic belief, although some commentators claim it means simply "after death." Paul apparently uses the term in II Cor. 12:4 to signify heaven. (See Eschatology; Hell; Immortality; Limbo; Purgatory; Resurrection of the Dead.)

Paradox is originally a Greek word which meant "that which is against common opinion." The word has been variously used, however, to refer to: (1) the strange and unbelievable; (2) an expression which is at one and the same time both true and false; (3) a proposition that has mutually contradictory subjects and predicates though appearing to be intelligible; (4) a peculiar type of wise saying like "he who loses his life will find it." The interpretation of logical P.es has been an important feature of modern logic.

The term has played an important role in some contemporary Prot. THEOLOGY influenced by Kierkegaard (1813-55). Although Kierkegaard himself had a very elaborate justification of the use of the concept, its use is now often defended because it is said to point to the inability of man's reason to grasp the infinite nature of GOD. All true theological doctrines, therefore, are alleged to be paradoxical: "the Eternal has come into time," "the Infinite has been embodied in a single man," etc. A P., in short, is a formulation in which two contradictory categories or sentences are juxtaposed, but which claims to be required by the reality in question. Kierkegaard argued that P. especially has the power to awaken and sustain passion, hence is peculiarly appropriate as an object of FAITH. Critics, however, have insisted that P. is a refuge for irrationalism and obscurantism and, therefore, should be avoided by theologians. Paul Tillich (1886-) argues for the original Greek meaning of the word and insists that it has nothing to do with irrational or nonsensical propositions. (See Dialectical; Neo-Reformed Theology.)

Parousia is the Greek word used in the N.T. to mean both "coming" and "presence." It has become a technical term in Christian ESCHATOLOGY for the second coming of Christ in his glory in order to judge the "quick and the dead" and to establish the KINGDOM OF GOD. The two meanings of the word, however, are still reflected in two somewhat differing interpretations of the second coming of Christ that have competed with one another throughout the course of Christian history. One interpretation stresses the visible coming of Christ that will bring a world full of evil to an end and will establish a reign of peace and order (see Millennialism). The second interpretation stresses the presence of Christ in the CHURCH, after the reign of which the world and its history will be brought to a close. Each of these interpretations, in turn, have variants, the most extreme of which stand in almost outright contradiction to one another. The N.T., with the exception of the Fourth Gospel, is more or less dominated by the first view, it being believed that the "end of the age" is at hand and that Christ will soon come and establish his messianic reign. The earlier letters of Paul reflect this belief. The most explicit and extreme version of it is found in the Book of Revelation, which has always been the document to which certain Christian groups have appealed to support their beliefs concerning the immediately expected end of the world. This belief also seems to have been quite characteristic of the early church generally and is found in most of the early Christian literature. It has emerged again and again in the history of the Christian church and has frequently led to SCHISM and the founding of sects convinced that the end of the world is at hand and that they have been called out to witness to it. The second view tends to spiritualize the P. of Christ and to minimize, where it does not ignore, a cataclysmic end to the present order of EXISTENCE. The Fourth Gospel is representative of this view. Although the author believes that Jesus Christ will return to earth after his death, this return is spoken of as Christ's presence with those who see in him the truth. This emphasis is further developed by such early Christian writers as Origen (c.185-c.254), who rejects the literalistic hope of a second coming and defends the idea of a transformation of existence into a higher order of being after an indefinite period of growth. St. Augustine (354-430) also tends to minimize a second coming of Christ that will issue in a millennial reign and speaks rather of Christ's continual coming in the church, although it is also true that Augustine believed that this reign of the church would ultimately be climaxed by the end of history. In general, neither Roman Catholicism nor classical Protestantism has emphasized the P., although it has remained as a part of their doctrinal teaching.

The doctrine of the P. of Christ has constituted a problem for Protestantism since the rise of BIBLICAL CRITICISM. The belief all but disappeared in LIBERAL PROTESTANTISM, it being incompatible generally with the belief in progress and the IMMORTALITY of the SOUL. The neo-Reformed theologians generally re-emphasized the importance of eschatology and, hence, the P., but they tried to avoid the literalism of traditional belief. For the most part, they have argued that the P. is a SYMBOL expressing the conviction that history has an end and a goal and that this fulfillment of history involves a judgment on sin, a judgment the Christian must interpret in the light of the REVELATION in Christ. (See Apocalyptic Literature; Chiliasm; Eschatology; Judgment, Final; Millennialism; Resurrection of the Dead.)

Patripassianism when used strictly refers to a particular doctrine that flourished in the early 3rd century. Emphasizing the deity of Christ, certain theologians (Praxeas, fl. *c.*200; Noetus, fl. *c.*200) asserted that GOD was born, suffered, and died. Since this view makes no distinction between the PERSONS of the TRINITY it is also called MONARCHIANISM or anti-Trinitarianism or SABELLIANISM. Those who rejected P. insisted that God was not capable of suffering because he was impassible and, further, that a distinction had to be made between Father and Son. The term is now more generally used to refer to any view in which God is believed to take the sufferings of the world into his own life and experience. (See *Actus Purus*; God; Impassibility; Panentheism; Perfection, Theological; Theodicy.)

Patristics is the name given to the study of the life, literature, and thought of the theologians of the early CHURCH, who flourished from the 1st to, approximately, the 8th century. These theologians are sometimes called "the Fathers" (*patres*) of the church, and their writings are essential for understanding the development of Christian THEOLOGY and DOGMA as well as of ecclesiastical forms and liturgical practice. No brief description could adequately indicate the extraordinary variety of their concerns or the diversity of their styles and modes of thought. Some of them were engaged in defending Christianity against the attacks of pagan authors, others in seeking to define Christianity over against Judaism or various Greek philosophies and religions, still others in combatting heresies of all kinds or in constructing systems of doctrine that would exhibit the integrity of the CATHOLIC FAITH in its fullness or that would reconcile doctrinal views. Any division of the Fathers is, therefore, necessarily arbitrary. Traditionally, certain rough groupings have emerged: the Apostolic Fathers (fl. *c*.95-150), the Apologists (fl. *c*.150-200), the ante-Nicene Fathers (Greek and Latin) (fl. *c*.185-325), the post-Nicene Fathers (Greek and Latin) (fl. *c*.325+), culminating in the systems of John of Damascus (*c*.700?-753?) in the East and Isidore of Seville (*c*.560-636) in the West.

Pelagianism. Strictly, the term refers to the teachings of the British monk Pelagius (fl. 400-420?) and his school concerning the relationship between divine GRACE and the human will. Although his views now have to be reconstructed from the writings of his opponents, Pelagius seems to have denied the doctrine of ORIGINAL SIN. He argued that GOD would not command man to do what he was unable to do. The will, therefore, must be regarded as free to do good or evil. This freedom cannot have been lost by Adam. It is meaningful to talk about sin only as the quality of an action and not as a condition of the SOUL; therefore, Adam's disobedience had significance only for himself. The death Adam suffered was natural and in no way a punishment for sin. To the extent one can talk about the universality of sin, it must be attributed to habit and custom.

St. Augustine (354-430) rigorously attacked this position, taking Pelagius to mean that man can save himself and does not need grace. Pelagius denied this was his conclusion, but Augustine's position more or less became the orthodox one, so that "P" is now more loosely and pejoratively used by some to designate any view which champions FREEDOM OF THE WILL, or rejects the doctrine of original sin, or argues that guilt can only be properly attached to a free and conscious act. (See Anthropology; Freedom of the Will; Imputation; Semi-Pelagianism; Sin, Actual; Sin, Original.)

Perfection, Christian. Because of the injunction of Jesus "You, therefore, must be perfect, as your heavenly Father is perfect," various Christian groups have claimed that this P. is not a remote hope, to be realized only in the future life, but an obligation and a real possibility for this one. These groups have differed somewhat as to the content of this idea. In gnostic Christianity, P. was the release of the SOUL from the bondage of the flesh and was attained by means of an esoteric knowledge and illumination (*gnosis*). In PELAGIAN-ISM, P. was the culmination of vigorous moral education and discipline. Still other groups have defined P. in terms of mystical experience or ecstatic gifts of the Holy Spirit.

Because of these claims, often based on what seemed alien principles, the traditional position of the CHURCH since Augustine (354-430) has been that P. is perfect love and not possible in this life, except for the saints. The Prot. Reformers departed from this view only in denying it as a possibility even for the saints. Calvin (1509-64) wrote quite typically that "there still remains in a regenerate man a fountain of evil, continually producing irregular desires . . ." and that this warfare in man's being "will be terminated only by death. . . ." The Reformers did not deny that progress was possible in the Christian life; they simply denied one could ever claim to be perfect. In subsequent Protestantism, the undue stress on the notion that sin itself was not overcome in the believer but only that guilt was not imputed to him sometimes corrupted even this hope for progress, and it was against this notion that pietists and others revolted.

One of the few to work out the idea of P. on evangelical principles was John Wesley (1703-91), and this idea is often regarded as the unique contribution of Methodism, which he founded. Wesley regarded P. as "pure love reigning alone in the heart and life" and as a real possibility for every Christian who had first been justified by FAITH. While he viewed love as God's law, he also believed that P. was a gift of GRACE. Although a long period of effort might precede it, P. was given instantly. With it was also given an ASSURANCE, just as one was given an assurance of JUSTIFICATION, although this assurance was not in all cases equally clear.

Controversies have always marked perfectionist groups: (1) whether P. is sinlessness or not and (2) whether it is attainable in this life. Wesley's views are unequivocal on the latter issue. P. is possible in this life, although only a few may attain it. On the former point, however, Wesley's views are less clear, partly because of his definition of sin as a "voluntary transgression of a known law." P., he argued, was compatible with errors and with "involuntary transgression." Since the Reformers did not limit sin to voluntary transgressions or acts, it is difficult to know whether Wesley and they are saying the same thing or not. They would, however, have been disturbed by any claim that the inbred sin of our nature is entirely overcome in this life. (See *Agape* and *Eros*; Anthropology; Assurance; Law and Gospel; *Ordo Salutis*; Sanctification.)

Perfection, Theological. P. is a term traditionally predicated of GOD by Christian theologians because it means "completely whole" or "lacking any defect." It must be remembered, however, that the same term frequently means different things to different people and a study of the history of Christian THEOLOGY reveals this to be true of the concept of P. (1) For those who consider any characteristic of finite BEING to be a defect (i.e., individuality), divine P. will be synonymous with pure being and with something that lies beyond all predication. (2) For those who consider only certain but not all aspects of finite being to be defects (like change or mutability), P. will be the possession of those positive predicates in an absolute degree. Both ideas of P., it is clear, are closely linked with the idea of absoluteness in the sense of excluding the possibility of change in any respect.

Both of these traditional ideas of P. have been criticized by some contemporary Prot. theologians and by some philosophers of religion. Emil Brunner (1889-), for example, insists that the idea of P. is itself purely a formal and empty idea and presupposes some standard other than REVELATION by

179

which God can be measured. He insists that the only P. of which the Bible knows anything is the P. of "love in its fullness," which is not a speculative idea. Karl Barth (1886-) argues (1) that the traditional idea of P. rests on the *analogia entis* (see Analogy, Way of), and (2) that it has been too determined by the idea of the absolute simplicity of the divine being. Barth rejects the way of analogy as the source of the knowledge of God and insists that revelation discloses the richness and multiplicity of the being of God. Barth speaks, therefore, of the individuality and diversity of the divine P.s. Philosophers of religion, like F. R. Tennant (1866-1957), have argued that the idea of P. as pure being is meaningless, because, by virtue of excluding any positive predicates, the idea is indistinguishable from nothingness. It has also been argued, by Charles Hartshorne (1897-), as well as by Tennant, that the idea of P. as including all positive predicates in an absolute degree may be a self-contradictory idea, and that it certainly is if one tries to include all the traditional predicates in it. Some traditional predicates, it is alleged, are incompatible with others. For example, it is literally impossible for a perfectly compassionate being to be impassible or unmoved by another's suffering, just as it is impossible for a being to be at once omniscient, compassionate, and perfectly blissful. Neither Hartshorne nor Tennant rejects entirely the idea of P.; they only insist that it must be more clearly specified in degree and kind. Hartshorne defines a P. as an excellence such that rivalry or superiority on the part of any conceivable individual is impossible, although this is not incompatible with an increase in that specific excellence. For example, God cannot be excelled by any other being in his enjoyment of all the creatures that do or will exist. But in so far as the creatures that do not yet exist will add a real increment to his enjoyment, that excellence will be increased. God is perfect in that he is that being than which no other being could conceivably be greater but which himself could become greater in another "state." P. is thus severed from absoluteness and requires, furthermore, discrimination among the attributes or perfections and their relation to one another. (See Analogy, Way of; Attributes of God; Being; God; Impassibility; Omniscience; Theism; Theodicy.)

Perichoresis is the term used in the doctrine of the TRINITY to refer to the mutual interpenetration of the PERSONS of the godhead, so that although each person is distinct in relation to the others, nevertheless, each participates fully in the BEING of the others. The being of the godhead is thus one and indivisible. The same term is also used in some christological theories to indicate the interpenetration of the divine and human. (See *Communicatio Idiomatum*). Synonyms for P. are coinherence and circumincession. (See Appropriations; Christology; *Communicatio Idiomatum*; Hypostatic Union; Person; Procession; Theandric Acts; Trinity.)

Perseverance. Apart from its general meaning, the term technically refers to the Calvinistic doctrine that those whom GOD elects by his ETERNAL DECREE and regenerates by the Holy Spirit are so preserved by divine GRACE that, although subject to temptation and sin, they never "lose the grace of adoption" or "forfeit the state of JUSTIFICATION" or "commit the sin unto death." In short, believers are guided and preserved to the end and may be assured of that fact. The doctrine was the object of a great dispute between Arminians and Calvinists, the former arguing that the doctrine was not contained in Scripture and led to ANTINOMIANISM and PRIDE. It is contained both in the canons adopted against the Arminians by the Synod of Dort in Holland (1618-19) and in the Westminster Confession (1646), the most important Calvinist confession of faith. (See Assurance; Election; Faith; Predestination.)

Person. In traditional THEOLOGY, P. is a technical term (*terminus technicus*) that probably originated with Tertullian (150?-225?), who created the formula "three persons in one SUBSTANCE" to describe the TRINITY. His usage probably reflects that of Roman law and the theater. In the former, a *persona* was a legal entity or party to a contract. In the latter, it was a role throughout a drama and, therefore, was used of the mask worn by the actor. Neither usage identifies a P. as a self-conscious being as modern usage does. One actor (a modern P.) could play several *personae* (or roles) just as a legal corporation (*persona*) could be made up of several persons in the modern sense of the word. Tertullian argued that GOD was one with respect to his BEING (nature or substance) but three with respect to the exercise of his sovereignty. Jesus Christ was one P. (or entity) having two natures (divine and human).

Boethius' (c.480-c.524) definition of a P. as an "individual substance with a rational nature" had an important influence on medieval theology and approaches more nearly the modern meaning of the term. It was so applied by St. Thomas (c.1225-74) to man as a unity of body and SOUL. It is a matter of some dispute whether this meant that Thomas then held a social conception of the Trinity, i.e., three self-conscious persons in the godhead. Probably not. Both Thomas and Augustine (354-430) regarded the P.s of the Trinity to be individuated by their relationships to one another within one divine "consciousness," hence their reliance on the analogies of memory, understanding, and will for interpreting the Trinity.

Modern Prot. theology has been influenced by the Western philosophical tradition since Descartes (1596-1650) and Locke (1632-1704) more than by the medieval terminology. In the former tradition, a P. was regarded as a thinking, willing being who is the subject of rights and who can perceive the obligations in a rational moral order. In so far as a P. was regarded as a self-conscious being (a personality), 18th- and 19th-century theologians found it especially appropriate as a SYMBOL for God. It should be noted, however, that the term P. was used by moderns to signify the unity of God whereas the older classical theology used it to point to the distinctions within God. For this reason, "three persons in one substance" became increasingly strange to modern ears; even more so because Prot.s after the 18th century turned their backs on the medieval theological and philosophical tradition and its terminology.

Philosophy in the 19th and 20th centuries has been characterized by a series of profound explorations into the nature of human EXISTENCE. Idealism, the so-called philosophy of life (*Lebensphilosophie*), and EXISTENTIALISM, together with modern psychology, have all influenced modern Prot. theological conceptions of P. Space does not permit any adequate indication of the nuances of meaning the term now possesses, but these might be noted: (1) a P. refers to the unique unity of will, imagination, reason, bodily desire that expresses itself in decision and cultural forms; (2) a P. is radically conditioned by his past (or history), so that his thoughts, ideas, value judgments, and language are only intelligible in terms of a specific historical context; (3) nevertheless, a P. by virtue of memory, imagination, and freedom transcends history in the sense of not being merely a product of history; (4) a P. can best be talked about not in terms of substance and attributes, soul and its activities, but in terms that express "lived existence" and the unique qualities of that existence, such as ANXIETY, concern, responsibility, etc.; (5) the distinctive fulfillment of a P. occurs in relationships of mutuality, openness, and responsibility, in an I-THOU relationship. A P. comes to self-knowledge with other persons and is, therefore, essentially social. This understanding provides, it is claimed, the most illumination for the Biblical ideas of COVENANT and AGAPE. (See Anthropology; God; Historicity of Human Existence; Personalism; Spirit–Holy Spirit; Theism; Trinity.)

Personalism is a term applied somewhat loosely to any philosophy in which PERSONS are regarded either as the sole or highest form of reality and, therefore, as possessing intrinsic value. However, the designation indicates very little because of the various conceptions of personality actually held by philosophers and the various possible world views called P. This accounts for the number of adjectives which historians of philosophy have felt obligated to employ to specify further the point of view in question: atheistic P., theistic P., teleological P., pantheistic P., panpsychist P., absolutistic P., phenomenological P., etc.

The term, however, has come to be used in America to describe a type of THEISM most systematically developed by Borden Parker Bowne (1847-1910), a very influential American writer and professor. Bowne's two major interests were EPISTEMOLOGY and METAPHYSICS. So far as the latter was concerned, he believed that only the idea of personality satisfies the requirements necessary for a true conception of reality. The relationships of things constituting the universe required, he thought, a self-existing, absolute person. A GOD so conceived must in some sense be temporal, in contrast to the God of classical theism. Moreover, this personal being must be regarded as moral and history seen as the unfolding realization of his will.

This type of P. profoundly influenced the general character of LIBERAL PROTESTANTISM in America and accounts in large part for its rationalistic temper, its anti-supernaturalism, its opposition to obscurantism, its anti-Trinitarian ethos, and its general confidence in progress. The personalistic tradition continued in Boston for years, modified somewhat by the PHILOSOPHY OF RELIGION of Edgar Brightman (1884-1953), who advocated the view that God is limited or finite. (See God; Liberal Protestantism; Theism.)

Phenomenology is a term closely associated with the philosophy of Edmund Husserl (1859-1938), although it has acquired a more general meaning as a designation for a certain method of investigation of certain fundamental human activities, like religion and art. Husserl's own philosophy was preoccupied with highly technical, logical and methodological problems. To oversimplify, he sought a completely objective and scientific philosophical method. The aim of his philosophy was to establish the basic structure of consciousness and the conditions of any possible experience. To do this, he believed that the investigator of any type of experience must attempt to apprehend the universal ESSENCES or structures given in the phenomena of that experience. He can do this only if he suspends or "brackets" his own beliefs and presuppositions and attends rigorously to the phenomena themselves as they appear in the experience being investigated. In the P. of religion, for example, the investigator does not judge the beliefs of a religion to be true or false; rather he suspends his own judgment and tries to see the world as the believer sees it. In this way, he hopes to describe the structures of the religious consciousness in general. Husserl's ideas had an important influence on some existentialist philosophers, such as Martin Heidegger (1889-) and Karl Jaspers (1883-), as well as on certain scholars of religion, such as Rudolf Otto

(1869-1937), Max Scheler (1874-1928), G. van der Leeuw (1890-1950). (See Existentialism; Holy.)

Philosophy of Religion is a type of philosophy that appeared in the 18th century and is a product of the Enlightenment. It may be divided into two distinct but related enterprises that are sometimes encompassed within the concerns of the same philosopher and sometimes not: (1) the analysis and evaluation of religious experience and belief, (2) the construction of a philosophy or ONTOLOGY. In the 19th-century idealism, it was quite characteristic, for example, for the philosopher to interpret the SYMBOLS of the Christian religion as imaginative ways of expressing ideas that could be apprehended more truly by reason. In the 20th century, however, the emphasis has often fallen on the analysis and evaluation of religious experience and belief in general. Common concerns have been the nature of religious knowledge, the relation of religion and science, the relation of religion to morality and art, and, most recently, the nature of religious language.

Pneumatology is derived from the Greek words *pneuma* (spirit) and *logos* (discourse). In classical philosophy, it refers to the discussion of the nature of the SOUL or the self. In Christian THEOLOGY, it refers to that section of theology dealing with the Holy Spirit.

Positive Theology is the name sometimes given to that type of THEOLOGY concerned with historical fact, tradition, and the DOGMAS and doctrines of the CHURCH in contrast to NATURAL THEOLOGY, which is concerned with principles derived from reason and experience.

Positivism originally was the name given to a philosophic and religious movement founded in the 19th century by the French philosopher Auguste Comte (1798-1857). It has now come to denote a more general and widespread position not directly dependent on Comte's views. Comte used the word "positive" in contrast to "conjectural" and called for a "positive" philosophy, the aim of which was to coordinate known facts, in contrast to a "speculative" philosophy, the aim of

185

which was to deduce causes. Comte formulated the famous Law of Three Stages to describe how the mind of man progresses from a theological to a metaphysical stage before arriving at the last and final positive stage.

The more general use of the term P. reflects this suspicion of all speculations not controlled by fact and sense experience. Positivists argue that all true knowledge consists either of matters of fact or logic and mathematics. In this sense, P. is a thoroughgoing EMPIRICISM.

Postlapsarianism. See Predestination.

Postmillennialism. See Millennialism.

Potentiality. See Actuality.

Pragmatism initially designated a theory concerning the meaning of words, a theory originated by the American philosopher C. S. Peirce (1839-1914). Convinced that a good deal of abstract METAPHYSICS was "gibberish" due to a lack of clarity concerning the meaning of words, he argued that the rational meaning of a word or expression "lies exclusively in its conceivable bearing upon the conduct of life; so that, since obviously nothing that might not result from experiment can have any direct bearing upon conduct, if one can define accurately all conceivable experimental phenomena which the affirmation or denial of a concept could imply, one will have therein a complete definition of the concept, and there is absolutely nothing more in it." To say something is "soluble," for example, is to imply the experiments one would conduct in order to confirm or deny that statement.

This basic idea and the term P. were borrowed and developed by William James (1842-1910) and John Dewey (1859-1952) but with a fundamental—some critics would say confusing—shift in meaning. Whereas Peirce thought of P. as a theory of meaning, James and Dewey converted it into a theory of truth. But there is a difference between establishing the meaning of an expression and its truth. P., therefore, became identified with the notion that whatever satisfies one's purposes is true, a notion that has obvious implications in religion and ethics. P. did, as a matter of fact, have an important influence on religious thought in the early 20th century, especially on R.C. MODERNISM.

Predestination is often identified with foreordination, the idea that before the CREATION of the world, GOD determined (foreordained) all that would come to pass in it. Technically, however, P. is narrower in scope and refers specifically to God's will or ETERNAL DECREE respecting the destiny of intelligent creatures. There are two main ways in which the doctrine has been formulated, each of which, in turn, has two variants. Supralapsarianism (antelapsarianism) is that starker form of the doctrine which holds that even before the creation and fall (*lapsus*) of man, God eternally willed some men to salvation without any consideration of their MERITS or worthiness. Infralapsarianism (sub- or postlapsarianism) is that form of the doctrine—some would call it the milder form—which holds that God's decree is subsequent to the fall; that is, after the fall of man, God elects to save some who would otherwise have perished. The infralapsarian argues that the supralapsarian view is not consistent with the love and JUSTICE of God, who would not condemn some men to damnation before their creation and the exercise of their freedom. The supralapsarians argue that the infralapsarian position is logically and theologically indefensible because an omnipotent and omniscient deity necessarily foreordains all that happens, even the fall. In later Calvinism, a further distinction was sometimes made within each of the above positions, especially within infralapsarianism, a distinction having to do with the divine will respecting damnation. Some held that God both elects some to salvation and others to damnation, hence the term "double P." Others argued that although God elects some to be saved, he simply "passes over" the remainder and has no positive will respecting their destiny, hence the name "single P."

Until Augustine (354-430), the doctrine of P. was relatively undeveloped. Out of his reflection and polemics he concluded that (1) all men since Adam are utterly lost in sin, (2) only GRACE can enable the human will to have FAITH, (3) God's grace is irresistible, (4) it is given only to a limited number of men, the others perishing. Augustine's views regarding the necessity and prevenience of grace were adopted by the Second Council of Orange (529), although it avoided endorsing his views on P. and explicitly rejected "double P." Roman Catholicism in general has not endorsed any particular doctrine on the matter and officially tolerates both the Molinist view, the gift of divine grace is given in the light of God's foreknowledge of free human cooperation, and the more rigorous Thomistic view, although even the latter does not approach the harshness of the Calvinistic view.

Most of the Prot. Reformers embraced "double P." in principle, although it is not altogether clear whether or not they were also supralapsarians. Calvin (1509-64) most systematically developed and defended the doctrine. Sympathetic interpreters claim that his view was based less on the view of the divine majesty and OMNIPOTENCE than on the Biblical theme that God elects men in Jesus Christ. At any rate, he fully embraced the doctrine that "eternal life is foreordained for some, and eternal damnation for others" and that neither ELECTION nor rejection has any reference to human righteousness. Calvin's position was rejected by the Arminians, and it was against the latter that the Calvinist doctrine was reaffirmed in the canons of the Synod of Dort (1618-19) and in the Westminster Confession (1646).

Contemporary neo-Reformed theologians, especially Karl Barth (1886-) and Emil Brunner (1889-), argue that the Calvinistic doctrine is not Biblical, although it represents an attempt to do justice to the Biblical idea of God's free election. Brunner argues that the Augustinian and Calvinistic doctrines were corrupted by an abstract, philosophical idea of God's omnipotence that substituted mechanical cause-effect analogies for personal ones. Barth argues that the sole object of Christian faith is God's disclosure of himself as being "for man" (i.e. electing man) in Jesus Christ and that it is theologically erroneous to posit the possibility of a hidden decree of condemnation (double P.). Barth and Brunner do not themselves agree as to the implications of their views, but both are united at least in asserting that God reveals himself as gracious, i.e., as willing the universal salvation of man. (See Arminianism; Covenant; Decrees, Eternal; Determinism;

Election; Foreknowledge; Freedom of the Will; Grace; Justification; Omniscience; Omnipotence; Soteriology.)

Pre-existence of Christ is an expression for the conviction that the life of Jesus Christ is rooted in the being of GOD. The term P.O.C. has always been misleading, for it suggests the pre-existence of the man Jesus. The CHURCH, however, has never endorsed that idea. Pre-existence refers to the existence of the "eternal Son" or LOGOS which, in the fullness of time, was made flesh or, to use the technical language of traditional THEOLOGY, was joined to a human nature and made one PERSON in a HYPOSTATIC UNION. (See Christology; *Homoousion*; *Logos*; Person; Wisdom; Word of God.)

Pre-existence of Souls refers to the belief that every SOUL possesses a career before its embodiment in this life. It is a belief found in many forms in many religions, although there is considerable variation as to the type and nature of the prior existence the soul is believed to have had. Strictly speaking, it is not to be identified with a belief in transmigration, although they are closely related. Early Christian theologians, who were strongly under the influence of Greek philosophy, must have been strongly tempted to embrace the idea, and some did. The most famous of them was Origen of Alexandria (*c*.185-*c*.254). Convinced that SPIRIT was indestructible, he saw the material world as created for the discipline and purification of free spirits who had fallen and been banished. Origen's doctrine was condemned, however, and the doctrine is viewed as heretical. (See Immortality; Resurrection of the Dead; Creationism; Soul; Spirit—Holy Spirit.)

Premillennialism. See Millennialism.

Prevenient Grace. See Grace, Prevenient.

Pride is the first of the so-called SEVEN DEADLY SINS and has generally been regarded by theologians as the root of all sin. By P. is not meant a sense of achievement for what one has created or done (what common sense means by P.), but the defiant rejection of limitation and creatureliness and, thus, the self-elevation of man into the divine (Tillich). In Pauline theology, P. is the opposite of FAITH, since faith is but the acknowledgment that one's own life is a fragile gift. There is, therefore, no basis for boasting before GOD. Contemporary Prot. theologians, especially Reinhold Niebuhr (1892-), have analyzed the nature and effects of P. in both individual and social life with great imagination. (See Faith; Sin, Actual; Sin, Original.)

Priesthood of All Believers is the phrase symbolic of one of the basic and distinctive principles of the Prot. Reformation. Luther (1483-1546) thought of it as a correlate of the doctrines of JUSTIFICATION by FAITH alone and of the liberty of the Christian believer. Like other Prot. affirmations, this one has a positive and a negative meaning. Positively, it means that just as every Christian has an inner liberty of CONSCIENCE that makes him a "lord over all," so, too, every Christian is a priest or "servant of all." By this Luther meant not simply that every man has his own direct access to Christ but that all Christians are "worthy to appear before GOD to pray for others and to teach one another the things of God." Negatively, this means not only a rejection of the medieval tradition that practically identified priesthood with the administration of the SACRAMENTS but also constitutes an attack on the conception of the priesthood as constituting a special class in the eyes of God with a special power and a higher morality. Luther insisted that the public ministry was simply a matter of practical function or VOCATION. It followed that it was not a higher or more religious form of life with a special standing in God's eyes. The Anabaptists, that other part of the Reformation too frequently forgotten, took the phrase to mean the complete abolishment of any functional distinction between clergy and LAITY. No believer was believed to have any status or function not fully shared by all. (See Faith; *Fiducia*; Justification; Law and Gospel; Vocation.)

Process Philosophy is the name frequently given to the META-PHYSICS of Alfred N. Whitehead (1861-1947), which has had an important influence on some philosophers of religion and theologians. The name reflects the fundamental conviction of Whitehead that process, or becoming, is the basic and inclusive ontological category rather than BEING or SUBSTANCE, as in classical Western philosophy and THEOLOGY. To make unchanging substance or being the "really real," Whitehead maintained, leads to a static conception of reality and to insurmountable philosophical and theological problems. Reality is not made up of unchanging substances, which have "accidental" relationships, but of processes, or events, or "occasions of experience" that have relatively enduring abstract structures or forms. These occasions of experience are essentially related to other processes in an ordered web of relationships that constitutes a cosmic organism, which is itself continually changing and in the grip of "creative advance." By "creative advance" Whitehead means that the entire process of becoming composed of actual entities constitutes an advance in richness and value, that the passage from past to future is only possible because the actual occasions and the boundless wealth of potentiality join together again and again to form new aesthetic unities. The world is an ever-growing totality of experience.

Three ideas are especially worth noting so far as the importance of P.P. for theology is concerned. The first is that Whitehead argues that subjectivity is the principle of all being, that all actual entities from the lowest grade of organism to the highest have a kind of self-relatedness and a relatedness to other antecedent actualities that can only be properly analyzed in terms of the principle of subjectivity. Thus, he rejects the idea of inert matter. Secondly, GOD, in Whitehead's system, is not an exception to all the categories which characterize finite being, as he is in classical philosophy by virtue of being defined as ACTUS PURUS; rather, God is the chief exemplification of all the truly universal categories. Thus, in so far as being in principle is marked by process and abstract identity, God, too, is in the process of change, although he, too, has a purely abstract ESSENCE as does any individual being. God, as an actual entity, includes all other actual entities in his own life and, thus, his experience is enriched by theirs. Classical theology, of course, cannot accept this idea, and it is just the forever fixed and static character of the divine being which Whitehead believed makes classical philosophy at once metaphysically false and religiously unproductive. There are those interpreters of Whitehead who, like Charles Hartshorne (1897-), argue that "Whitehead is, in the Western world at least, the first great philosophical theist who, as a philosopher, really believes in the God of religion," i.e., God as a PERSON. These interpreters argue that the classical idea of an unchanging God is a texture of contradictions and, moreover, is not the God of Biblical piety. Because of this, they continue, theologians have either had to give up metaphysics if they wanted to do justice to the anthropomorphic SYMBOLS of religion, or they have turned to metaphysics and been unable to illumine the life of piety. The result, it is concluded, has been unfortunate for both metaphysics and religion. (See *Actus Purus*; Analogy, Way of; Being; God; Historicity of Human Existence; Impassibility; Metaphysics; Omniscience; Panentheism; Perfection, Theological; Substance; Theism.)

Procession. In the traditional doctrine of the TRINITY there is assigned a special order of relationships among the three PERSONS. The Father is the eternal origin, the LOGOS is "from the Father," and the Holy Spirit is, in the Western version of the doctrine, "from the Father and the Son" (see *Filioque*). The term P. is the technical word for the derivative relationships of the Son and Holy Spirit, so that theologians speak of three persons but only two P.s.

More technically, however, the term P. has been applied only to the Holy Spirit to distinguish its manner of origination from that of the Son. The Son is "begotten" or "actively generated" while the Spirit originates by "passive spiration" and is the only person who, technically speaking, "proceeds," in contrast to "is begotten." (See Appropriations; Filiation; *Filioque*; Generation; *Perichoresis*; Person; Spirit–Holy Spirit; Trinity.)

Prolegomena is a Greek word literally meaning "the things said beforehand" and is often applied in systematic THEOLOGY

to those issues a theologian feels it necessary to discuss before
he turns to theology proper, for example, the general nature
of systematic theology, the relationship of theology to other
disciplines (like philosophy), the problems of truth and
authority, etc. (See Epistemology; Natural Theology; Revelation; Theology.)

Proofs for the Existence of God. A recurring phenomenon in
the history of Western philosophy and Christian THEOLOGY
has been the attempt to demonstrate the EXISTENCE and nature
of an intelligent and benevolent deity. However simple the
arguments may appear on the surface, philosophical analysis
has shown that the presuppositions of and issues raised by
them are extraordinarily complex: What constitutes the nature
of a proof? What are the limits and validity of the idea of
causality? Is existence a predicate? Is perfection a meaningful term? Is an infinite regress logically possible? Must what
human beings necessarily think be necessarily so? It is not
surprising that the literature on the P.F.E.G. is enormous
and technical.

There are a number of such arguments, and each has
several variations. A frequently used classification divides
them into the *a priori* (an argument in which the conclusion
follows necessarily from the definition of the terms and,
as in the case of mathematics, no appeal to experience is
needed to confirm the conclusion as true) and the *a posteriori*
(an argument which starts from experience and posits something to explain that experience). The most famous *a priori*
argument is called the ONTOLOGICAL ARGUMENT and is usually
associated with the name of St. Anselm of Canterbury (1033-
1109), although variations on it may be found in the works
of Descartes (1596-1650), Leibniz (1646-1716), and others.
Since this argument is discussed elsewhere in this handbook
(see Ontological Argument), this article will restrict itself to
the *a posteriori* arguments, even though it has been argued by
Immanuel Kant (1724-1804) and others that the *a posteriori*
arguments necessarily presuppose the *a priori* one.

The classical exposition of the *a posteriori* arguments is to
be found in the writings of Thomas Aquinas (*c*.1225-74).

(1) The argument from motion (*ex motu*): We observe that some things in the world are in process of change, which technically may be regarded as the passage from potentiality to ACTUALITY. All such change, however, requires some prior actuality, and since this cannot go on *ad infinitum* there must be a perfectly actualized First Mover, i.e., GOD. (2) The argument from efficient causation (*ex causa efficiente*): Nothing we know in the universe can be the cause of itself, for then it would exist before itself, which is impossible. Nor can there be an infinite series of efficient causes. Therefore, there must be a first efficient cause, i.e., God. (3) The argument from contingency (*ex contingentia mundi*): We find in nature things that come into existence and perish, i.e., are contingent and not necessary. If everything were capable of not being, there must have been a time when nothing actually existed. In that case, however, nothing would have come into existence, since nothing can be the cause of itself. Therefore, there must exist a NECESSARY BEING (one whose very nature it is to exist), i.e., God. (4) The argument from the degrees of goodness (*ex gradibus*): All comparative judgments of better or worse presuppose some absolute standard of judgment. The things we judge to be better or worse participate in that absolute standard, i.e., God. (5) The argument from design (*ex gubernatione rerum*) or the teleological argument: All the inanimate processes of nature are adapted for the realization of some end or goal. Since inanimate objects have no intelligence of their own, and since the appeal to chance explains nothing, and, further, since the only other demonstrable agent of purpose is mind or intelligence, there must be a supreme intelligence who is the cause of this adaptiveness and order in nature.

In addition to these famous arguments, there are others which appeal to such things as: the fact that all men everywhere believe in the existence of gods (the *consensus gentium*); the fact that the world can be known, i.e., the correlation between mind and reality; the fact of moral experience and that the world provides the stage for significant moral effort; the fact of beauty; the fact of religious experience. All of these arguments, however, presuppose the principle of causality, the impossibility of infinite regress, and that like effects have like causes, or the principle of analogy. (See Analogy, Way of). It is not surprising, therefore, that critics of the P.F.E.G. should concentrate on the criticism of these presuppositions. It is generally acknowledged that the most devastating critics were David Hume (1711-76) and Immanuel Kant.

Hume's criticisms have achieved a peculiar kind of immortality by virtue of the manner in which he chose to put them, an extremely witty series of dialogues in which his own position is not easily discerned. The point made there is that the idea of cause is not valid if it is used to argue for a cosmic intelligence. We infer a watchmaker from a watch only because in repeated situations we have come to see that the latter requires the former, that is to say, our idea of what kind of effects are related to what kind of causes arises only after repeated experiences. No single experience of an event, on the other hand, offers any basis for asserting it to require a certain kind of cause, and in advance of such repeated experiences no legitimate inference can be drawn. Even if we knew what we meant when we talked about the world as an effect (for who observes the world?), no one has ever seen worlds being made by world makers. Given no stable this-kind-of-effect-requires-this-kind-of-cause relationship, therefore, one could as well argue that the world was created as an experiment by some minor deity or a committee of them. Indeed, it is conceivable that there may be an infinite regress of causes. If it be argued that we must stop somewhere, it may be replied that we should stop simply with the world as it is. But even if one grants the existence of a cause, this would at best argue for a finite deity, since there is no basis for believing a cause must be greater than its effect.

Kant's arguments are not as readily understandable as Hume's, since they are bound up so closely with his EPISTEMOLOGY, but like Hume he attacked the legitimacy of the extension of the principle of causality beyond experience. He argued that the idea of causality is only legitimate within experience and is not when extended beyond it. Furthermore, Kant argued that the *a posteriori* proofs really presuppose the *a priori* one, and that this argument makes the mistake of thinking "existence" to be a word that functions like a predicate. Kant insisted that the mind was simply not capable of reasoning beyond experience, since there are no sense data which we can organize and form with our concepts. The idea of God, to be sure, serves important theoretical and moral functions, but the existence of God cannot be demonstrated, although one may believe in God on FAITH.

Not all philosophers or theologians regard these criticisms of Hume and Kant as devastating, but since their time very few have ventured to offer any simple version of the old arguments without a preliminary and elaborate justification of the idea of cause or an analysis of the idea of infinite regress. For this reason, the defenders of the arguments today tend to become involved in what Kierkegaard (1813-55) called a "galloping parenthesis," and the arguments themselves have lost that simple cogency which once served to indicate self-evidence. Furthermore, the rise of the sciences and the philosophies of the sciences have introduced new complexities and problems. The theory of evolution, for example, alters somewhat the problem of explaining adaptation, just as it also raises questions about the economy of nature. So, too, the philosophy of science has raised questions about the relation of scientific theory to so-called natural laws as well as interesting questions about the nature of explanation in general. The Prot. theologians of the last generation have tended to retreat from a discussion of these technical questions and, not wanting to erect their systems on foundations so infirm, have largely confined their efforts to showing the relevance of Christian faith for social and ethical issues and the understanding of human nature. It was, for example, almost accepted as axiomatic by the neo-Reformed theologians that theology has no legitimate interest in the P.F.E.G. Recently, however, others have argued that theology cannot remain insulated from philosophy, and that no theology can continue to appeal to REVELATION without the same sort of questions arising about that appeal as arise about the P.F.E.G. Consequently, one hears increasingly of philosophical theology and, within the circle of those who practice it, the P.F.E.G. are once more being discussed in dialogue with contemporary philosophy of all sorts. (See Apologetics; Being; God; Metaphysics; Natural Theology; Ontological Argument; Theism.)

Propitiation in general means to appease the wrath of deity by offering some acceptable sacrifice and, therefore, to atone. The term has been used to render the Jewish word *kaphar* and its derivatives, which occur often in the O.T., as well as the Greek terms *hilaskomai* (Heb. 2:17), *hilasterion* (Rom. 3:25), and *hilasmos* (I John 2:2, 4:10), all of which refer to the significance of the death of Christ in the N.T. The idea of P. lies at the heart of one theory of the ATONEMENT that has been prominent in Latin Christianity as well as in Prot. ORTHODOXY. This theory holds that the divine wrath against sin requires a satisfactory penalty, because God's JUSTICE would be compromised were he simply to forgive sin without exacting punishment. Since men themselves are unable to pay the penalty, GOD makes it possible through Jesus Christ, who, by virtue of his two natures in one PERSON, is able to accomplish a work of infinite value. He makes P. for man's sin.

This entire theory has been subjected to a radical criticism by many contemporary Prot. theologians, especially Gustaf Aulen (1879-). They argue: (1) the theory rests on a mistaken view of the use of the Greek words above; (2) it violates the sense of Scripture where the language of sacrifice refers to God's self-giving and mercy and not to an appeasement of his wrath; (3) it either introduces an untenable split between the work of Christ and God or it reduces forgiveness to a divine transaction; (4) it has no relevance to contemporary understandings of reconciliation and justice. (See Atonement; Expiation; Grace; Imputation; Justification; Righteousness of God; Satisfaction.)

Protestant Principle is a term especially to be found in the writings of Paul Tillich (1886-), although he regards it as but a name for a universal principle that, while embodied in the Prot. Reformation, is effective in all periods of history and is implicit in all great religions. The P.P. may be negatively expressed as the protest against any absolute claim made for a finite reality, whether it be a CHURCH, a book, a SYMBOL, a PERSON, or an event. Positively it may be expressed as the confession that GRACE is not bound to any finite form, that GOD is the inexhaustible power and ground of all BEING, and that the truest FAITH is just that one which has an element of self-negation in it because it points beyond itself to that which is really ultimate. It is the embodiment of this P.P. that makes the cross the center of true Christian faith, Tillich argues, for Jesus is the Christ just because He "sacrificed himself as Jesus to himself as the Christ," because he did not draw men to himself but pointed beyond himself to God. Although many other theologians also have this idea at the core of their THEOLOGY, Tillich has made it the basis for his THEOLOGY OF CULTURE and his critique of Protestantism as a historical reality. He has even extended its meaning into the intellectual sphere. He insists that just as the P.P. means that one is justified as a sinner, it must also mean that one is justified even though a doubter. "Neither works of piety nor works of morality nor works of the intellect establish unity with God. They follow from this unity, but they do not make it." (See Faith; *Fiducia*; Grace; Justification; Neo-Reformed Theology; Righteousness of God; Word of God.)

Providence traditionally has encompassed three closely related ideas: the divine preservation (*conservatio*) by which GOD sustains all creatures in their distinctive natures and powers; the divine cooperation (*concursus*) by which God not only sustains but actively concurs in these creatures' action in such an intimate way that every action of these beings can be ultimately explained only by reference to both their and the infinite's action; the divine government (*gubernatio*), by which God fulfills his purpose for the creatures by guiding them.

The divine preservation is closely linked to the act of CREATION itself and has not been the subject of as much debate as the divine *concursus* and *gubernatio*. For the idea of concurrence raises all the issues of the relation of primary to secondary causation, issues peculiarly thorny with respect to human action. Thomists, for example, traditionally have argued that God's infinite action is adapted to the nature and needs of each kind of creature so that it is different in, say, animals than in free, intelligent beings. Nevertheless, free actions have been regarded as also divine actions. "God," writes Thomas Aquinas (*c.*1225-74), "is a cause to us not only of our will but also of our willing." The followers of Molina (1535-1600), on the other hand, believe that this prejudices human freedom and argue that the divine concurrence does not influence the will directly but simply is the general and continuing assistance enabling the will to produce any act whatsoever. Calvinists rejected the idea of concurrence altogether and insisted that God's activity is so direct and so arouses the creature that the latter's activity may be said to be God's activity, although they (the Calvinists) added the rhetorical flourish "this by no means does away with human freedom." Arminians rejected the Calvinist view and, in effect, embraced the Molinists' position. More recently, Karl Barth (1886-) has claimed that all these traditional alternatives labor too much under the abstract idea of causality and do not take sufficiently seriously God's coexistence with his creatures.

In ordinary piety, the idea of P. has been most identified with the third idea, the divine government. This idea has seemed to many to be the most natural implication of the Biblical view of history as well as religious experience. Yet it is just this idea that seems difficult for modern man to understand, far less to reconcile with certain fundamental ideas—the idea of physical law, radical freedom, and the lack of a discernible pattern in history. In the 19th century, the idea of progress seemed to some to be an acceptable way of interpreting this aspect of P. but this was unconvincing after two world holocausts. Some theologians have insisted that history must be interpreted as the prophets interpreted it, as God's mighty acts. But unlike the prophets, these theologians are too aware of the ambiguity and complexity of modern history to point to any particular acts as God's, and their theology is, therefore, unconvincing. Still other theologians have argued that the idea of a plan or a purpose for history is itself an unbiblical idea, that history remains ambiguous to the end and that it is just this insight that is preserved in the apocalyptic imagery in the Bible. (See Covenantal Theology; Foreknowledge; Freedom of the Will; *Heilsgeschichte*; Miracle; Predestination; Theodicy.)

Purgatory. According to R.C. doctrine, all baptized souls who have died without repentance for venial sins or who have not paid their punishment for sins the guilt of which has been removed, go to a "place" called P. P. is not, despite popular misunderstanding, a period of probation. It is for those who already are partakers of supernatural grace and, therefore, destined to be saved but who, for the reasons stated above, cannot enter heaven directly. The sufferings of P. are said to be embraced by the believer with joy because the soul wants to do all in its power to serve the Almighty and to hasten the day of final bliss. Prot.s reject the doctrine of P. for several reasons: (1) that it is without Scriptural foundations; (2) that it retains the idea of a punishment after forgiveness; (3) that it implies that the satisfaction of Christ is not fully sufficient; (4) that it vitiates the Gospel of a complete forgiveness of sins. (See Beatific Vision; Eschatology; Hell; Immortality; Judgment, Final; Paradise; Resurrection of the Dead; Soul.)

Pyrrhonism is a word loosely used to designate extreme skepticism. Pyrrho of Ellis (365-275 B.C.) was a Greek philosopher who denied the possibility of certain knowledge and believed that the realization of this fact would lead to inner peace.

R

Ransom Theory. See Atonement.

Rationalism. Often used quite loosely, the word usually signifies any theological or philosophical position which values reason as the ultimate arbiter and judge of all statements. It is also sometimes used to designate those systems of thought laid out in a logical and deductive fashion, whether they make reason the ultimate arbiter of religious truth or not. For example, the Prot. Scholastics are sometimes called rationalists even though they believed that Christian truth was supernaturally revealed and not capable of being established by reason, because they organized that truth in a highly logical and rationalistic fashion. (See Scholasticism.)

Realism. See Nominalism.

Real Presence is used generally to refer to the actual presence of Christ in the sacrament of the EUCHARIST. Among those who affirm the R.P. there have been disagreements about the mode or nature of that presence. (See Consubstantiation; Eucharist; Sacrament; Transubstantiation.)

Recapitulation comes from the Latin *recapitulatio* which means literally "summing up." It is used in connection with a certain type of CHRISTOLOGY and SOTERIOLOGY that has had an important place in the history of Christian thought. This type was most thoroughly elaborated by one of the most important theologians of the early CHURCH, Irenaeus of Lyons (*c.*130-*c.*200). His view was that the eternal and divine LOGOS became fully man in Jesus Christ, who, unlike Adam, was perfectly obedient through every stage of his human life from birth to death. Thus, he so summed up or recapitulated all that GOD intended perfect humanity to be that he represented man to God in a new way. He perfectly fulfilled human nature as no other man had done and so raised man to a new level of BEING. (See Christology.)

Redemption means quite generally restoring or saving or getting back. So understood, it is an idea that is at the heart of many religions, the difference among them being how that from which men need to be redeemed is conceived and how, therefore, they can be redeemed. Characteristic of Biblical religion is the idea of sin as rebellion against the will of the creator and the corresponding idea of GRACE and forgiveness. These two basic motifs have been variously interpreted in the history of Christian thought. (See Alienation; Atonement;

Christology; Covenant; Election; Faith; Grace; *Heilsgeschichte*; Justification; Revelation; Sanctification; Sin, Actual; Sin, Original; Soteriology.)

Regeneration means literally "rebirth" and is the term used to signify the actual renewing of the self which, according to Christian THEOLOGY, occurs with the reception of GRACE. How this takes place has been the subject of much discussion in the history of Christian thought. In Roman Catholicism it is associated with the SACRAMENTS; in Protestantism with the gift of the Holy Spirit. (See Baptism; Church; Election; Eucharist; Faith; Grace; Justification; Sanctification.)

Religionsgeschichtliche Schule means literally "history of religions school" and is applied to a small but influential group of O.T. and N.T. scholars and theologians—Herrmann Gunkel, Wilhelm Bousset, Johannes Weiss, William Wrede, Ernst Troeltsch—who flourished around the turn of the century. Basically, their aim was to analyze and interpret the origins, Scriptures, and nature of Christianity as one would any other historical movement, to see it in the context of its environment rather than as an absolutely unique or supernatural reality isolated from its immediate surroundings. In this way they believed it possible to understand how and why Christianity borrowed elements from other religions as well as to see how these elements were fused into a new synthesis. Bousset and Weiss, for example, were interested in the non-Jewish origins of the messianic and apocalyptic ideas and their influence on the N.T. Their historical work, as well as that of others, had a profound effect on subsequent Biblical scholarship, especially FORM CRITICISM. Even when the results of the R.S. were modified or corrected, their basic historical method was accepted. Ernst Troeltsch (1865-1923) was frequently regarded as the theologian of the group. He argued that Christianity could not, in the light of these researches, be considered as an absolute religion. He regarded it as only one of the ways in which men experience the divine, although for Western culture it was a practical absolute since it was so much a part of that culture. The neo-Reformed theologians challenged Troeltsch's theological interpretation even though they acknowledged the fruitfulness of much of the historical work of the R.S. (See Biblical Criticism; Form Criticism; Historicity of Human Existence; Inspiration of the Bible; Word of God.)

Religious *a Priori* is a term that has played an important role in the PHILOSOPHY OF RELIGION since Friedrich Schleiermacher (1768-1834). Most generally, it refers to something like an inherent capacity in man for religion that is the presupposition of all particular and concrete religions. Schleiermacher had argued that all religions represent a peculiar and unique formation of a feeling of absolute dependence. This feeling appears, for example, in one form in a religion like Judaism and in another form in Christianity. There is no such thing, Schleiermacher argued, as religion in general. There are only specific religions. But each religion presupposes a religious capacity or R.A.P. Since Schleiermacher, others have developed theories of the R.A.P. but interpreted it in different terms. Rudolf Otto (1869-1937), for example, speaks of the *sensus numinus* as a "faculty of divinization." (See Holy.)

Resurrection of Christ. The earliest Christian community was based on the conviction that GOD had raised the man Jesus from the dead and exalted him "to the right hand of the Father." So central was this conviction that it is frequently made the content of FAITH in the N.T. (I Cor. 15:3f; Rom. 1:1-4; 8:34; Phil. 2:9-11; Col. 2:15). The reason for this centrality is not altogether clear so long as the R. is viewed, as it has so often been in the history of Christian thought, primarily as the basis for believing in IMMORTALITY. In the N.T., the R. is regarded as the decisive REVELATION and vindication of the sovereignty of God the Creator, his victory over the "powers" of sin and death. These "powers" are viewed in a quite literal—one might even say mythological—way: SATAN is "the god of this world" (II Cor. 4:4); the "ruler of this world" (John 12:31; 14:30; 16:11); the "prince of the power of the air" (Eph. 2:2). Satan is not alone but is accompanied by demonic "principalities and powers" (Rom. 8:38; I Cor. 15:24,26; Col. 1:16; 2:10,15; Eph. 1:21; 3:10; 6:12; I Pet. 3:22) and "elemental spirits of the universe" (Gal. 4:3,9; cf. Col. 2:8,20). The R. represents a defeat of these demonic powers and is a disclosure, therefore, of God's sovereignty over the world. This is the meaning of the eschatological symbolism, because the manifestation of God's sovereignty is the coming of the KINGDOM OF GOD and is the beginning of the end of the age. So understood, the R. is not regarded as one MIRACLE alongside of others, although they also were "signs of the times," but a cosmic act to be compared with CREATION itself. The R. is the basis for confidence that God is Lord over creation, which is another way of talking about faith, because faith is confidence in God who calls into EXISTENCE the things that are not. The aim of the R. is, then, the aim of all revelation, namely, to awaken faith. Thus, Paul can echo the earlier confession that Jesus was "raised for our JUSTIFICATION" (Rom. 4:25). The central actor in the R. is God, not Jesus. But because Jesus is the representative of God and because the aim of his life, which was to awaken faith, comes to full expression in the R., he has been exalted and "given a name above every name." The R. stands in closest connection, therefore, with the exaltation; indeed, some N.T. scholars have argued that the two beliefs were one and the same in the earliest CHURCH: to say Jesus was raised was to say he had been exalted and made Lord (Phil. 2:9-11). Finally, because the R. is regarded as the disclosure of God's power over the powers of sin and death, it is the basis for the confidence in the possibility of a present life free from the dominion of these powers. Thus, the author of the Fourth Gospel can have Jesus say, "I am the resurrection and the life" (John 11:25), and Paul can put the belief in the R. in closest approximation to the participation in the new life (Rom. 6:5-14). The imagery of death and R. becomes the imagery of human faith as such: being dead in sin and being liberated to a new life.

Although the R. is the central core of N.T. belief, it has, in the history of Christian thought, frequently been relegated to a minor role, to an appendage of the doctrine of the INCARNATION or of the ATONEMENT. In ORTHODOXY, both Prot. and R.C., it functions largely as the basis for confidence in eternal life or as one of the offices of Christ, though a minor one.

Because of the nature of the belief, BIBLICAL CRITICISM has

posed more questions about the R. than about any of the central affirmations of belief. There are certain ironies in this situation. (1) In so far as Biblical criticism was conceived and nurtured by LIBERAL PROTESTANTISM, it was a child of the hope that historical inquiry might establish a firm and non-miraculous core of belief in the N.T.—perhaps the personality and teachings of Jesus. But it was just this same Biblical research that disclosed the centrality of the R. and, moreover, how determinative the eschatological elements were in the preaching of Jesus. (2) The orthodox, however, could scarcely take comfort in this embarrassment of the liberal, for it was also clear that their own interpretation of the R. had little in common with the earliest R. belief in the victory over Satan and his legions, or in the new age that had dawned. (3) The more historical research inquired into the documents concerning the R., the clearer it became that there were two types of early traditions: appearance stories and empty-grave stories. The appearance traditions appear to be the earliest, especially the one given by Paul in I Cor. 15. The empty-grave traditions appear to be later. Furthermore, the appearance traditions apparently conflict, one being located in Galilee, the other in Jerusalem. Most interesting, however, is the fact that the earliest appearances were to believers only, and, in Paul's case, seemed to have been such that they can only be described as "non-fleshly." This, in turn, raised the questions (1) whether the R. need be interpreted in a literalistic sense and (2) what its significance for present faith is.

This latter question has especially concerned Rudolf Bultmann (1884-), who argues that the R. cannot be viewed as a visible, objective historical fact. The mythological language is meant to express, he claims, the eschatological dimension of the cross, i.e., that the meaning of the cross is a meaning that can be made effective only by preaching its significance for the present. Theologians have reacted quite diversely and violently to Bultmann's views, and contemporary THEOLOGY offers a wide spectrum of interpretation of the R. Some argue that its significance lies in the victory of Christ over death and insist on a bodily R. Others argue that the R. is God's disclosure of his sovereignty over physical death and history but prefer to be silent concerning the mode of the R. Still others argue that the R. is not historical in the literal sense of the word, but is a SYMBOL for the victory over ALIENATION and estrangement that was won in Jesus of Nazareth. (See Christology; Faith; Soteriology.)

Resurrection of the Dead. The basis of Christian FAITH and hope in the N.T. is the RESURRECTION OF CHRIST in which the true believer participates. This hope finds expression in the SYMBOL "resurrection of the *soma*" (body) rather than in the continued existence of the SOUL (see Immortality). For the Biblical writers made no distinction between soul and body as did later theologians under the influence of Greek thought. *Soma* or "body" denoted man's existence as a whole PERSON capable of relating himself to other persons rather than the physical body in contrast to soul. Man is not regarded as a soul having a body but as being a body capable of a certain quality of life (*psyche*). The R.O.T.D. means, therefore, the transformation and rebirth of the entire person.

Since faith itself is such a transformation, it is not surprising that the R.O.T.D. was spoken of not merely as a future event but as one that is happening now. In so far as BAPTISM is regarded as incorporation into the death and resurrection of Christ (into his *soma*), the man of faith is already sharing in the risen life (Rom. 6:1-11). Thus the believer can already be said to have eternal life (John 11:17-27; 14:18-21; I John 3:14). Even though the R.O.T.D. is not merely future, however, it has some reference to the future as well as to the FINAL JUDGMENT of GOD and the complete and entire transformation of the person. Thus Paul can write that the already resurrected believer still exists under the external mark of death (I Cor. 15:22-26; II Cor. 4:7-12) and that the present new life is to be seen as a down payment or guarantee or seal of the future hope (II Cor. 1:22; 5:5). But this hoped-for future resurrection is not to be regarded as the release of a SPIRIT from the prison house of the body, as in Greek thought and GNOSTICISM, but a complete and final transformation of the self that frees it from the power of sin. It is the REGENERATION of a *soma* ruled by sin and the LAW (a fleshly body) into a spiritual *soma*, one ruled by obedience to God.

Subsequent Christian THEOLOGY tried to synthesize this idea with the Greek idea of the immortality of the soul and, in consequence, stressed only the futuristic element in the resurrection belief. As a result, the traditional Christian idea neglects these important Biblical emphases: (1) the psychosomatic unity of man; (2) the R.O.T.D. as a giftlike "new creation" rather than a birthright due to the immortality of the soul; (3) the R.O.T.D. as transformation that occurs in the present as well as the future. (See Eschatology; Immortality; Intermediate State; Judgment, Final; Resurrection of Christ; Soul.)

Revelation translates the Greek word *apokalypsis* and literally means "an uncovering, a laying bare, making naked." However much theologians have differed concerning what is revealed, this formal meaning of R. remains the same. So understood, R. presupposes (1) that someone or something is hidden and (2) that this someone or something has not been discovered but, rather, disclosed. Although R. is a technical term, it is not specifically a Christian concept nor, surprisingly, does it often occur in this sense in Scripture. In fact, there is no developed concept of R. in either the O.T. or N.T., it being a result of later reflection on the message of the CHURCH. This is not to say that the O.T. and the N.T. do not have a number of images and SYMBOLS for the disclosure of GOD's will and purposes. But, just because this basic understanding is cloaked in images and symbols, the texts do not provide a self-evident control over the interpretations of theologians. Consequently, a theologian's interpretation of R. often reflects a prior understanding of the idea which he then seeks to find justified in the texts.

It is commonly said that there are two basic models for understanding R.: (1) R. as a disclosure of a series of supernatural truths; (2) R. as a disclosure not of propositions but of God himself. The former, it is alleged, is characteristic of R.C. and Christian ORTHODOXY generally, while the latter is the Biblical and truly Prot. understanding. This distinction, however, is too rough-hewn and does not exhaust the alternatives. The first model conceals the fact that there are two kinds of knowing: one in which the language of ESSENCE and nature seem appropriate; the other in which personal symbols are.

Although these are related they are by no means identical. It is one thing, for example, to claim one knows the essence of a friend and by that mean the relationship between his intellect and will or the brain and consciousness. It is quite another thing to say that one knows a friend in terms of how he characteristically behaves or what his deepest commitments are. So, too, it is one thing to claim to know God's essence and it is quite another to claim that God is trustworthy. Furthermore, to know God in either of these senses cannot simply be contrasted with knowing God himself.

Generally speaking, most CATHOLIC and many Prot. theologians interpret R. as the disclosure of supernatural truths not otherwise attainable by the reason. Certain metaphysical propositions about the divine essence (i.e., the doctrine of the TRINITY) constitute revealed knowledge and are, therefore, preserved as DOGMA. FAITH is largely defined in terms of assent to these. Sometimes, especially in Prot. Scholastic, COVENANTAL, and HEILSGESCHICHTE THEOLOGY, the stress is laid less on the revealed essence of the divine than on his cosmic plan for history. But this is merely a difference in emphasis, not in basic conception of R. Luther (1483-1546) represented a radical departure from this model, although it may be argued that he did not see all of its consequences. R., for Luther, was not a disclosure of some hidden essence or of a plan for history, but the disclosure of the RIGHTEOUSNESS OF GOD, his mercy. God does not deal with man in terms of rewards and punishments but in terms of mercy and forgiveness. Thus, Luther could at one and the same time say that God's essence remains hidden but that his "heart" is laid bare in Christ, i.e., that R. adds nothing to our store of metaphysical knowledge although it transforms our self-knowledge. This is not to say that faith does not involve knowledge or assent or belief but that, in the context of personal language, the assent involves a different kind of decision than the acceptance of doctrine. It is trust or FIDUCIA. In this sense, Melanchthon's (1497-1560) formula well represents this side of Luther's thought: "To know Christ is to know his benefits." A similar understanding, though not so radical, is to be found in Calvin (1509-64).

The last two centuries have witnessed a fundamental break

with the propositional view of R. This break has sometimes been formulated as follows: R. is not the disclosure concerning truths about God but the living God himself. But this formula, like the previous one, actually conceals two alternatives: (1) R. as a word for the mystical experience of the HOLY that may find all words inadequate or even be expressed irrationally; (2) R. as the creation of an I-THOU encounter between God and a particular man. These alternatives actually may be antithetical, although there are certain superficial similarities between them.

Contemporary NEO-REFORMED THEOLOGY has been characterized by a lively discussion over the nature of R. Rejecting the idea of R. as the disclosure of certain metaphysical truths, it has, in general, tended to identify R. with an I-Thou encounter between God and man. It is not easy to see, however, how this is to be related to the idea of a final R. in Jesus Christ, for how does one have an I-Thou encounter with a past event? Other theologians, therefore, have turned to the *Heilsgeschichte* model and regarded R. as "God's mighty acts in history" that reveals a plan of salvation. It is questionable, however, whether the Bible has as its fundamental question the meaning of history, and it is also not clear how having a philosophy of history helps one live in the present as a forgiven man. Existentialist theologians like Rudolf Bultmann (1884-), therefore, equate R. not with a knowledge about God but a present confrontation with one's own unauthenticity and the new possibility of life given in the KERYGMA. This view, however, rests on the PARADOX that R. must be received to be R. and, therefore, raises the question again of the significance of past historical events. Paul Tillich (1886-) defines R. as the manifestation of the ultimate ground and meaning of human EXISTENCE in which this ground does not cease to retain its mysterious character. Thus, Tillich attempts at one and the same time to reject the propositional view of R. and to do justice to history and to avoid the I-Thou model. Karl Barth (1886-), fearing that all of these alternatives surrender the view of R. as objective knowledge about God, has tried to unite person language and essence language, although many believe his work is in that respect an individual *tour de force* and that Protestantism can never go back to the orthodox formulas once it has seriously entertained Luther's distinction between knowing God's nature and knowing his disposition toward us. (See Faith; God; Grace; I-Thou; Justification; *Kerygma*; Law and Gospel; Righteousness of God; Soteriology; Word of God.)

Righteousness of God. In the O.T. the Hebrew words *tsedeq* and *tsedaqah* have two closely related meanings: (1) the inexorable will of GOD for JUSTICE and rectitude and (2) the exercise of that will on the behalf of the helpless, poor, and weak. In so far as the first meaning is equivalent to our word "justice," the R.O.G. may be translated "the justice of God." But the word "justice" has traditionally meant "to give every man his due," and this fails to communicate the element of mercy, compassion, and active intervention on the behalf of the weak that is contained in the second meaning. The 8th-century prophets, for example, appealed to the R.O.G. not as a norm for abstract justice but as God's active demand for concern for the needy and intervention in their behalf.

In the N.T. the word *dikaiosune*, which occurs chiefly in the letters of Paul, is usually rendered "righteousness," while the verb form of it is usually rendered "to justify." The term is sometimes used in the ethical sense, as it is in the O.T., but more often and significantly it is associated, where it is not identified, with salvation and life. The R.O.G. is said to be revealed in Jesus Christ apart from the LAW (Rom. 3:21 f.) and men are made righteous (or justified) through FAITH. The R.O.G. is, then, not so much God's abstract character of BEING but his redemptive, saving will as manifested in Christ. It is necessary to understand this duality of meaning in order to understand Luther's (1483-1546) theological protest against Rome. Medieval theologians generally regarded the R.O.G. as God's retributive justice by virtue of which he rewards the good and punishes the wicked, a meaning implicit in the Latin *iustitia*, which was used in the Latin Bible (the Vulgate) to translate the Hebrew and Greek words above. This idea, Luther wrote later, terrified him and even aroused hatred in his heart for God, because it meant that God always stood over man as a judge and lawgiver, thereby making it impossible to love him or to have joy and confidence in him. Luther's new faith was born when he thought through the implications of Paul's assertion that the Gospel of Jesus Christ reveals the R.O.G. and that the just man lives by faith. The R.O.G., then, was not God's abstract justice, Luther concluded, but his sheer goodness and GRACE whereby, without waiting for man to deserve his favor, he confers it. It was not a problem of reconciling God's justice and his mercy but of redefining his justice in terms of his mercy. The R.O.G. *is* his compassion and grace. Some interpreters of Luther argue that this new exposition of Rom. 1:17 was the basis of a genuinely new doctrine of God. The upshot of Luther's view was to deny that a man's relationship to God was in any way dependent on his good works or his MERITS. God treats men as righteous (justified) even though they remain sinners. R.C. theologians argue that this doctrine ignores the cooperating will of man and interprets justification as something external to the SOUL, i.e., a mere act of forgiveness and not a real REGENERATION and SANCTIFICATION of the believer. Prot.s reply that it is precisely the unconditional nature of God's justifying act that enables man to overcome his despair and guilt. It gives man the freedom and joy which are the basis for regeneration and new life. Furthermore, it is argued, this grace cannot be understood as confined to or given only in the SACRAMENTS. (See Conscience; Election; Faith; God; Grace; Imputation; Justice; Justification; Law and Gospel; Protestant Principle; Revelation; Sanctification; Word of God.)

S

Sabellianism. See Modalism.

Sacrament. A S. is a rite in which it is believed GOD's saving GRACE is uniquely active. Although St. Augustine (354-430) defined a S. as a "visible sign of an invisible reality," and this definition is accepted by both Prot. and R.C. theologians, this does not sufficiently distinguish those signs which the

CHURCH has believed to be divinely ordained or indicate how one should understand the relation of the invisible reality to the visible sign. Both issues separate R.C.s from Prot.s and some Prot.s from one another. R.C., E.O., and the more CATHOLIC churches celebrate seven S.s (BAPTISM, Confirmation, Marriage, Ordination, Penance, the EUCHARIST, and Extreme Unction), while Prot.s usually celebrate two (Baptism and the Eucharist). The reason for this difference is that Prot.s regard two only as having explicit Biblical sanction.

Apart from the question of the proper number of S.s, it is not so easy as is often supposed to make generalizations concerning the differences between R.C. and Prot. sacramental THEOLOGY in general, in contrast to noting differences over the interpretation of specific S.s. If, for example, it be said that R.C.s stress the objective power of the S.s while the Reformers stressed subjective FAITH, it must be noted that R.C.s insist that a S. does not produce GRACE if there is an obstacle to it in the SOUL, just as it must also be said that Luther (1483-1546) insisted that Jesus Christ is bodily present "in, with, and under" the elements of the Lord's Supper. Or if it be said that R.C.s believe the S.s to be valid only if properly performed, it is also true that many Prot. theologians have insisted that the mark of the true church is that the S.s are properly administered. Historically, some Prot.s have been closer to some R.C.s than either have been to other Prot.s. Nor is R.C. theology so monolithic as is popularly supposed.

The complexity of the matter, however, should not blind one to the genuine differences in the understanding of grace and faith underlying R.C. and Prot. theology of the S.s. In general, R.C.s regard the S.s as themselves the channels (means) of SANCTIFYING (habitual) GRACE. The relationship of the priestly office to this grace is so conceived that it is possible to speak of VIRTUES being infused and lying dormant until later activated or, as in the case of Baptism, Confirmation, and Ordination, of indelible characteristics being conferred upon the recipient. The Prot., on the other hand, generally does not understand grace after the analogy of a medicine, so that it can be spoken of as infused if the requisite conditions are objectively present. Grace, he believes, is the divine favor and can only be received, therefore, by active faith. This means, in effect, that while the S.s, rightly administered, proclaim and, therefore, "embody" the promise of God, this grace cannot be restricted to the S.s. And if faith is not present, the S.s are not effective at all. Calvin (1509-64) saw clearly the logic of the view that grace refers to the favor of God. He regarded the function of the S.s, therefore, to be precisely the same as that of the WORD OF GOD. The S.s confirm, proclaim, and seal the promise of God to be gracious and "communicate no grace from themselves, but announce and show, and, as earnests and pledges, ratify, the things which are given to us by the goodness of God."

Even if one argues that to liken the S.s to the Word of God is to say that they, like the Word, must objectively communicate grace, it is also true that the S.s are not necessarily the sole means of grace in the R.C. sense, nor are they efficacious in that sense. The Prot. cannot speak of infused or dormant virtues, nor can he conceive of an indelible character conferred by a S., nor can he imagine a S. to be efficacious simply if no positive obstacle exists in the will of the recipient, i.e., if, as in Roman Catholicism, the recipient only has a virtual intention.

The R.C. believes that the Prot. view fundamentally destroys the authority of the S.s because it implies that the S.s are not necessary for salvation. The Prot. argues that the S.s, being a Biblically sanctioned form of the Word, are, in one sense, necessary but that they (the S.s) are not the only form of the Word. Furthermore, to suggest they are the only form of the Word means that the Word of God is not understood as proclamation aimed at faith. It is clear, therefore, that the fundamental difference consists in the respective conceptions of faith, grace, and the Word of God. (See Baptism; Church; Consubstantiation; Eucharist; *Ex Opere Operato*; Faith; Grace; Habit; Infusion; Justification; Merit; Real Presence; Righteousness of God; Sanctification; Transubstantiation; Word of God.)

Salvation. See Soteriology.

Sanctification. Based on the Latin word *sanctus*, which means HOLY, this term has been used traditionally to describe the process in which new life is imparted to the believer by the Holy Spirit and he is released from the compulsive power of sin and guilt and is enabled to love GOD and to serve his neighbor. Like other important theological concepts, the concrete meaning of this term is a function of a larger theological perspective.

In Roman Catholicism generally, there is no sharp division between JUSTIFICATION and S. as there is in some forms of Protestantism after the Reformation. SANCTIFYING GRACE is required to remit ORIGINAL SIN and to impart to the SOUL a new and higher disposition or VIRTUE that will make possible the salutary acts leading to final salvation, the BEATIFIC VISION of God. For the R.C., the entire life of the believer should be a growth from "grace to grace," FAITH leading to hope and CHARITY. Salvation is not achieved through faith alone. This growth in grace (or S.) is closely linked to the sacramental and penitential system of the CHURCH, for the remission and forgiveness of post-baptismal sins is essential for the final salvation or justification of the believer. Since it is believed that a special INFUSION of grace is necessary for the eradication of all sin, and since no one can be assured that he will never fall from grace, final forgiveness and, therefore, justification may be said to be identical with complete S.

Superficially, the views of the Prot. Reformers seem similar. Luther (1483-1546) and Calvin (1509-64) did not draw a sharp line between justification and S. either (see Justification), tending to interpret the new life as one aspect of justification. The difference between the Reformers' views and the R.C. view lies in the meaning attached to the formula "justification by faith alone through grace alone" (*sola fides sola gratia*). Faith was not regarded, as in Roman Catholicism, as intellectual assent to certain doctrines but as the basic orientation of the self that always had to be renewed. Faith had two aspects: (1) the deep inward appropriation of the forgiveness of sins through the death of Christ (see Atonement), and (2) the beginnings of a new life by virtue of the gift of the Holy Spirit. The former was prior, however, and justification was not regarded as contingent on or as a reward for the new life of the believer, although the former never occurs without the latter. The new life of inward freedom (S.) flows naturally from the knowledge that one is forgiven without any MERIT, and the sins that do occur during the Christian life are not counted against the man of faith.

The Reformers themselves did not develop an elaborate THEOLOGY concerning the relationship of S. to justification, although their writings abound with description of Christian freedom, the nature of Christian moral obligation, etc. Nor did they, like their followers, make a sharp distinction between justification and S. In general, their view was that while the compulsion to sin has been broken in the true man of faith, his life is, nevertheless, a day-by-day struggle with egoism and PRIDE. No perfection (see Perfection, Christian) is finally possible in this life and no action, however exalted, is without the taint of sin (Calvin).

It remained for subsequent Prot. groups, like the Pietists, to make S. their main concern, and it was John Wesley (1703-91), the founder of Methodism, who worked out the doctrinal basis for Christian perfection, his term for the kind of complete S. possible in this life. Considerable differences are to be found among Pietists concerning the nature of full S., ranging from extravagant to more moderate claims concerning what is called the "second blessing." In general, however, it is argued that the N.T. enjoins perfection, that it is possible in this life, and that it is compatible with error and even lapses due to transmitted evil. This perfection consists in an intimate union with the Holy Spirit and a life filled with a horror of sin and a love for the neighbor. Wesley's doctrine of perfection is complex (see Perfection, Christian) but his emphasis falls on the possibility of being granted in this life the gift of a "patient love of God and our neighbor, ruling our tempers, words and actions." Wesley's attitude toward "sinlessness" is debatable, but it seems clear that he did think that the believer could be sanctified in fact in this life and not just in principle. (See *Agape* and *Eros*; Faith; Grace; Imputation; Justification; Law and Gospel; Perfection, Christian.)

Sanctorum Communio. See Communion of the Saints.

Satan is the proper name in traditional Christian thought for the supreme power of evil. Derived from the Hebrew word meaning adversary, it only occurs occasionally as a proper name in the O.T. Since most of these occurrences, if not all, are believed by some scholars to be from post-Exilic times, it has sometimes been argued that the idea of a personified power of evil reflects the influence of Zoroastrian beliefs on the Hebrews, although it is conceded that the Hebrews did believe in intermediary and supernatural beings of some sort before this time. At any rate, the belief in demons and angels was widespread in N.T. times. In the N.T. itself, S. is the being who opposes GOD, tempts Jesus, is the leader of the kingdom of evil, and is responsible for sin. He is sometimes called Beelzebub and the devil.

The idea of S. played a particularly important role in the doctrine of the ATONEMENT propounded by the early Greek Fathers, but this theory was gradually replaced in Western Christendom by the SATISFACTION theory of Anselm (1033-1109). The idea of S. served chiefly to explain the fall and the existence of evil. He was regarded as a fallen angel who, with his legions, would finally be put down after one last fearful battle.

In LIBERAL PROTESTANTISM, the concept of S. was abandoned as a relic of a prescientific mentality and even the neo-Reformed theologians, although they often found some real meaning in the dramatic symbolism of the demonic, showed no inclination to resurrect the idea of a personal demonic being. (See Atonement; Descent into Hell; Hell; Millennialism; Theodicy.)

Satisfaction means generally to offer recompense of some sort for an injury or a crime committed. In Christian THEOLOGY, the idea has played an important role in the doctrine of the ATONEMENT and also in the theory of penance. In the doctrine of the atonement that has dominated Western Christendom since Anselm (1033-1109), the basic premise has been that man's sin has violated GOD's honor and JUSTICE and that these must be satisfied before man can be forgiven and judged righteous. Since no sinful man can render the proper S., it is done by the vicarious sufferings of the sinless God-man Jesus Christ, who accepted the burden of man's guilt and the corresponding punishment, death. An analogous idea of S. underlies the R.C. theory of penance, it being argued that even after contrition and confession it is necessary to remit temporal punishment, in contrast to eternal punishment, and so to make S. (See Atonement; Expiation; Imputation; Justice; Propitiation; Righteousness of God; Soteriology.)

Schism is a word technically referring to the willful act of separating oneself from the unity of the CHURCH. It is to be distinguished from HERESY. Heresy is the propounding of false doctrine. A S., on the other hand, need not involve doctrinal issues at all. In Roman Catholicism, a S. is a sin against love and not against the FAITH; hence, a bishop in S. may still ordain priests, just as a priest in S. may continue to celebrate the Mass. (See Apostasy; Heresy.)

Scholasticism is used somewhat generally to refer to a type of thinking that assumes some authority to be binding and which is devoted to the detailed and often artificially elaborate refinement and extension of it. If, for example, a modern theologian like Karl Barth (1886-) were to be accepted as having expounded the definitive system of doctrine and a group of disciples were to devote their scholarly lives to further refinements of that system, it would be proper to speak of a Barthian S. The term is more specifically applied to the medieval schoolmen, largely because their work was of such a character. After the 13th century, Aristotle (384-322 B.C.) was usually regarded as that authority, and it was sufficient to show that an opinion was consistent with his works to establish it as worthy of belief. This naturally involved excessive logical refinement and a general lack of originality. In the 16th and 17th centuries, a Prot. S. also developed with many of the same characteristics, although it is interesting to note how little these theologians appealed to the Reformers, in contrast to Aristotle.

Second Coming of Christ. See *Parousia.*

Self-Understanding is a term frequently found in the writings of contemporary Prot. theologians. It refers to the basic interpretation a man has of himself and his relationship to all of life, an interpretation that "stands under" and expresses itself in his action and speech. According to most existentialist theologians, a S-U. is rooted in a basic decision, hence, the term "existential S-U." is commonly used. The concept has proved useful in many areas, historical and cultural interpretation, philosophy, and THEOLOGY. In history, it has been argued that the aim of the historian is not so much to chronicle events as to discuss the intentions and purposes of past agents, their S-U.s. He does this best by sympathetically trying to see the world as they saw it, by reliving (W. Dilthey, 1833-1911) and rethinking (R. G. Collingwood, 1889-1943) their thought. In philosophy, it has been argued by Martin Heidegger (1889-) and others that every S-U. is a unique determination of certain universally human possibilities and that it is the task of philosophy to describe these. In theology, it has been argued that FAITH is basically an existential S-U. and that the task of theology is to clarify and articulate it. Rudolf Bultmann's (1884-) DEMYTHOLOGIZATION of the N.T. rests on the basic conviction that the task of N.T. interpretation is to expose the S-U. reflected in its stories and mythological thought forms and to show their contemporary relevance. Paul Tillich's (1886-) THEOLOGY OF CULTURE rests on a similar basis. (See Authentic Existence; Culture, Theology of; Demythologization; Existentialism; Faith; Hermeneutics; Historicity of Human Existence; Phenomenology.)

Semi-Pelagianism refers to a middle-of-the-road position on the problem of GRACE and the FREEDOM OF THE WILL between the extremes of the Augustinian position, on the one side, and of the Pelagian position, on the other. If Augustine (354-430) argued that sinful man could not even make the initial steps toward FAITH without God's grace, and the Pelagian insisted that faith was man's own free act, the S-P. asserted that man could of his own free will turn towards GOD and that God would then grant man the grace to continue in the new life. S-P. stands opposed to Augustinian teaching at a second point. Augustine held that God's grace was irresistible and that those whom God predestines and calls cannot, therefore, perish (see Perseverance). S-P. held that man is able to resist the grace proffered to him after he turns toward God. This controversy broke out shortly before Augustine's death and went on for about a century until, in 529, the Second Council of Orange decided to settle the matter. The statement adopted there explicitly condemns both Pelagianism and S-P. but the summary passages at the end of it are sufficiently non-Augustinian and ambiguous to raise doubts concerning the consistency of the document. The term S-P. is now often used more generally to refer to any view that insists on the ability of the will to cooperate with divine grace. (See Freedom of the Will; Grace; Pelagianism; Perseverance; Predestination; Synergism.)

Sheol is the name given in the O.T. to the region where the SPIRITS of the dead abide. There were probably definite ideas about S. in popular Hebraic belief, but it is noteworthy how inexplicit the texts of the O.T. are on the matter. What can now be said about S. must be constructed from passing references and allusions, for example, the story of Saul and the witch of Endor (I Sam. 28). The spirits in S. seem to possess only a shadowlike, powerless, flaccid type of EXIST-ENCE. Furthermore, all departed spirits seem to go there, and it appears to have little to do, therefore, with rewards and punishments. In some strata of the O.T., S. seems even to be removed from the presence of Yahweh, and there is no hope of deliverance from S. Toward the end of the O.T. period, the idea of resurrection gradually seized the Hebraic imagination, with the exception of Sadducees. The reasons for this are difficult to determine and probably involved many factors, not least of which was the idea of GOD's ultimate vindication of the righteous individual in contrast to the nation. At any rate, the idea of S. was gradually absorbed into and supplanted by the notions of heaven and HELL. (See Descent into Hell; Hell; Immortality; Resurrection of the Dead; Soul.)

Similitudo Dei means the "likeness of God" and is, according to some R.C. teaching, to be distinguished from the IMAGE OF GOD (*imago dei*) which Adam also possessed before the fall. The S.D. refers to those supernatural graces Adam possessed and which he was deprived of when he sinned, while the image of God refers to his natural endowments of reason and free will that remained intact even after the fall. The Prot. Reformers rejected this distinction because they believed it was based on a misinterpretation of what is merely poetic parallelism in Gen. 1:26. They insisted that the image of God designates man's ORIGINAL RIGHTEOUSNESS that was lost in the fall. This loss consequently distorts the entire being of man. (See Depravity, Total; Image of God; Original Righteousness; Sin, Original.)

Simul Iustus et Peccator means literally "simultaneously justified and a sinner" and is the Latin phrase used to express the Reformers' doctrine of JUSTIFICATION by FAITH alone: although still a sinner, man is forgiven (justified) by GOD. (See Faith; Imputation; Justification; Sanctification.)

Sin, Actual. In both the R.C. and Prot. orthodox traditions, A.S. is usually defined as any act, which includes thoughts as well as deeds, done in conscious and deliberate violation of GOD's will as expressed in the revealed or NATURAL LAW. A.S.s arise from the state of ORIGINAL SIN, but are to be distinguished from the latter. Guilt is regarded as properly imputed to all A.S. where there is no repentance.

R.C. moralists have distinguished between two forms of A.S.: MORTAL AND VENIAL SINS. The older Prot. theology rejected this distinction but classified sins according to whether they were voluntary or involuntary, external or internal, of omission or of commission. Generally, this type of classification has all but vanished among contemporary Prot. theologians, presumably because of the distaste for CASUISTRY. In NEO-REFORMED THEOLOGY there has generally been a concern to show the elements of PRIDE and egoism in all human action and to relate these, in turn, to the compounding of freedom and limitation in human nature. Consequently, it may be said that this THEOLOGY is less concerned with a typology or classification of sins than with a general illumination of the human situation. (See Anthropology; Anxiety; Freedom of the Will; Image of God; Sin, Original; Theodicy.)

Sins, Mortal and Venial. R.C. teaching distinguishes between M. and V.S. The former are against the final end of the LAW, the love of GOD, and, being deliberate and grave, are worthy of eternal damnation. The latter, though serious, do not destroy the relationship with God. The Prot. Reformers rejected the distinction between M. and V.S., largely because they tended to view sin as opposite to FAITH, not to VIRTUE. They acknowledged that certain sins were, humanly speaking, more serious than others, but they argued that all transgressions of the Law were equally damnable in the sight of God, the difference being that God pardoned the sins of believers. It is questionable whether such a position is fully consistent, since if sin is the opposite of faith and not virtue it is doubtful whether one can talk about individual sins or the difference between those of believers and unbelievers. Subsequently, Protestantism was driven to make new and numerous kinds of distinctions among sins: sins of omission and commission, inward and outward, sins of weakness and besetting sins, etc. (See Faith; Imputation; Justification; Law and Gospel; Perfection, Christian; Pride; Sanctification; Sin, Actual; Sin, Original.)

Sin, Original. In the classical Christian tradition, O.S. refers to the universal and hereditary sinfulness of man since the fall of Adam. It is contrasted with ACTUAL SIN, which is a self-conscious violation of GOD's law. Whether the idea of universal sinfuless is to be found in the O.T. is a matter of debate, but it appears in the O.T. Apocrypha and is presupposed, where it is not explicit, in the N.T. Although the idea that this universal sinfulness was in some sense inherited seems common among the earliest CHURCH theologians like Justin Martyr (c.100-c.165), Irenaeus (c.130-c.200), Tertullian (150?-225?), and Origen (c.185-c.254), there were important enough differences among them to justify the judgment that it was Augustine (354-430) who definitively formulated the doctrine and connected it with Adam's sin. His view subsequently dominated ORTHODOXY. In it, man and the angels possessed a freedom either to accept the order of CREATION in which they existed, or to rebel. Some angels rebelled and then seduced man. Since submission to the order of creation would have meant self-fulfillment, rebellion against it necessarily involved the loss of the happiness of those who fulfill their own essential nature. The creatures were self-condemned to ignorance and to insatiable desire and CONCUPISCENCE. The order which should have obtained between reason and passion was disturbed and man found himself prey to every passing fancy and mood. In Augustine's thought, O.S. is not merely a psychological state but a metaphysical one; that is, man's fall was a fall in the order of BEING. Once having fallen, therefore, man cannot by his own efforts regain his former status in being. This is expressed in Augustine's notion that before the fall angels and men possessed the ability not to sin (*posse non peccare*) as well as the ability to sin (*posse peccare*) but that after the fall they possessed only the latter. Adam's sin, then, has corrupted the entire human race and it is a mass of sin (*massa peccati*) and justly subject to damnation. By this Augustine means not only that man inherits a tendency to sin but that he inherits guilt. How this comes about is not so clearly stated by Augustine, since he accepted the idea that every SOUL is freshly created by God (see Traducianism; Creationism). What he does say implies some kind of mystical representation and participation of the entire race in Adam and this, generally, has been the keystone in the arch of the traditional doctrine.

The doctrine of O.S. was generally rejected by liberal Prot.s as being incompatible with scientific knowledge (man's origins were brutish, and a moral state like Adam's is the consequence of a long process) as well as moral insight (a man can justly be regarded as guilty only for his own self-conscious acts). The liberals argued that the doctrine, so far as it contained any truth at all, pointed to the remnants of man's animal ancestry or to the social and corporate power of evil. Neo-Reformed theologians were more appreciative of the doctrine, although agreed that it had to be disentangled from what they believed to be its literalistic absurdities. Reinhold Niebuhr (1892-), for example, argued that the doctrine cannot be fully rationalized but that it preserves better than any alternative the PARADOX of the inevitability of sin and man's responsibility for it. It should be called, therefore, a MYTH, which, though not literally true, expresses a truth about human existence. Paul Tillich (1886-) interprets the SYMBOL as pointing to the fact that the exercise of freedom inevitably leads to estrangement from one's essential being. (See Anthropology; Anxiety; Concupiscence; Conscience; Depravity, Total; Fallenness; Freedom of the Will; Image of God; Imputation; Justification; Original Righteousness; Sanctification; *Similitudo Dei*; Soteriology; Soul.)

Sins, Seven Deadly. According to tradition they are: (1) pride, (2) covetousness, (3) lust, (4) envy, (5) gluttony, (6) anger, (7) sloth or *accidie*.

Social Ethics. See Ethics, Social.

Social Gospel is the name given to the central idea of a widely influential movement within American Protestantism in the late 19th and early 20th centuries. Its greatest spokesman was Walter Rauschenbusch (1861-1918) a Baptist minister and, later, theological professor. His premise was that personal EXISTENCE is basically social and that a relevant Christianity would "bring men under repentance for their collective sins" and would proclaim a corresponding social salvation. He appealed to the demand for JUSTICE that was characteristic of the Hebrew prophets and to the centrality of the KINGDOM OF GOD in the teachings of Jesus. This Kingdom, Rauschenbusch argued, is a goal toward which God is working in this world, not an other-worldly goal. The S.G. movement was characterized by a sharp criticism of the injustices, especially economic, of the social order and by a program for more revolutionary social action on the part of the CHURCHES. Because the S.G. was so closely identified with the tenets of LIBERAL PROTESTANTISM, the belief in progress, and the attribution of sin to evil social institutions, and because of its erroneous identification of Jesus' teaching about the Kingdom of God with these tenets, it was severely criticized by orthodox and neo-Reformed theologians. The latter, nevertheless, believed that the Reformatory drive of the S.G. was valid if stripped of its utopian elements and based on a more Biblical understanding of man. In this form, the influence of the S.G. still lives on. (See Justice; Liberal Protestantism; Neo-Reformed Theology.)

Socinianism. A post-Reformation movement of the late 16th and early 17th centuries that flourished in Poland and later spread to the Low Countries and England. It is said to have been the forerunner of Unitarianism because of its rationalistic and ethical tone as well as its anti-Trinitarian content. Because S. is most often noted for its polemic against the orthodox doctrines of the TRINITY, the PRE-EXISTENCE OF CHRIST, ORIGINAL SIN, and the SATISFACTION theory of the ATONEMENT, it is important to emphasize that it rejected these doctrines primarily because it believed them to be unbiblical as well as irrational. The Socinians accepted the finality of REVELATION in Jesus Christ but they thought these orthodox doctrines to be false. Their argument against the satisfaction theory of the atonement is typical: if GOD was absolutely sovereign, he could forgive man in any fashion he saw fit. Furthermore, the remission of sins and satisfaction are mutually exclusive, because if God forgives sin no satisfaction is necessary, and if satisfaction is necessary, forgiveness is an illusion. Adolf von Harnack (1851-1930), the noted church historian, concluded that S. played an important role in restoring to the individual believer the freedom to examine the Biblical texts for himself.

Solipcism is the view that only the self with its perceptions exists and that all other realities depend on that self and have no independent reality of their own. Sometimes the term is used more loosely for the view that all that is finally certain is the EXISTENCE of one's own self, and that the existence of an external world is but a matter of blind faith.

Soteriology. Derived from the Greek words *sozein* (to save) and *logos* (discourse), the term traditionally denotes that part of Christian THEOLOGY concerned with the doctrine of salvation, hence with (1) the work of Christ, his ATONEMENT; (2) the doctrines of JUSTIFICATION and SANCTIFICATION and the presupposition of those doctrines, the doctrine of sin; (3) the means of GRACE; and (4) man's final destiny.

There have been two basic perspectives in the history of Christendom so far as conceiving of salvation is concerned, one of which is characteristic of Roman Catholicism and the E.O. churches, the other which is more characteristic of Protestantism generally. Each perspective has certain presuppositions, leads to certain emphases, and casts up a certain kind of language. In the former, salvation is basically regarded as the deification of man by participation in supernatural grace. In this view, man's destiny is nothing less than participation in the divine life. Hence, the SACRAMENTS and the CHURCH play a decisive role, since they are the divinely appointed instruments for mediating the "medicine of immortality." So, too, the language of nature and supernature, of BEING, is crucial in all discussions of man, sin, the person of Christ, the church, the sacraments, justification, and sanctification. In Protestantism, salvation is conceived basically in terms of a restoration of a broken personal relationship. In this view, man's true destiny is not so much deification as the forgiveness of sins and personal communion with GOD. Grace is not thought of as a medicine so much as the divine favor. Hence, the importance of the sacraments and the church consists primarily in their communication of the WORD OF GOD, which at once calls for repentance, promises the forgiveness of sins, and liberates man so that he may be a responsible creature and serve the neighbor in love. The language of this perspective, therefore, is not so much that of nature and supernature but of personal existence, and words like promise, COVENANT, faithfulness, righteousness, word, forgiveness, sonship and love are decisive. If the former view is concerned primarily with the doctrine of the INCARNATION, the latter is preoccupied with the ATONEMENT. Although there is considerable overlapping of these two perspectives in the history of Christendom, these two fundamentally divergent emphases underlie a considerable number of the basic disagreements concerning the nature of man, Christ, and the justification and sanctification of the believer, and illumine the extremes of each position. In the CATHOLIC churches, the monastic tradition represents one extreme, a life ordered around prayer and the sacraments. In the Prot. tradition, the moralization of all belief and the reduction of faith to moral conduct constitute an extreme. The former can regard all social responsibility as expendable so long as the sacraments remain; the latter can regard all sacraments as nothing if personal responsibility is not the outcome. (See Church; Christology; Election; Faith; God; Grace; Image of God; Justification; Atonement; Priesthood of All Believers; Revelation; Righteousness of God; Sacrament; Sanctification; Word of God.)

Soul has, in traditional Christianity, referred to the originative seat of reason and will in the human PERSON. Created by GOD, it is regarded as a spiritual entity that survives physical death. This concept of the S. was the product of a long and complex history, and it is precisely because of the reinterpretation of this history that the idea of the S. has become a subject of controversy among contemporary theologians.

There is no developed conception of the S. in either the O.T. or the N.T. and, consequently, little agreement on the matter among theologians until the Middle Ages. The Hebrew, unlike the Greek, regarded man as a living body and had no distinctive word to designate body in contrast to S. The N.T., on the whole, is closer to the Hebrew than the Greek, although there are a few allusions suggesting the possibility of a separate existence for the S. With the emergence of Christianity into the Graeco-Roman world, theologians tried to establish a *rapprochement* with Greek philosophy, especially Platonism. At the heart of Platonism, however, was the idea of an indestructible, immortal S., the salvation of which consisted in being liberated from the body. The attempt to weave this thread into the fabric of Christianity taxed the ingenuity of the theologians: If Platonism regarded the S. as divine and indestructible, the Christian regarded it as created and, in some sense, mortal; if Platonism viewed the body as the source of evil, Christianity affirmed the goodness of the body and interpreted evil as a perversion of the will; if the Platonist hoped for IMMORTALITY, the Christian looked for the RESURRECTION OF THE DEAD. In general, the Greek idea triumphed, although the creeds continued to contain the remnants of the old Hebraic anthropology.

Thomas Aquinas (*c.*1225-74) effected the most impressive synthesis of Greek and Hebraic notions, largely by virtue of his reliance on Aristotle (384-322 B.C.) rather than Plato (*c.*427-347 B.C.). Aquinas rejected the Platonic idea of the S. using the body the way a pilot uses a ship and regarded S. and body as but two distinguishable factors in one SUBSTANCE or person. Nevertheless, he argued, the S. can survive the body, although this is not its natural state. Thus the S. will be rejoined to the body after the resurrection.

For the most part, this general understanding was accepted by the Prot. Reformers and their successors, the only points of disagreement being over the details of the future state of the S. (see Purgatory, Limbo). In LIBERAL PROTESTANTISM, the doctrine of immortality was especially treasured, partly because of its consistency with philosophical idealism, and the idea of resurrection was quietly discarded as an unnecessary and embarrassing appendage.

The neo-Reformed movement was characterized by a basic suspicion of all ideas rooted in Greek philosophy and, especially, the idea of the immortality of the S. It was believed to be unbiblical and, in general, to lead to a depreciation of the body and bodily experience. For those theologians influenced by EXISTENTIALISM the idea of the S. was an OBJECTIFICATION that was philosophically inadequate. As a result, the literature of this movement is replete with discussions of "the self" but little is to be found concerning the S. For the most part, the SYMBOL of the resurrection of the body was renovated, although there are considerable differences of opinion as how this symbol should be interpreted. (See Anthropology; Creationism; Existentialism; Historicity of Human Existence; Hell; Image of God; Immortality; Judgment, Final; Limbo; Person; Pre-existence of Souls; Purgatory; Resurrection of the Dead; Soteriology; Traducianism.)

Speaking in Tongues. See *Glossolalia.*

Spiration. See Procession.

Spirit—Holy Spirit. *Pneuma* is the Greek word most frequently translated in English as "spirit" and, like the English word, it has an extraordinary number of related meanings. In the Bible, these meanings cluster around two poles, the spirit as a term for distinctively human life and for the dynamic activity of GOD.

In the O.T., it is God's Spirit (*ruach*) that acts in CREATION, motivates leaders, imparts WISDOM, discernment, and holiness, and that inspires the prophets. In short, the Spirit of God is the power and presence of God in the world and, especially, in the history of Israel. It is the Spirit of God that vitalizes man so that man also may be said to have spirit or *ruach*. Spirit, then, becomes a term for the distinctive powers of man (intelligence, will, and emotion) and is synonymous with "SOUL" and "heart," which were the terms for the seat of human action and life.

In the N.T., *pneuma* has roughly the same two meanings, the distinctive qualities of human life and the creative activity of God, although the latter comes to predominate because the N.T., in general, is written in the conviction that in and through FAITH in Jesus Christ, which is itself the work of the Spirit, the Holy Spirit has come with unique and extraordinary power. Paul, for example, uses the term *pneuma* along with other terms (*soma* = embodied existence; *psyche* = human vitality; *nous* = "mind"; *kardia* = "heart") to indicate the distinctive EXISTENCE of man as a willing, striving being who is always "living for" someone or some purpose. But mostly, Paul employs *pneuma* in reference to the peculiar redemptive power of God at work in Jesus Christ and in the lives of those who surrender their own claims to righteousness and accept God's graciousness.

The distinctive emphases of various writers of the N.T. concerning the Holy Spirit are too numerous and complex for discussion here. In general it may be said that the Holy Spirit (1) is the motivating power in the birth, life, and RESURRECTION OF CHRIST; (2) is believed to be a miraculous power, so that MIRACLES and other extraordinary phenomena are attributed to it; (3) is given to man with faith in Christ and is, therefore, not a natural possession but a gift empowering the faithful to live free from the compulsion to sin; (4) is continuous with the "Spirit of Christ"; (5) is something that manifests itself in a new form of life characterized by joy, peace, patience, goodness, faithfulness, gentleness, and self-control; (6) is the author of special and diverse gifts, such as prophecy, teaching, ecstatic utterance (*glossolalia*); but, above all (7) is that which is active in the love of the neighbor (AGAPE) and, hence, is the basis for the unity of the CHURCH.

There is, properly speaking, no doctrine of the Holy Spirit in the N.T., although the specific language about it provided the materials for later theological elaboration. Christological controversies preoccupied most of the theologians of the early church, and although it was assumed by the orthodox parties that the Holy Spirit was a coequal and coeternal HYPOSTASIS or PERSON in the godhead, the doctrine of the Holy Spirit did not become the basis for controversy until the late 4th century. As in the controversy over the LOGOS, some theologians, called Macedonians and *pneumatomachi*, denied the full divinity of the Holy Spirit. Their views were condemned at the Council of Constantinople in 381, and the formula of three coequal persons in one godhead was accepted as the orthodox one in the West. The relations between the Holy Spirit and the other two persons became a later object of controversy between Eastern and Western Christendom. (See Appropriations; Filiation; *Filioque*; Generation; *Hypostasis*; Modalism; Monarchianism; *Perichoresis*; Person; Procession; Soul; Trinity.)

Sublapsarianism. See Predestination.

Subordinationism is that view of the TRINITY in which the divine LOGOS is regarded as subordinate to the Father, or the Holy Spirit is regarded as subordinate to both. Any subordination of one of the PERSONS in the Trinity is judged to be heretical by those churches which accept the classical creeds. (See Arianism; *Homoousion*; *Logos*; Person; Procession; Trinity.)

Substance is a term that has had a long and extraordinarily complex history in Western philosophy and, hence, THEOLOGY.

In 3rd-century Western Christendom, it was, after long debate, finally chosen, rightly or wrongly, as the appropriate term to translate the Greek word *ousia*, which was used by Plato (*c*.427-347 B.C.) and Aristotle (384-322 B.C.) to signify primarily the defining characteristics of a thing, the pattern or form that persists throughout its career.

In subsequent Western theology and philosophy, the term came more and more to signify the permanent, unified, causal reality of a thing in contrast to its changing ACCIDENTS or qualities, or, more loosely, to signify the thing itself in contrast to its modifications. This is how the term is used primarily in Thomistic philosophy. Whether the Thomistic usage corresponds to the Aristotelian is a subject for debate among historians of philosophy. At any rate, the Thomist can speak of a world of S.s and mean by that a world of existing, enduring, concrete entities. The distinction between S. and accidents was particularly important in interpreting the doctrine of TRANSUBSTANTIATION.

Still later, a S. was defined as that which required nothing else for its EXISTENCE, a definition that led Spinoza (1632-77) to argue that there was and could be only one reality fulfilling that definition, namely, GOD. It followed that all other beings were but modes or ATTRIBUTES OF GOD. The course of modern philosophy since Locke (1632-1704) has been marked by other modifications of the meaning of this ancient term, modifications too numerous and complex to permit a simple summary statement here, and the most influential schools of contemporary philosophy have attacked the concept of S. itself. Process philosophers, like Whitehead (1861-1947), reject the idea of an underlying, enduring reality in contrast to its modifications. They argue that change or process is primary, although every changing entity has certain abstract features. Positivists reject the idea as unverifiable, or as a confusing way of speaking about characteristics that can be better talked about in some other way. Existentialists believe the concept is particularly inappropriate for dealing with human existence. Consequently, contemporary Prot. theologians have all but abandoned the notion as having any valid theological use. When it is not dismissed as speculative and unbiblical, it is attacked as a static category peculiarly inappropriate to denote personal existence. (See Being; Essence; Existence; Existentialism; Metaphysics; Non-Being; Positivism; Process Philosophy; Soul.)

Sufficient Grace. See Grace, Sufficient.

Summum Bonum means literally "the highest good" and is a crucial concept in those types of ethics (called teleological) concerned with a definition of the highest good for which men strive. In classical Christian THEOLOGY, the S.B. has been regarded as the union of the SOUL with GOD.

Supralapsarianism. See Predestination.

Symbol. This word, like the word MYTH, is one impossible to define without already prejudicing discussion to some degree. In general, a S. is a picture, word, or thing that bears a certain meaning or meanings for an individual or a group. A flag, a number, a cross, a picture of a fish, a word, may be a S. Since man is a creature whose very nature is to communicate meanings, he may be defined, as the philosopher Ernst Cassirer (1874-1945) has pointed out, as a symbol-making animal (*animal symbolicum*). These meanings may be of the most diverse types, although they tend to fall into certain perennial kinds: religion, art, science, myth. In recent times, anthropologists, literary critics, art historians, psychologists, philosophers, and theologians have been especially concerned with the uses and principles of symbolism, and highly sophisticated theories have been elaborated, not all of which can be reconciled with one another.

Philosophers of religion and theologians have naturally been concerned with religious symbolism. There is, first of all, the question whether religious symbolism exemplifies any characteristic that sets it apart from, say, artistic symbolism. It seems clear that this question cannot be answered by inspecting the S.s themselves. Whether a S. is religious or not depends on its function or use. Is there, then, any one function or use called religious, and does such a function tend to generate any special kind of symbolism? There are those who call a S. religious if it bears an ultimate concern. Others see religious S. as attempts to express man's feelings of awe in encounter with the HOLY. Still others see religious symbolism as a highly expressive form of language unifying theoretical, artistic, and valuational elements. Still others argue that religious S. as attempts to express man's feelings of awe in sense of the mystery of life.

The question of the function of religious symbolism passes naturally into the question whether any particular symbolic affirmation has any theoretical meaning, implicit or explicit. This question is particularly important for theologians in so far as they view their task to be the interpretation of religious symbolism. Traditionally, Christian theologians have held that human language about GOD cannot be literal, on the one hand, nor can it be simply equivocal on the other. They have regarded it as analogical, and on this basis have translated religious S.s into some sort of metaphysical language. Those who find this approach unconvincing have offered three alternatives: (1) religious S.s do not have any theoretical import at all but are ways of expressing certain attitudes or feelings; (2) religious S.s are grounded in REVELATION and no justification except FAITH in the revelation can be given for them; (3) religious S.s are images taken from one sphere of historical experience and used to relate oneself to the divine mystery which cannot be otherwise known. The divine can be experienced for oneself through them but they cannot be forced on another person or culture. (See Analogy, Way of; Holy; I-Thou; Myth; Natural Theology; Perfection, Theological.)

Symbolics refers quite generally to the study of Christian SYMBOLS, which are of many sorts. Sometimes it refers more particularly to the study of the creeds and confessions of the CHURCH, which are also called symbols. In ancient times, a messenger was frequently required to match one half of a bone or an earthen dish with another half that had been sent on ahead independently in order to prove that he was the true messenger. Such a thing was called a *symbolon*. The term later became applied to any authenticating password and, therefore, to the creeds or confessions which were regarded as indicating one had the proper doctrine and belonged to the group.

Syncretism is the attempt to combine teachings and doctrines from different and apparently divergent traditions; for example, from Roman Catholicism and Protestantism, or from Christianity and, say, Buddhism. The term is often applied to certain historical periods and cultures, which are characterized by the mixture of different ideas and cultural elements. ⟶ GNOSTICISM

Synergism literally means "working together" and is used to denote the views of those theologians who stress the cooperation of the human will with divine GRACE in contrast to those who, like Augustine (354-430), Luther (1483-1546), and Calvin (1509-64), insisted that man can do nothing unaided toward his own salvation, not even accept grace. There are various forms of S., ranging from PELAGIANISM to the more subtle formulations characteristic of Roman Catholicism. Neo-Reformed theologians, who have been influenced by EXISTENTIALISM, argue that both the synergists and their opponents have not yet rid themselves of an impersonal concept of grace and that the problem disappears when FAITH is regarded as a personal response to a prior and personal act of God. (See Arminianism; Determinism; Election; Existentialism; Freedom of the Will; Grace; Pelagianism; Predestination.)

Synoptic Problem. One of the problems of BIBLICAL CRITICISM has been to devise an explanation for the fact that there is some identical and a great amount of similar material contained in the first three gospels of the N.T., as well as materials peculiar to each. The Fourth Gospel is not concerned because it differs markedly in content, style, and thought from the other three. Because almost the whole of Mark is contained in Matt. and Luke, and because it appears that the latter two used Mark's outline of Jesus' ministry, there emerged the Two Source Hypothesis as an answer to the problem. According to this, there are two basic sources for what we now have in the Synoptics: the Gospel of Mark, or something approximating it, and another nameless and unknown source sometimes referred to as Q, which contained a collection of the sayings of Jesus. Matt. and Luke, it is believed, used Mark; then each combined the sayings of Jesus according to his own fashion, and added his own materials. These latter materials are sometimes said to be independent sources as well, and are referred to as M. (for Matt.'s peculiar source) and L. (for Luke's peculiar source), but this is a matter of some debate. In this fashion it was thought that the striking agreements as well as the differences among the writers could be accounted for. There have been many variations on this general theory but the basic hypothesis is widely shared.

Synteresis. See Conscience.

T

Teleology is derived from the Greek words *telos* (end or goal) and *logos* (discourse). Sometimes it is used quite generally to refer to the adaption of means to ends and sometimes more particularly to refer to that branch of philosophy concerned with ends or final causes. In the former sense, the idea has played an important role in METAPHYSICS, ethics, and THEOLOGY, for the adaption of means to ends in organic life generally has been the basis for a philosophy of nature as well as one of the most popular arguments for the EXISTENCE of an intelligent deity. (See Proofs for the Existence of God.)

Theandric Acts. According to orthodox christological doctrine there were in Jesus Christ two natures and two wills in perfect harmony. The question arose whether one could distinguish those actions which were purely human, those which were divine, and which were a unity of both, i.e., T.A.

CATHOLIC doctrine, on the whole, does so distinguish actions proper to each nature and calls T.A. those in which the divine acts as the principal cause and the human acts as the instrumental cause. Scholastic theologians of the Reformed tradition argued for a more intimate union, claiming that what Christ did as divine or human is done by the one whole Christ. Luther's doctrine of the COMMUNICATIO IDIOMATUM is even more radical. (See Christology; *Communicatio Idiomatum*; Hypostatic Union.)

Theism refers to a system of thought in which is postulated the EXISTENCE of one unified, perfect being that, although distinguished from the cosmos, is the source of it and continues to sustain it in its forms and powers and, in some sense, providentially guides it. So understood, T. is usually contrasted with PANTHEISM, in which, roughly speaking, GOD is a name for the unity of the cosmos taken as a whole, and DEISM, in which God is regarded as the creator of the cosmos and the establisher of its physical and moral order though exercising no continuing providential guidance over it. It is commonly said that in pantheism the deity is wholly immanent, in deism that it is wholly transcendent, and in T. that it is both transcendent and immanent. Since T. does not preclude the intervention of God in the natural and historical order, it has been favorably regarded by most Christian theologians and has been the dominant tradition in Western PHILOSOPHY OF RELIGION until recent times.

Since T. depends, for the most part on METAPHYSICS and became closely allied with NATURAL THEOLOGY, it has been widely challenged and rejected by many contemporary neo-Reformed theologians. Paul Tillich (1886-) rejects it not for these reasons but because, he charges, T. regards God as one being, albeit the greatest, among others. This, he insists, prejudices the absoluteness of God who, properly, must be regarded as being-itself. Another modern philosopher of religion, Charles Hartshorne (1897-), has argued, however, that the one term "T." actually conceals several possible ideas of God. He has delineated at least seven logically possible doctrines: (1) There is a being in all respects absolutely perfect or unsurpassable. (2) There is a being who is absolutely perfect in some respects, relatively perfect (unsurpassed) in others. (3) There is a being absolutely perfect, relatively perfect, and imperfect, each in some respect. (4) There is a being absolutely perfect in some, imperfect in all other respects. (5) There is a being absolutely perfect in no respect, relatively perfect in all. (6) There is a being absolutely perfect in no respect, relatively perfect in some, and imperfect in the others. (7) There is a being absolutely perfect in no respect but imperfect in all respects. This classification, Hartshorne claims, is exhaustive. Classical T. is an instance of (1) and ATHEISM of (7). Hartshorne believes he can show the metaphysical and religious superiority of (2). His alternatives at least serve the function of showing that the one term "T." is too rough-hewn for precise philosophical discussion. (See Attributes of God; Creation; Deism; God; Immanence; Panentheism; Pantheism; Perfection, Theological; Proofs for the Existence of God; Theodicy; Transcendence.)

Theodicy is derived from the two Greek words meaning "deity" and "JUSTICE" and refers to the attempt to justify the goodness of GOD in the face of the manifold evil present in the world. The problem exists for any THEISM that attributes both power and goodness to the deity. It may be expressed in a famous dilemma: either God is able to prevent evil and will not, or he is willing to prevent it and cannot. If the former, he is not merciful; if the latter, he is not omnipotent. The problem of explaining evil, which occurs as early as the philosophy of Plato (c.427-347 B.C.), takes on an especially paradoxical form in Christianity because the latter affirms at one and the same time that the CREATION is good and that God is especially revealed in an "evil" event, the crucifixion.

An inspection of the traditional answers to this problem reveals that they usually involve many complex philosophical problems, for example, the meaning of such terms as "possibility" and "impossibility," "freedom," and "NATURAL LAW," as well as wider considerations concerning the relationship between REVELATION and reason. Any simple description of the alternatives, therefore, will necessarily seem superficial. With that qualification in mind, certain classical solutions, all of which have important variants, may be briefly noted. (1) The evil in the world is to be attributed to sin or rebellion against God by another deity or by a creature, whether an angel or a man. (2) Evil is a necessary aspect of any finite order in which there are free beings and a relatively stable physical order. (3) Evil is really an illusion of finite or temporal experience and would be seen not to exist from the standpoint of ETERNITY (*sub specie aeternitatis*). (4) There is no theoretical answer to the mystery of evil and it can only be seen as an occasion for obedience and childlike trust in the goodness of God despite the appearances.

In general, these answers either attack one horn of the dilemma (usually OMNIPOTENCE) or appeal to mystery. Alternatives (3) and (4) require no explicit qualification of the omnipotence of God, but pay the price of providing no theoretical solution at all: (4) by confessing that there is none, (3) by appealing to a perspective (*sub specie aeternitatis*), which no finite mind, in the nature of the case, could have. Alternative (1), except where it depends on the belief in an intrinsically evil power, can probably be reduced to a variant of (2), since it presupposes the freedom of the creatures (even SATAN is believed to be a "fallen angel") and, therefore, implies that revolt is an intrinsic possibility for such creatures. Indeed, most of the attempts to provide a theoretical justification within Christendom have taken some form of (2). Within this general alternative, three different types of emphases are apparent: (a) those which stress the self-limitation of God in creation, and (b) those which deny that abstract omnipotence is a meaningful term and redefine it, and (c) those which assert that God definitely is limited. Those (a) which stress the self-limitation of an omnipotent God (an assertion which itself is a problematical one) are particularly troubled by the amount of evil in the world, for if God can easily lift the limits he has imposed on himself, in what sense can he be called merciful? It is no accident, therefore, that this solution frequently makes use of alternative (4), the appeal to mystery and childlike faith. Those (c) which stress the limited nature of God are often criticized on the grounds that such a limited being ought not to be called God because he is not worthy of worship. This criticism is not so much a philosophical one as it is an objection that the solution does not do justice to certain traditional Christian beliefs, to which it has been frequently replied that reason should be preferred to blind confidence in ORTHODOXY. There are those (b), however, who argue that the insights of Christian faith itself require a redefinition of omnipotence, or more precisely, that the Biblical witness requires one to think of God's power in terms of his love and that this requirement dictates a severe qualification of the traditional understanding of omnipotence. Certain neo-Reformed theologians, therefore, reject the idea of God in classical theism and, in effect, imply that evil is a necessary risk involved in the creation of free beings. It is characteristic of this same theology, however, not to deal with the metaphysical problems that arise by virtue of its position, i.e., the problem of "natural evil," the meaning of "possible" and "power," etc. For the most part, appeal is made to the Biblical witness or to CHRISTOLOGY. It is interesting, therefore, that a philosophical criticism of classical theism has been developed by some philosophers of religion, especially Charles Hartshorne (1897-), influenced by the PROCESS PHILOSOPHY of Alfred N. Whitehead (1861-1947). This position, in effect, argues that it is impossible to solve the problem of evil within the framework of the classical conception of God as an omnipotent, impassible, but merciful being. It is argued that not only is omnipotence a meaningless term but that it is incompatible with mercy as the dilemma suggests. Consequently, it is necessary to develop a more adequate ontology which does justice to both active power and receptivity. Hartshorne maintains that omnipotence can only mean the power to determine the conditions that maximize the opportunities for desirable decisions by finite creatures. This necessarily entails risks, for the greater the opportunity for joy, creativity, and happiness, the greater the possibility of tragedy. This argument has been often advanced in the past but Hartshorne's solution differs most radically from other theodicies by virtue of his insistence on the idea of divine suffering. The tragedies of existence are themselves known and felt as tragedies within the divine life. His argument, in effect, is that the force of the dilemma cited at the beginning of this article depends on an acceptance of the idea of omnipotence and the thought of a deity who disinterestedly observes the sufferings of the creatures. He rejects both. (See Attributes of God; God; Panentheism; Pantheism; Theism.)

Theologia Crucis means literally "theology of the cross" and was used by Luther (1483-1546) to express his conviction that the GRACE of GOD could only be apprehended in the humble and "despised man" Jesus of Nazareth. It was this, he believed, that comforted the heart in contrast to contemplating the naked majesty of God, which could only strike terror into it. T.C. was to be contrasted, then, with a *theologia gloriae* (a theology of glory).

Theology comes from the Greek words *theos* (deity) and *logos* (discourse). Narrowly considered, T. has to do only with the EXISTENCE and nature of the divine. Broadly considered, it covers the entire range of issues concerning man's relationship to GOD. Neither consideration necessarily limits T. to Christian T., although the terms are often used synonymously in the Western world.

In so far as it involves a systematic and rational clarification of FAITH through the use of technical concepts and logic, Christian T. is a peculiar synthesis of Hebraism and the Greek philosophic spirit. The O.T. and N.T. have, to be sure, an implicit understanding of human existence before God, but this understanding is rarely the object of refined theoretical reflection. When Christianity emerged into the Graeco-Roman world, its best thinkers tried to make their beliefs intelligible to that world, and they inevitably turned to the language and concepts of Greek philosophy. There were, however, Hebraic elements that did not easily accommodate themselves to Greek philosophical terminology, just as there were Greek presuppositions of the language that were alien to Hebraic thought. Consequently, there has been a tension between the two from the very beginning, a tension that has been relaxed in certain epochs but which has come to the fore in others. There are some systems of Christian T. so philosophical in mode that they are unintelligible without a prior understanding of their Greek philosophical antecedents. This is true, for example, of some of the early CHURCH theologians like Clement (*c.*150-*c.*215) and Origen (*c.*185-*c.*254) of Alexandria, Thomas Aquinas (*c.*1225-74), and many of the medieval Schoolmen. On the other hand, there have always been those theologians who have tried to assert the independence of T. from Greek, especially Aristotelian, philosophy, for example, Tertullian (150?-225?), Luther (1483-1546), and Calvin (1509-64).

The beginning of the modern historical period in the West was characterized by the break of philosophy from its slavish dependence on its Greek forebears, especially Aristotle (384-322 B.C.), on the one hand, and by its declaration of independence from T. on the other. These phenomena were complicated by the rise of the natural sciences. Since that time, the relationship between philosophy and T. defies any simple description because there have been many kinds of philosophy and, in Protestantism at least, many sorts of T. Protestantism, more than Roman Catholicism, has been marked by experimentation in T., and its theologians have become infatuated with certain brands of philosophy in one generation, like Kantianism or idealism, only to become disillusioned and hostile in another. The contemporary period, especially, is confusing in this respect, some theologians claiming to reject philosophy altogether, others making alliances with such divergent philosophies as EXISTENTIALISM, logical POSITIVISM, ANALYTIC PHILOSOPHY, and PROCESS PHILOSOPHY.

Christian T. has always served to clarify and criticize the faith of the churches, and this naturally is reflected in various specialized functions with specific names. Curricula in theological seminaries frequently are organized around these. Historical T. is the study of past theological systems. Systematic T. is, as the name suggests, the systematic organization and discussion of the problems that arise in Christian faith. In so far as systematic T. is guided by the doctrinal standards of the church, it is frequently called "dogmatics" or "dogmatic

T." The special concentration on the ethical implications of T. is called "moral T.," especially in the more CATHOLIC churches, or "Christian ethics" in the Prot. communions. Practical T. has as its aim theological reflection on the "practical" tasks of the church: preaching, education, the care of souls, the structure of church life, worship, and the like. Biblical T. may be regarded in a sense as a type of historical T., but because the study of the Bible has always had a normative significance in Protestantism it is regarded as a special field. In addition to these somewhat traditional designations, there have been others created to suggest distinctive emphases. Apologetic T., for example, was a fashionable name a few decades ago for the attempt to show the validity of the Christian faith. This term has tended to fall into disrepute, however, and one hears more commonly these days of philosophical T. This term is usually used by those who are convinced that T. must use philosophical terminology or who are interested in problems common to both T. and philosophy.

Theonomy. See Heteronomy.

Theopaschites means literally "those who believe that GOD suffered" and was applied to those monophysites who opposed the Chalcedon Creed (451). The formulas "God has suffered" and "God was crucified" were ancient ones in the CHURCH, but when the monophysite patriarch of Antioch, Petrus the Fuller (d.488), attempted to modify an ancient liturgical formula, the Trisagion, to include "who was crucified for us," a complicated controversy ensued, the upshot of which, as Adolf von Harnack (1851-1930) notes, "gave the name 'Theopaschitian' a permanent place in . . . [ORTHODOXY'S] collection as a heretical name." (See Christology; Monophysitism.)

Theophany refers to the temporal and spatial manifestation of GOD in some tangible form. Theophanies are said to occur in many religions, and because this is so many Christian theologians have taken pains to argue that the INCARNATION of God in Christ is not a T. in this sense. (See Christology.)

Theotokos means literally "the bringer or bearer of God" and was applied to the Virgin Mary by some of the early Greek Fathers. In the 5th century, those who emphasized the complete humanity of Jesus attacked the use of the term but it was maintained by the Council of Chalcedon (451). In the R.C. CHURCH, the customary term is *Dei Genetrix* or "Mother of God," which has a different emphasis than "bearer of God."

Traducianism refers to that theory held by some theologians according to which the SOUL is not newly created in each PERSON (CREATIONISM) but is generated by the union of the parents. Sometimes this GENERATION was viewed in a somewhat material way (material T.) and sometimes in a spiritual fashion (spiritual T.). T. professed to be an answer to how ORIGINAL SIN could be inherited. It is regarded as heretical in the R.C. church, which believes that each individual soul is created by a unique act of GOD. (See Soul.)

Transcendence is derived from the Latin words meaning literally "to surpass" or "go beyond." As a metaphor, it easily conveys a number of varied although related meanings. An inspection of the history of philosophy and THEOLOGY reveals that the precise significance of the term in any particular work must be determined from the context. In general, however, the term has been used in Christian theology in three closely related ways. (1) It has been used to designate any ideal or thing or being that "stands over against" the knowing subject. It conveys "otherness." One may say, for example, that an ideal transcends EXISTENCE in the sense that it "hovers beyond" the subject who aspires to it but does not achieve it. Or one may say that another self is transcendent in the sense of confronting one as an autonomous and independent center of consciousness. Or one may use the term, as Kant (1724-1804) did, to refer to those objects that lie beyond or surpass human modes of perception and cognition altogether and, thus, are unknowable. (2) The term has been used to signify that which stands "over against" all finite BEING as such, hence a term for GOD, the ground and source of all being. T. then designates God's unique mode of relationship to the world. He is said to transcend the world in the sense that his being is not identical with or his power not exhausted by the realm of finite being (see Theism, Deism, Pantheism, and Panentheism). This conception of T. is implied in the attribute "holiness" and, more mythologically, in the spatial and temporal SYMBOLS of heaven and ETERNITY. The polar opposite of this meaning is IMMANENCE. When this idea of T. has been radicalized, as it has been in neo-Platonic philosophy, certain forms of mysticism, and in some of the early forms of NEO-REFORMED THEOLOGY, it has led to the view that the deity is "wholly other" and, therefore, unknowable by the unaided natural mind. (3) The term "T." has been used to designate certain categories that necessarily characterize any conceivable or possible being. In Scholastic philosophy six such categories were named transcendentals: reality (*res*), being (*ens*), truth (*verum*), goodness (*bonum*), being something (*aliquid*), and unity (*unum*). Although not all metaphysicians agree on this list, most agree that there are certain categories that must be presupposed in all human thought about reality and cannot be denied without self-contradiction, and in this sense these categories are transcendent. It is interesting to note that this meaning of T. contains one aspect of the meaning of immanence, for the very fact of the universal presence (immanence) of these categories in any conceivable being constitutes their T. And for this reason, it is alleged, it is meaningless to say God is "wholly other," since these categories must either apply to God literally or analogically. (See Analogy, Way of; Attributes of God; Being; Immanence.)

Transubstantiation refers to the R.C. DOGMA that the SUBSTANCE of the elements of bread and wine is transformed by GOD's power into the substance of the body and blood of Jesus Christ directly upon the words of the priestly consecration in the Mass. Against any view that regards these elements as mere SYMBOLS of Christ's body, or as seals of FAITH, or as unchanged elements along with which Christ is really present (see Consubstantiation), the R.C. asserts that the substance of each element is wholly transformed into both the body and blood of Christ.

No dogma is perhaps so misunderstood by non-R.C.s. Either

it is interpreted as the simple conversion of one matter into another or it is identified with the Thomistic interpretation of it. The R.C. argues not that the qualities of bread and wine are changed, which, unfortunately is what the common man means by substance, but that the inner substantial reality underlying its appearances has been transformed. To be sure, R.C. theology has in the past leaned heavily on the Thomistic distinction between substance and ACCIDENTS to make this point clear. The substance of anything, it is claimed, is not perceptible to the senses but can only be grasped by the intellect. It is this inner reality that is transformed, not the accidents that are perceptible to the eye. Thomistic philosophy has also been brought into service to explain the related idea of concomitance, that since the substance of Christ's body and blood is indivisible, the faithful may take only the bread and still receive the whole Christ. But, however that may be, there are many R.C. theologians eager to insist that the CHURCH is not bound to the Thomistic categories but only to the dogma that T. takes place. (See Consubstantiation; Eucharist; Sacrament.)

Tridentine. Pertaining to the R.C. Council of Trent (1545-63), called to reform the CHURCH in the face of the spread of Protestantism. Its doctrinal utterances were made with a view to what it believed were Prot. errors, and its position, therefore, made almost impossible a *rapprochement* between the two bodies.

Trinity. The doctrine of the T. states that in the BEING of the one eternal deity there are three eternal and essential distinctions, traditionally named Father, Son, and Holy Spirit. In Western Christendom, the classical formula has been "three PERSONS in one SUBSTANCE" (*una substantia et tres personae*); in Eastern Christendom, "three HYPOSTASES in one being" (*treis hypostaseis, mia ousia*). The doctrine did not crystallize until the 4th century, although Trinitarian language is found in the N.T. and in the primitive CHURCH. This crystallization was precipitated by several factors, the two most important being the reflection on the relation of Christ to GOD and the necessity of combating radical views which, like Marcion's (*c*.100-*c*.160), asserted that the creator and redeemer were not one but two gods, or which, like Arius' (*c*.250-*c*.336), asserted that the Logos was neither fully human nor fully divine. By virtue of the identification of the pre-existent Christ of Johannine and Pauline thought with the Greek concept of the *Logos*, Christian THEOLOGY was inevitably led in a speculative direction, that is, to defining the relation of the *Logos*, or eternal Son, to the divine origin, or Father. This inevitable tendency was increased when less circumspect minds advanced solutions that were clearly untenable. The monarchians or modalists so emphasized the unity of God that all distinctions were rejected and it was said that the Father suffered and died. The subordinationists insisted that the *Logos* was a creature of God, which in effect undermined the belief that God was incarnate in Christ. These theological controversies were extraordinarily complicated by political and ecclesiastical rivalries. Moreover, the Eastern parties were laboring on the matter with a Greek vocabulary while the Western parties were using Latin, a situation still further confused by the fact that there was no fixed terminology in either Greek or Latin. Men first had to agree what they meant and then to translate that into terms which themselves not agreed upon. The aim of the orthodox party in the East, led by Athanasius (*c*.295-373), was to preserve the unity of God and the coequal status of the Father, Son, and Holy Spirit. For years this party was unable to agree on the precise terminology until a reconciling formula and interpretation were provided by the Cappadocians. It was "one *ousia* (or being) in three *hypostases*" (distinctions in being). This formula appealed to the Western theologians because it seemed parallel to Tertullian's (150?-225?) earlier Latin formula, three persons in one substance.

Although the doctrine has always been alleged to be a mystery, theologians have not hesitated to try to clarify it. The orthodox view since Augustine (354-430), whose work determined subsequent thought on the matter, has been that there are three significant distinctions within the one divine reality. These distinctions are called persons or hypostases and are coeternal and coequal. In each of them the divine nature is fully and undividedly contained. Even though the persons are in the closest possible unity with one another and interpenetrate one another (see *Perichoresis*), each has a peculiar character when viewed in relation to the others. The Father is not begotten but is said to be ingenerate. The Son is begotten eternally and proceeds by FILIATION. The Spirit proceeds by spiration from both the Father and the Son (see *Filioque*). Sometimes certain qualities and activities are assigned to one of the persons (see Appropriations), but this has been qualified by the traditional notion that every one of the persons shares fully in all the activities and operations of the others, for example, in CREATION, REDEMPTION, and SANCTIFICATION. It is important to note that no important Christian theologian has argued that there are three self-conscious beings in the godhead. On the contrary, Augustine's favorite analogy for the triune god was one self-consciousness with its three distinctions of intellect, will, and the bond between them.

In so far as the doctrine of the T. has been a speculative theory concerning the internal life and being of God rather than a doctrine aimed at the threefold activity of God, it has tended to be relegated to the periphery of the thought of those theologians most concerned with the immediate problems of FAITH and unfaith. The Reformers, for example, did not doubt the doctrine, but they primarily emphasized the triune structure of the Christian confession: faith in the creator who reveals himself in Jesus Christ whose spirit dwells with the believer. The most radical overhaul of the doctrine occurred in LIBERAL PROTESTANTISM, however, where it was taken as axiomatic that theology was necessarily limited to immediate religious experience. Even though the so-called neo-Reformed theologians rejected the liberal theological program, they insisted, nevertheless, that the doctrine was not revealed and that it was justified only as a reflection on the structure of the "encounter" with God in Jesus Christ. It was not regarded as a statement about the divine nature itself. Emil Brunner (1889-) calls it a protective doctrine. Karl Barth (1886-) is the notable exception to this generalization. He argues that although the doctrine is, to be sure, not revealed, God discloses himself as he really is in Christ, and this is triune. The doctrine is, he concludes, the central and unique doctrine of Christian dogmatics. There has been a renewed interest in it because of Barth's work. In general, two analogies have been used: the social and the personal. The critics of the former argue that it verges on TRITHEISM. The critics of the latter argue that it does not justify the three distinctions. (See Appropriations; *Hypostasis*; *Logos*; Modalism; Monarchianism; Person; Procession; Trinity, Economic.)

Trinity, Economic. Theologians have traditionally noted distinctions made with respect to GOD's being considered apart from his activities in the world (*ab intra*) and distinctions made with respect to God's activity or operations (in Greek, *oikonomia*) in the world. The terms "essential" or "immanent" Trinity refer to the former and "economic" to the latter.

Tritheism is an extreme form of Trinitarianism. It asserts the EXISTENCE of three separate and distinct centers of consciousness sharing the abstract and common nature of deity. It denies the unity of deity as it has been conceived in orthodox Trinitarian THEOLOGY. (See Trinity.)

U

Ubiquity means generally being present everywhere and, thus, is one of the ATTRIBUTES OF GOD. Luther (1483-1546) also attributed U. to the exalted Christ (see Ascension) when, in controversy over the EUCHARIST (see Consubstantiation) he insisted that Christ is bodily present in the sacramental elements. (See Omnipresence.)

Universalism. See *Apocatastasis*.

Universals. See Essence; Nominalism.

V

Virgin Birth of Christ traditionally refers to the miraculous birth of Jesus by Mary, i.e., without the benefit of a human father. Its theological significance has always been to protect the deity of Christ, the incarnation of the divine Logos in human flesh. Originally, the doctrine had nothing to do with the belief that sexual intercourse was sinful or was the means of transmitting ORIGINAL SIN, although both of these ideas soon crept into popular thinking and more sophisticated theological thought. Its original meaning was undoubtedly to testify to the conviction of the earliest CHURCH that Jesus Christ was the unique coming of GOD into human life, that he was the Messiah. With the rise of BIBLICAL CRITICISM, doubts arose concerning the authenticity of the accounts in Matt. and Luke, the only references to the V.B.O.C. in the Bible and which are difficult to reconcile with one another. Liberal Prot. THEOLOGY, which was suspicious of all MIRACLE stories and which saw no relationship between this one and the religious significance of Christ, rejected it. Fundamentalists and orthodox theologians reacted somewhat violently, and saw in the V.B.O.C. the crucial test of Christian belief. They elevated it, therefore, to a position of importance it probably never had before. Neo-Reformed theologians generally accepted the idea that the N.T. accounts were legendary but argued that this fact did not necessarily diminish the theological importance of Jesus Christ as the decisive REVELATION of God. They insisted that the V.B.O.C. was not an essential article of belief but a SYMBOL expressing the confession that Jesus Christ was the final disclosure of the divine will.

Virtue. According to R.C. teaching, a V. is a HABIT or a disposition of right conduct. V.s may be either acquired by education and repetition or they may be infused. Those V.s aimed at the perfection of human nature without respect to its supernatural end are called natural V.s. Those V.s which have to do with man's supernatural destiny are called supernatural or theological V.s and, because they cannot in the nature of the case be acquired by human effort, must be supernaturally infused into the SOUL by means of SANCTIFYING GRACE. The four principal (cardinal) natural V.s are prudence, JUSTICE, fortitude, and temperance. The three theological virtues are FAITH, hope, and CHARITY (see *Agape*). The theological V.s grow with grace and, when they find expression in good works, MERIT further increase in grace. Prot. THEOLOGY, on the whole, has rejected the idea of V. Particularly obnoxious was the R.C. teaching that faith is a "habit" and that good deeds performed by the faithful merit further graces. (See Faith; Grace; Habit; Image of God; Infusion; Merit; Sacrament.)

Vocation has had two meanings in Christian THEOLOGY, the call to repentance and FAITH, and the call to serve the neighbor in the world. This article deals with the latter, especially as it is related to daily work. The O.T., on the whole, takes a very positive attitude toward work. Although Gen. 3:14-19 has frequently been interpreted to mean that work is a divine curse, the previous verses in which Adam is given dominion over the earth cannot be ignored any more than the innumerable passages throughout the O.T. in which honest work is praised and viewed as GOD's intention for man. This positive attitude reflects a general affirmation of daily life characteristic of the O.T. In so far as the N.T. is Hebraic in substance, work is also valued and idleness condemned. There is, however, very little theological reflection on the religious significance of daily work in the N.T., largely because most of it was written in the expectation of the immediate end of the world and the PAROUSIA. In the Middle Ages, there was a marked tendency to distinguish between sacred and secular work, the former having to do with the monastic and priestly life, the latter with non-ecclesiastical life. Although the non-ecclesiastical V.s were not altogether devalued in religious significance because they reflected God's NATURAL LAW for the restraint of sin in a fallen world, the truly religious service of God could best be performed, it was believed, in the CHURCH. The ascetic, monastic life was, for example, regarded as a higher calling than the married estate with its sexuality and filial duties. Consequently, there was in the Middle Ages no impressive theological reflection on the religious significance of serving the neighbor through one's daily work.

Whether or not the medieval CATHOLIC synthesis also devalued daily work and the secular professions by virtue of its elevation of monasticism and the priestly office is a matter of debate. Some scholars insist that it did, while others point out that the organic view of society, which was such a dominant idea in that synthesis, suggests that every role in that organism, from peasant to king, was essential to the health of the organism and, thus, to be valued. However that may be, social historians generally agree that the Reformers contributed a unique idea of work to Western culture which had revolutionary social consequences, for the Reformers argued that no distinction can be made between sacred and profane work; indeed, that profane work was far more useful and pleasing in the sight of God than the ascetic, monastic, and priestly work. Luther's (1483-1546) views were based on the distinction between a man's "person" and his "office." The former referred to his relationship to God, the latter to his relationship to other creatures. The justified person fulfilled the command to love his neighbor through the roles or callings or stations he had in life. These stations (for example, husband, wife, businessman, milkmaid, etc.) were concrete embodiments of the natural law, and to neglect these responsibilities was to disobey the will of God. The impact of Luther's view was (1) to deprive churchly or religious V.s of any special MERIT, and, in fact, to criticize them as irresponsible if they seduced one away from one's concrete, daily duties, and (2) to interpret all useful secular V.s as having a positive religious meaning.

Some historians believe Luther's view was reactionary because he gave religious sanction to the idea that every man must simply remain in the V. to which he had been born. Calvin (1509-64), on the other hand, actually developed a positive interpretation and critique of the usefulness of certain

V.s in contrast to others. Furthermore, it is sometimes argued, Calvin put a premium on worldly success in one's V. as an indication that one had been divinely elected and, thus, provided a tremendous incentive that prepared the way for the "work ethic" of modern capitalism. Other scholars question this; but, whatever the case, it is usually agreed that the Reformation's positive evaluation of secular work as the service of God introduced a dynamic factor into Western society.

With the rise of modern technology and mass production, it was increasingly difficult to see how the average laborer could regard his boring and routinized work as the service of God, especially if he was being exploited by his boss. When Karl Marx (1818-83) argued that labor in capitalistic theory was regarded by the employer as simply an expendable means of production, his views constituted a tremendous challenge to Prot. and R.C. ethicists alike. In England in the middle 19th century, the Christian Socialists responded to this challenge as did, somewhat later, the leaders of the SOCIAL GOSPEL movement in America and Popes Leo XIII (1810-1903) and Pius XI (1857-1939). Ironically, the fundamentalists, who regarded themselves as faithful to the principles of the Reformation, were indifferent to or defended the injustices of the new capitalist order. Since these reform movements, theologians and ethicists have devoted an extraordinary amount of effort to interpreting V. from a Christian point of view. They have written about property, the role of the state, the rights and duties of labor and management, marriage, war, and most related issues. R.C.s still deal with these matters in terms of natural law theory; Protestants, in general, in more pragmatic terms and in the light of a relatively defined common good. (See *Agape* and *Eros*; Ethics, Christian; Ethics, Social; Justice; Law and Gospel; Natural Law; Social Gospel.)

W

Wisdom is used in the Bible in two contexts, human and divine. In the former, it has a wide range of meanings: human skill, practical knowledge, magic, ability to coin wise sayings, and meditation on the Law. In the latter, it refers to the infinite W. of GOD in CREATION and in the guidance of the destinies of peoples and nations. In the later O.T. period, there was a tendency to talk of this W. as if it were independently real, a tendency which made it natural for later Christian theologians to identify W. with the LOGOS or second PERSON of the TRINITY. This was facilitated by St. Paul's assertion that Jesus Christ "is the W. of God" (I Cor. 1:24) and the Johannine claim that Jesus Christ is the embodiment of the eternal *Logos* which was in the beginning with God and was God (John 1:1-16). (See Christology; *Logos*; Person; Pre-existence of Christ; Word of God.)

Word of God is a particularly important expression so far as understanding Prot. THEOLOGY, classical and modern, is concerned. It is used in close connection with Jesus Christ, the Bible, preaching, and the SACRAMENTS, each of which is often referred to as the W.O.G. In Luther's (1483-1546) thought, the W.O.G. is the term for the concrete expression of the divine love or mercy. In this sense, he uses Jesus Christ and W.O.G. interchangeably, since he believed that Jesus Christ was the ultimate and final REVELATION of the divine will. But since the Gospel (and even the LAW when rightly interpreted) witness to the true meaning of Jesus Christ, they also may be said to be the W.O.G. And since the Bible contains this witness, it, too, may be called the W.O.G., as may also preaching and the sacraments. For Luther the W.O.G. is not a static concept. It is the real inner meaning of Jesus Christ, the Bible, preaching, and the sacraments, and it gives them their present significance for man. This is why the only proper response to the W.O.G. is FAITH or trust (FIDUCIA), because the aim of the W.O.G. is to awaken a response in the heart of the one who hears it. Unless one realizes, wrote Luther, "that Christ is born . . . and has died for me, then the preaching or the knowledge of the story of Christ is useless."

NEO-REFORMED THEOLOGY is based upon a similar understanding and, therefore, is sometimes called a "theology of the W.O.G." Karl Barth's (1886-) *Church Dogmatics*, for example, is a monumental attempt to see theology as an exposition and interpretation of the divine revelation or W.O.G., as revealed in Jesus Christ, the Scriptures, and the proclamation of the CHURCH. Other neo-Reformed theologians, like Emil Brunner (1889-), Rudolf Bultmann (1884-), and Friedrich Gogarten (1887-) have also utilized this expression in a fundamental way. They argue that this highly symbolic formula best expresses the insight that God "encounters" or "addresses" man, that revelation is more like an "event" than the disclosure of certain supernatural and abstract truths or doctrines. In this way, these theologians believe they avoid the errors of FUNDAMENTALISM as well as of Roman Catholicism, for both of these, they insist, identify the W.O.G. with some proposition or doctrine that requires intellectual assent. (See Church; Faith; Grace; Hermeneutics; Law and Gospel; *Logos*; Revelation; Sacrament; Soteriology.)

Works. See Justification; Merit; Righteousness of God.